The Complete Idiot's Reference Card

W9-DGC-912

The Days

Sunday	*Zuntik*
Monday	*Montik*
Tuesday	*Dinstik*
Wednesday	*Mitvokh*
Thursday	*Donershtik*
Friday	*Fraytik*
Saturday	*Shabes*

The Months

January	*Yanuar*
February	*Feber*
March	*Merts*
April	*April*
May	*Mey*
June	*Yuni*
July	*Yuli*
August	*Oygust*
September	*September*
October	*October*
November	*November*
December	*Detsember*

Question Words in Yiddish

Word	Meaning	Example	Translation
Far vos?	Why?	*Far vos shlofst du?*	Why are you sleeping?
Ven?	When?	*Ven kumst du aheym?*	When are you coming home?
Vi azoy?	How?	*Vi azoy tust du dos?*	How do you do that?
Vi vayt?	How far?	*Vi vayt forst du?*	How far are you going?
Vi lang?	How long?	*Vi lang vartst du?*	How long are you waiting?
Ver?	Who?	*Ver kumt?*	Who's coming?
Vos?	What?	*Vos iz dos?*	What is this?

alpha books

Words You Can't Do Without

English	Yiddish	Example	English
yes	yo	Yo, ikh kum.	Yes, I'm coming.
no	neyn	Neyn, ikh vil nit ….	No, I don't want ….
thanks	dank	A dank far di Matone.	Thanks for the gift.
here	daw	Ikh voyn daw.	I live here.
there	dorten	Dorten iz kalt.	There it's cold.
to	tsu	tsu zen mayn khaver	to see my friend
from	fun	Fun vanet kumt ir?	Where are you from?
with	mit	kave mit milkh	coffee with milk
without	on	on a dayge	without a problem
in	in	in a shif	in a boat
on	oyf	oyf a trep	on a step
near	noent	noent tsu mir	near to me
far	vayt	vayt avek	far away
in front of	far	far mayn hoyz	in front of my house
behind	hinter	hinter der tir	behind the door
inside	inveynik	Inveynik iz varm.	Inside it's warm.
outside	in droysen	In droysen iz finster.	Outside it's dark.
nothing	gornit	Es iz gornit mit gornit.	It's nothing with nothing.
many	sakh	a sakh tsores	many problems
few	veynik	veynik kroyvim	few relatives
enough	genug	Genug iz genug.	Enough is enough.
too much	tsu fil	Ikh veg tsu fil.	I weigh too much.
good	gut	Dos esen iz gut.	The food is good.
better	beser	Es ken zayn beser.	It could be better.
best	best	Vos iz best?	What's best?
bad	shlekht	Zayn hunt iz shlekht.	His dog is bad.
worse	erger	Es ken zayn erger.	It could be worse.
again	vider	Es regent vider.	It's raining again.
also	oykh	Er vil oykh kumen.	He also wants to come.
now	itst	Itst iz di tsayt.	Now is the time.
immediately	teykef	Ikh kum teykef.	I'm coming immediately.
soon	bald	Bald iz sumer.	Soon it's summer.
as soon as possible	vos gicher	Vos gikher, als beser.	The sooner, the better.
later	shpeter	Shpeter iz tsu shpet.	Later is too late.
slowly	pamelekh	Er geyt tsu pamelekh.	He's going too slowly.
quickly	gikh	Koom gikh.	Come quickly.
look out	hit zikh	Hit zikh far'n ayz.	Watch out for the ice.
listen	hert	Hert vos ikh zog.	Hear what I say.
stop	oyfheren	Amol muz men oyfheren.	Sometimes you've got to stop.

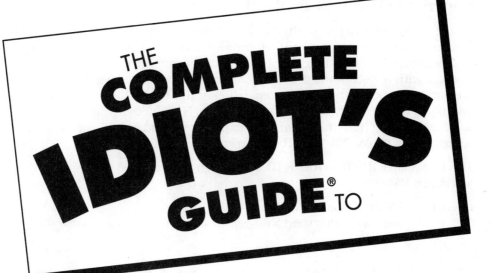

THE COMPLETE IDIOT'S GUIDE® TO

Learning Yiddish

by Rabbi Benjamin Blech

alpha
books

Macmillan USA, Inc.
201 West 103rd Street
Indianapolis, IN 46290

A Pearson Education Company

Copyright © 2000 by Benjamin Blech

International Standard Book Number: 0-02-863387-3
Library of Congress Catalog Card Number: Available from the Library of Congress.

02 01 00   8 7 6 5 4 3 2

Interpretation of the printing code: The rightmost number of the first series of numbers is the year of the book's printing; the rightmost number of the second series of numbers is the number of the book's printing. For example, a printing code of 00-1 shows that the first printing occurred in 2000.

Printed in the United States of America

Publisher
Marie Butler-Knight

Editorial Director
Gary M. Krebs

Product Manager
Phil Kitchel

Associate Managing Editor
Cari Luna

Acquisitions Editor
Amy Zavatto

Development Editor
Michael Koch

Production Editor
Michael Thomas

Copy Editor
Krista Hansing

Illustrator
Jody P. Schaeffer

Cover Designers
Mike Freeland
Kevin Spear

Book Designers
Scott Cook and Amy Adams of DesignLab

Indexer
Lisa Lawrence

Layout/Proofreading
John Etchison
Donna Martin
Gloria Schurick

Contents at a Glance

Contents

Introduction

Languages are normally identified with a land. French and France, Spanish and Spain, Chinese and China are all inseparable partners. Yiddish, however, is different. Yiddish doesn't have a geographical home. Yiddish isn't defined by boundaries.

Yiddish is a language created not for a country, but rather for a people. A Yid is another name for a Jew, and Yiddish is the way Jews learned to communicate with each other as they found themselves scattered to the furthermost points of the earth. Yiddish may, in fact, be the first international tongue, a language that recognizes no limitations of national borders and that freely considers itself a citizen of the world. To learn Yiddish is also like learning no other language. That's a promise I make to you as you set out on a project that I guarantee will bring you immeasurable rewards.

Isaac Bashevis Singer, the Nobel prize–winning Yiddish writer, playfully told an interviewer after he received his prestigious award, "Ghosts love Yiddish, and as far as I know, they all speak it. I am sure that millions of Yiddish-speaking corpses will rise from their graves one day, and their first question will be, 'Is there any new book in Yiddish to read?'" What Singer tried to convey is the agelessness of a tongue that has the capacity to link modern man with countless previous generations.

For many centuries, Yiddish was the language of a persecuted and oppressed people who almost miraculously managed to maintain their faith and their optimism. Yiddish was the language of the People of the Book who felt a special kinship with God and created what is often referred to as a holy tongue. Yiddish was the language of survivors who mastered the ongoing skill of survival. Yiddish not only reflected a culture, but it was instrumental in energizing it and allowing it to thrive and to prosper.

As a language spoken for almost a thousand years, Yiddish found a way to merge the wisdom of Solomon with the wit of Sholom Aleichem, the insights of the Bible with the observations of Sigmund Freud, the keen intellectualism of the scholars with the common-sense, down-to-earth musings of the simple Jew whose daily struggle for bread made him "street smart" far beyond his contemporaries.

To learn Yiddish, in short, is to become familiar with a very special outlook on life. "Dress British, think Yiddish" was a Madison Avenue slogan some years back. The way you dress will only change you on the outside. The way you think, however, can turn you into a different person. Think Yiddish, and you'll be wiser. You'll be happier. And, yes, of course, you'll be funnier.

Ironic, isn't it, that from a people who have suffered more than most others throughout history we find the greatest wellspring of humor. Jewish comedians dominate the American scene, and they don't hesitate to sprinkle their shtick with Yiddish expressions. I'll leave it to psychologists to figure out the profound reason for the link between this language and laughter. Whatever it is, though, learning Yiddish will grant you the gift of humor in addition to all its other benefits.

I can't guarantee that you'll be ready to become a stand-up comedian when you finish this book. But I do know that you're going to laugh a lot as you read through these pages. You'll also be very pleased with yourself as you experience the joy that comes with learning—a joy multiplied many times over as you realize you're building a bridge to a glorious past with a people known for their unique insights into life and the meaning of existence.

And Here's What You'll Find Inside

The book is divided into seven parts. Before we begin, I'd like to give you a quick overview:

Part 1, "Getting to Know Yiddish," introduces you to the language. You'll learn how Yiddish was born, why it almost died, and how it miraculously sprang back to life in the twentieth century. You'll find out how Yiddish differs from Hebrew and why Jews felt it necessary to create yet another way to communicate in addition to the language of the Bible they all knew and the language of the various lands in which they lived. You'll find out about the remarkable time known as the Golden Age of Yiddish, and you'll meet some of the people responsible for the tremendous burst of literary creativity that helped shape modern Yiddish.

Part 2, "So Let's Get Started Already," gets you going with the basics. You'll become familiar with the alphabet, crucial words you need for simple conversation, as well as expressions that allow you to enjoy social settings and be a polite guest. In this section, you'll also learn how to talk about time, the moments of our days and our years that define all of life.

Part 3, "Home, Sweet *Heym*," introduces you to the members of your family, acquaints you with the rooms of your house and what's in them, and teaches you how to talk about all those delicious foods that came out of your mother's kitchen.

Part 4, "On the Town," teaches you how to get around in Yiddish, from restaurants to movie theaters, to shopping expeditions, to trips and vacations.

Part 5, "That's Life," helps you deal with life's emergencies, opportunities, and obligations. From a visit with the doctor to career counseling, to conversations with and about God, you'll become an expert not only in the necessary words, but also the rules of grammar that will permit you to express yourself comfortably and clearly.

Part 6, "The Popular, the Powerful, and the Profound," teaches you put-downs and curses, blessings and good wishes, proverbs and wise sayings, and perfect descriptions for all the interesting characters you'll ever have the good fortune to meet. From this section you'll come away with a profound appreciation of the way Yiddish allows for expression of the most delicate shades of meaning and the most insightful observations.

Part 7, "**Yiddish Selections,**" will entertain you and enlighten you as you have the opportunity to read excerpts from beautiful and famous Yiddish passages. You'll also chuckle as you see what famous English selections sound like when they appear in Yiddish. Finally, you'll get a chance to see what makes Yiddish so funny as we bring the book to a close with a chapter on Jewish humor. A number of exercises are appended as a concluding chapter to ensure that you fully understood everything you learn in this book.

As a Bonus

To make reading this book an even more enjoyable experience, you'll find little sidebars scattered throughout—boxes of interesting and helpful information. These include:

A Gut Vort

Vort is Yiddish for word. Every time I use a word in the text you might not be familiar with, this sidebar will explain it and shed a little bit more light on its meaning.

Wise Sayings

A Yiddish proverb has it that, "A quotation at the right time is like bread in a famine to the famished." So many wise people of the past have succinctly expressed ideas in memorable fashion. When these quotes help to clarify and expand on an idea in the text, they'll appear, with attribution, in this sidebar.

With a Shmaykhel

Shmaykhel is Yiddish for "smile." Tell me the truth: What's life without laughter? Whenever the text reminds me of a good story, an anecdote, or anything that can elicit a chuckle, I'll share it with you in this sidebar.

Oy Vey

Oy vey means watch it, be careful, look out. Jewish mothers say it all the time, almost like a mantra. In this book, I'll use it to give you special tips and warnings. You'll be glad you got them, and if you choose to ignore them—*oy vey!*

Khap a Nash

To *khap* is to grab, and a *nash* is to food what a stolen kiss is to love. I use "grab a *nash*" metaphorically for those sweet, delicious asides you'll enjoy, just like a tasty snack. This sidebar will have all the useful and interesting information, just a teeny bit off the topic, that I couldn't bear to leave unmentioned.

Now don't waste another minute. Start reading. Start learning. And, best of all, start enjoying. *Es iz tsayt ontsuhoyben.* (It's time to begin.)

Acknowledgments

I would like to extend a special thanks to the technical editor, Professor Jean Jofen, who heads the Yiddish Department at Baruch College, City University of New York. Her efforts helped to make this book far more readable and enjoyable.

Trademarks

All terms mentioned in this book that are known to be or that are suspected of being trademarks or service marks have been appropriately capitalized. Alpha Books and Macmillan USA, Inc. cannot attest to the accuracy of this information. Use of a term in this book should not be regarded as affecting the validity of any trademark or service mark.

Part 1
Getting to Know Yiddish

Like most people, you surely already know that Yiddish is a language spoken by Jews for many centuries. You realize that just like those who spoke it, who were scattered around the globe, Yiddish was not restricted to any one country or even any one continent. You're aware that Yiddish served as the international voice of a people noted for their wisdom, their wit, and their indomitable will to survive.

What you probably don't know, however, are many of the details of the remarkable history of Yiddish. Where does Yiddish come from? How does it differ from Hebrew? Why did Jews who studied the Bible in the original Hebrew feel it necessary to create a new language for themselves? Part 1 introduces you not only to the birth of Yiddish, but also to its phenomenal growth, its almost tragic death during the twentieth century, and its miraculous contemporary revival. You'll meet the giants who helped bring about a Golden Age of Yiddish in modern times, and you'll learn about the explosion of Yiddish creativity in literature and the arts. You'll be intrigued to learn how Yiddish "adopted" so many other languages as its own, and you'll be amazed to discover how much Yiddish you already know.

Like a matchmaker (so learn a little Yiddish already and call him a shadkhen*) who hopes you'll fall in love with his verbal description of a beautiful bride or groom, this section wants to introduce you to Yiddish in a way that will allow the two of you to have a passionate and loving relationship from this day forward.*

Chapter 1

So What Do You Think, Yiddish Is Dead?

In This Chapter

➤ The Golden Age of Yiddish

➤ The giants of Yiddish literature

➤ The rise of Yiddish theater

➤ Why Yiddish almost didn't survive

➤ The contemporary revival of Yiddish

➤ Why *you* should learn Yiddish

Yiddish and Mark Twain have a lot in common. When the famous American humorist was shocked to read his own obituary in a popular newspaper, he immediately sent the editor a note to the effect that, "The report of my death was greatly exaggerated." In spite of what the press said, Mark Twain knew he was alive and well. Yiddish, too, has been the subject of premature obituaries. Time and again, it has been written off as a language without speakers, a jargon unknown to modern Jews, a vernacular with only a past and no future. Yet, it continues to confound its pallbearers and mock its mourners. Yiddish somehow shares with the Jewish people a most remarkable secret: the secret of survival.

True, the twentieth century may have come close to bringing about the death of the once-blossoming language. The systematic mass slaughter of some six million Jews by the Nazis during World War II almost led to the extermination of European Jewish life. The Nazis wanted to destroy not only a people, but also a religion, a culture, and a way of life. Yiddish was an important part of that way of life. The number of Yiddish speakers was further reduced by official suppression in the Soviet Union and by the semiofficial antagonism (until recently) of Israeli authorities zealously guarding modern Hebrew.

Language, it has been said, is the key to a nation's heart. Thankfully, Jewish hearts still survive. And when you look and listen around you, you can hear more Jewish lips pronounce Yiddish words that link their speakers to a glorious past and ancient traditions, and to a way of looking at life that embraces wisdom and humor, profound insight and optimism, pious reverence and irreverent questioning.

In retrospect, Yiddish has probably had the most remarkable century ever to affect any language. From robust, vigorous health at the beginning of the 1900s, it languished almost at death's door half a century later. An incredible recovery soon followed, resurrecting a critical patient to good health, an excellent prognosis, and countless friends and admirers. So, how's that for a miracle?

Those Were the Days, My Friend

Jews and Yiddish have enjoyed a long and powerful relationship. Historians estimate that Yiddish was the language of two-thirds of the Jewish people for one-third of its history. Because Jews were exiled so often and forced to flee to the most far-flung places, Yiddish had spread to almost every corner of the globe by the beginning of the twentieth century. Before World War II, approximately eleven million people could understand, speak, and, for the most part, read the language.

Created almost a thousand years ago (you'll learn more about that in the next chapter), Yiddish gained its greatest acceptance and respectability with an intense burst of cultural creativity that began in the late 1800s. From Poland, from the *shtetls* of Russia, from sophisticated cities across Europe as well as burgeoning cultural centers in the New World, came journals, books, newspapers, magazines, and plays, as well as translations of Shakespeare and other classics—all written in the tongue that, as the American writer Leo Rosten (1908–1997) put it so beautifully, "never takes its tongue out of its cheek." The humor, irony, sarcasm, wit, and wisdom of Yiddish sprung universally into view. For many, this period of cultural blossoming is known as the Golden Age of Yiddish. It came to an abrupt end when millions of Yiddish speakers fell victim to the Nazi Holocaust.

A Gut Vort

Shtetl, "little town" in Yiddish, describes an Eastern European village in which many Jews lived in the early modern period.

The Three Giants of Yiddish Literature

Although Jews love to argue, when the topic of conversation turns to Yiddish literature everybody seems in complete agreement. Mendele Mokher Seforim, Sholom Aleichem, and Isaac Leibush Peretz—three brilliant authors who coincidentally decided at approximately the same time to dedicate their literary efforts to works in Yiddish—were not only the founders of modern Yiddish literature, but also were the most important popularizers of the language into which they breathed new life and meaning. The way they used words, the sayings they either created or preserved from their culture, and the intonations and the characters they created breathed new life and meaning into the Yiddish language and are still with us to this day in literally hundreds of Yiddish to English (I prefer the word *Yinglish*) adaptations.

Mendele Mokher Seforim—literally, Mendele, "the seller of books"—was the pen name of Shalom Jacob Abramowitsch (1835–1917). His need for a pseudonym tells us something about the low regard for people foolish enough to write in what was considered until then as nothing better than a poor dialect of proper German. A native of Byelorussia, Mendele wrote in Yiddish because he wanted to reach the masses. The language of the people, he felt, also deserved its scribes. Similar to what Ernest Hemingway and others later did for American literature, Mendele wrote short, pungent sentences that read on paper "the way people really talk."

A Gut Vort

Yinglish is another way of referring to Yiddish words and expressions that have become anglicized and are easily recognizable.

Mendele helped Yiddish develop its satirical edge and its wonderful ability to flesh out characters. In stories such as "Fishke the Lame" and "The Nag," he describes Jewish beggars and thieves, Jewish *shlemiels* and *shlemazels* (you'll find out more about these characters in Chapter 20, "Morons and Misfits"). Mendele also introduced us to the *beservaisers*, a special breed not of know-it-alls, but those who "know it all better."

In general, Mendele's themes of humor and irony, love and understanding for the little people, the innate nobility of the poor, and the optimism of those whose lives were defined by deprivation remarkably enough ended up shaping the very language itself.

Polish-born Isaac Leibush Peretz (1852–1915) also took the daring step of staking his reputation on works written in the language of common people. Peretz loved people—instead of writing them off, he decided to write for them.

Peretz's philosophy was simple: "I live—therefore I have a divine spark in me. All who live have it. Even he who denies God also has the divine spark. So has the blasphemer." To many, *that* sounded blasphemous. But Peretz wrote poetry, drama, stories, essays, novels, and plays with the power of genius and the passion of a missionary for a language in whose beauty he deeply believed.

Khap a Nash

Sholom Aleichem wrote his first Yiddish book when he was 17. This was a book of Yiddish curses, which the author said was inspired by his stepmother. As the language of an oppressed people, Yiddish proved rich enough to provide the author with hundreds of entries.

With a Shmaykhel

On Sholom Aleichem's tombstone in New York City is inscribed a poem he wrote in Yiddish to mark his final resting place. In translation it reads: "Here lies a simple Jew who wrote in Jewish-German for women. For plain folks he was a humorist and a writer."

However, the man who towers even above Abramowitsch and Peretz is the one who took the most famous of Jewish greetings for his pen name and turned every occasion when two Jews met each other into a moment when they would have to remember him. *Sholom aleichem*—literally, "peace be upon you"—is the Jewish version of "Hello." Well, hello then to you all, said Sholom Rabinowitz (1859–1916) as he transformed himself to Sholom Aleichem and created the original immortal characters we all recognize today from the Broadway musical *Fiddler on the Roof*.

Laughing Through Tears

Sholom Aleichem is known as the greatest humorist in all of Jewish literature. That's true—but only if you understand the word *humor* within its Yiddish connotation. Yiddish asks us to laugh so that we do not cry. Yiddish stresses the humor in every situation because the reality for Jews is most often too difficult to bear. Laughter is the only alternative to madness. For a Jew, it isn't just a pleasant diversion—it's the only way to maintain one's sanity. As Sholom Aleichem put it to a friend in a personal letter, "This is an ugly and mean world, and only to spite it we mustn't weep. If you want to know, this is the constant source of my good spirit, of my humor. Not to cry, out of spite, only to laugh out of spite, only to laugh."

It has been said that Yiddish doesn't only have words; it also has an attitude. The attitude is humor born out of necessity. It is Tevye, the milkman from *Fiddler on the Roof*, who smiles and jokes with God even as he continues to suffer from a world that will not allow him to be at peace with his faith. Tevye believes in God, though he doesn't understand His ways. Tevye remains optimistic even as the world crumbles about him. And the language of Tevye became the very soul of Yiddish.

Universal Yiddish

The really amazing thing about Sholom Aleichem's work is that even when it's read in English, you can still feel that it's Yiddish. It's almost impossible not to picture the intonations, gestures, and accent when we read Sholom Aleichem's version of a letter that one of his heroes writes to a distant cousin who left his home in the *shtetl*:

> Dear Yankel:
> You asked me to write at length, and I would like to oblige, but there is really nothing to write about. The rich are still rich, and the poor are dying of hunger as they always do. What's new about that? And as far as pogroms are concerned, thank God we have nothing more to fear as we've already had ours—two of them in fact, and a third wouldn't be worthwhile. You asked about Hershel. He's been out of work now for over a year. The fact is they won't let them work in prison. Mendel did a clever thing: He upped and died, some say of consumption, others of hunger. Personally, I think he died of both. I really don't know what else to write about, except for the cholera which is going great guns.

So, with pogroms, prison, cholera, and the poor dying of hunger, there is really nothing to write about. We can only laugh and weep, even as we are moved to repeat Sholom Aleichem's favorite expression, "Oy, es iz shver tsu zayn a Yid!" ("Oh, it's hard to be a Jew!")

Richer Than Rothschild

By the time you finish this book, you'll be able to quote Yiddish proverbs and wise sayings in the original. But you have to get a feeling for the style, content, and approach of popular Yiddish sayings by meeting them first in English. There's no better way to start you off than with these selections from Sholom Aleichem.

Wise Saying

"If a horse with four legs can sometimes stumble, how much more a man with only one tongue."

—Sholom Aleichem

A Gut Vort

Pogrom is a Russian term used to designate a violent, unprovoked attack on a Jewish community. Though the term took on this usage only in the nineteenth century, it has come to be applied to anti-Jewish attacks in earlier times as well.

Khap a Nash

The Rothschild family became internationally renowned for their business acuity as bankers in the nineteenth century. Meir Anshel Rothschild and his five sons helped shape the political map of Europe with their financial aid and turned themselves into the wealthiest Jews in the world.

➤ God will provide, but if only He will provide until He provides.

➤ Dying while you are young is a great boon in your old age.

➤ If the rich could hire the poor to die for them, the poor would make a very good living.

➤ Our rabbi is so poor that if he didn't fast every Monday and Thursday, he'd starve to death.

➤ When things don't get better, don't worry—they may get worse.

➤ It's no disgrace to be poor—which is the only good thing you can say about it.

➤ Adam was the luckiest man on earth—he had no mother-in-law.

➤ If I were Rothschild, I would be richer than Rothschild. First of all, I'd have all of Rothschild's money, and then I'd make a little bit more on the side as a tailor.

All these observations were really written in Yiddish—and they happen to be just as funny with English words.

The Play's the Thing

The Golden Age of Yiddish was blessed not only with books and belles lettres, but also with the flowering of Yiddish theater that brought the spoken word to delighted audiences around the world.

The first Yiddish theatrical performance took place in Jassy, Rumania, in October 1872. This performance of *Serkele* by Aharon Wolfsohn-Halle proved so successful when touring Russia that the Russian authorities banned all Yiddish theater in 1883, fearing that it would encourage revolutionary sentiment. This measure proved to be a great blessing in disguise because the newly formed acting troupes were now forced to emigrate to Paris, London, and other major cities of Europe—and even to New York. For the first time, Yiddish plays became international successes.

Abraham Goldfaden (1840–1908) is considered the father of the Yiddish theater. The titles of his comedies, *Shmendrik* and *Kuni Lemel*, became familiar words in many languages. This marked the beginning of a phenomenon that would see hundreds of Yiddish words adopted into other languages for their special flavor and their fine shadings of meaning.

Boris Thomashefsky (1868–1939), one of the most flamboyant Yiddish actors and a pioneer of the Yiddish theater in the United States, not only loved to appear in romantic, swashbuckling parts written especially for him, but he also popularized translations of classic plays such as Shakespeare's *Hamlet* and *Richard III,* and Goethe's *Faust.* "Tsu zayn oder nisht tsu zayn" became as familiar to Jews as the original "to be or not to be" was to their neighbors. Many Jews, in fact, could never be convinced that there was ever a greater dramatist than the Jewish playwright Shakespeare, who was so good, rumor had it, that his plays were even translated into English!

In 1912, Thomashefsky built the National Theater in New York, where Yiddish show business would flourish for several decades. This was soon followed by the Jewish Art Theater, founded in 1918 by Maurice Schwartz, Thomashefsky's rival for the title of the greatest Yiddish actor of the time. Schwartz was an impressive figure who loved wide gestures, overacted wildly, and, when bringing the audience to tears and enthusiastic applause after one of his deeply moving death scenes, would do an encore—this proved that it's possible for an actor to die twice in the same performance!

Schwartz toured North America, South America, Europe, Israel, and South Africa. His company had a repertoire of 150 plays from Shakespeare, Lope de Vega, Toller, and George Bernard Shaw to Sholom Aleichem. He played Oswald in Ibsen's *Ghosts,* Shylock in *The Merchant of Venice,* and, of course, the *Melech* (King) in *King Lear.* His fame even drew some of the most influential Broadway critics to his Yiddish performances, affording a measure of respectability to the language in the non-Jewish world that it had never previously enjoyed.

Some of those who achieved fame on the Yiddish stage were so warmly received by non-Yiddish audiences that they shifted their talents to English roles in plays and films for a much broader American audience. Bertha Kalich, Sophie Tucker, Molly Picon, and Rudolph Schildkraut are just a few of the popular figures who went from Second Avenue (the lower East Side site of Yiddish theater) success to Hollywood.

A Gut Vort

A **kuni lemel** is a close relative of a **shlemiel,** a **nebish,** a **shmendrik,** a **shmo,** and a **shlemazel**—but just a little bit different. All are misfits of sorts, pitiable but nonetheless loveable characters. It takes a psychiatrist with at least five degrees to sort them all out.

Wise Saying

Here's how Mel Brooks explained the link between Jews and comedy: "It comes from the feeling that, as a Jew and a person, you don't fit into the mainstream of American society. It comes from the realization that even if you are better and smarter, you'll never belong."

At the same time, another kind of bicultural Yiddish-English partnership was being created in a Jewish version of summer stock theater. Hotels in the Catskills and Poconos around New York (known as the Borscht Belt because of the many Jews who came to vacation there) served as a training ground for the countless comedians who would graduate to become some of the best-loved comics in American culture. Mel Brooks, Sid Caeser, Moss Hart, Danny Kaye, Phil Silvers, and a host of others began their careers with Jewish audiences for whom Yiddish words and phrases were not only permissible, but almost mandatory.

A Gut Vort

Nebish became a **neb,** or a nerd in English. A nebish is innocuous, helpless, and an all-around loser. A Yiddish proverb says, "Better ten enemies than one nebish."

Yiddish influence remained strong as these performers became national stars. More than 80 percent of the most famous humorists of twentieth-century America were Jewish, so you have to be a *meshugener* or a *nebish* not to understand why even American Indians, as Mel Brooks taught us in *Blazing Saddles*, can speak at least a few words of Yiddish.

Oy Vey—Why Yiddish Almost Died

As the Yiddish expression goes, "If it was so good, why was it so bad?" Jewish history is filled with sudden dramatic shifts from one extreme to another. For the Jews, the Golden Age of Spain came to a swift and unexpected end with expulsion. The glorious era of German Jewry was rapidly consumed by the flames of the Holocaust. Almost as unexpectedly, the very survival of Yiddish was threatened in the middle of the twentieth century for obvious reasons:

Wise Saying

"In its years of decline, Yiddish culture was more than ever an international culture, a fraternity of survivors across the globe."

—Irving Howe (1920–1993)

➤ Six million Jews perished during the Holocaust. Almost all of them represented the Yiddish-speaking majority of the Jewish people. With their death went the chief creative voices of a language that was born, raised, and refined on European soil.

➤ The persecution of Jews in the Soviet Union, both during the Stalin era and during the consecutive Communist years, managed to successfully remove a great deal of ethnic and religious consciousness. Only total assimilation was rewarded in the Russian system, and Yiddish, the former language of millions of its Jewish inhabitants, condemned its speakers as social pariahs.

➤ The excesses of hatred on the European continent ironically found an unlikely accomplice in the freedom of the New World. Freely accepted in the United States as they never were before, Jewish immigrants considered Americanization not only a right, but a sacred duty.

➤ To become "a real Yankee" and speak American English was a way of reciprocating well-deserved love to a land whose Statue of Liberty so kindly welcomed the "huddled masses yearning to breathe free," as the Jewish poet Emma Lazarus put it. In a world of *pogroms* and brutal anti-Semitism in Poland and Russia, Jews needed the security of their own tongue and the isolation of their own language. The blessings of freedom and the ideal of a society as a melting pot of different cultures made English as the common language of the land far more attractive.

➤ To top it all off, in a bittersweet turn of events, Yiddish was forced to confront perhaps its greatest threat to survival because of the blessing of the birth of the State of Israel. Established in 1948, the new Jewish state adopted Hebrew as its official language. Going back to the Bible and the prophets for its inspiration rather than the tongue used by its people in the years of their exile, Israel's decision miraculously resurrected Hebrew into a living language while casting doubt on the continued viability of a way of communicating that had served Jews so well for centuries.

Wise Saying

"Yiddish came to have the same effect on many American Jews that Kryptonite had on Superman—it was a piece of the place they came from and therefore the one thing they could not abide."

—Jonathan Rosen, associate editor of *Forward*, a Yiddish daily newspaper

With a Shmaykhel

On a bus in Israel, an old woman is talking to her grandson in Yiddish. "Why don't you speak to him in Hebrew?" another passenger loudly criticizes. "What *chutspe*," the grandmother shouts back. "You want my grandson he shouldn't know he's a Jew?"

The big question Yiddish had to face after the 1950s was whether it could survive so many blows—and so many blessings.

L'Chayim—To Life: The Modern Rebirth

Dank Got (thank God), the years that followed proved Yiddish to be indestructible. When Isaac Bashevis Singer was asked in 1994 why he didn't write in Hebrew, he explained simply: "If Yiddish was good enough for the Baal Shem Tov (founder of the Hassidic movement), for the Gaon of Vilna, for Rabbi Nachman of Bratslav, for millions of Jews who perished by the hands of the Nazis, then it is good enough for me." And writing in Yiddish, Singer was awarded the Nobel Prize for Literature.

In his acceptance speech in Stockholm in 1978, Singer probably best captured the reasons why Yiddish simply would not die:

> The high honor bestowed upon me by the Swedish Academy is also a recognition of the Yiddish language—a language of exile, without a land, without frontiers, not supported by any government; a language which possesses no words for weapons, ammunition, military exercises, war tactics; a language that was despised by the gentiles and emancipated Jews. Yet … one can find in the Yiddish tongue expressions of pious joy, lust for life, longing for the Messiah, patience, and deep appreciation of human individuality. There is a quiet humor in Yiddish and a gratitude for every day of life, every crumb of success, each encounter of love.

Wise Sayings

"Yiddish wasn't just words, you see, it was an attitude. It was sweet and sour. It was a shrug and a kiss. It was humility and defiance all in one."

—Erica Jong, American author (1942–)

Yiddish *had* to survive. It would continue to serve as a living memorial for all those who cherished it in generations past, and for a way of life that is no more.

Yiddish is still spoken today by more than four million people. Some ultra-Orthodox Jews use it as their everyday language even in Israel, so as not to profane the holiness of Hebrew by secular, everyday usage. In many streets of Jerusalem, New York, Montreal, Paris, and around the world, you can still hear it. Many children of second-generation Americans are turning to Yiddish for a deeper understanding of their roots.

Yiddish language and literature courses are offered today in many colleges and universities, including the University of California at Los Angeles, McGill University in Montreal, Oxford University in England, Queens University in Belfast, and the Hebrew University in Jerusalem. Community centers, synagogues, and adult education programs in a large number of cities also have initiated Yiddish classes in response to public interest. Columbia University, the Hebrew University, and the City University of New York even have programs leading to a Ph.D. in Yiddish. Imagine how proud immigrants of half a century ago would be if they knew that knowledge of the language that they were ashamed of speaking in the United States could now be reason for someone to be granted the glorious title of "Doctor."

Nestled in a rolling apple orchard on the Hampshire College campus in Amherst, Massachusetts, a cluster of wooden buildings that resembles an Eastern European *shtetl* is today home of the National Yiddish Book Center. Founded by Aaron Lansky in 1997, its existence is vivid testimony to the renewed interest, involvement, and love for Yiddish that seems to be growing ever stronger. As Lansky once said, "It is common sense that we cannot throw away an entire literature, that we cannot discard a millennium of our history, that we cannot forget or purposely ignore where we have come from and still expect to know who we are and where we may yet go from here." The Center has nearly one and one-half million books in Yiddish carefully stored and catalogued.

The Top Ten Reasons to Learn Yiddish

So, because he has such a nice Jewish first name, I'll copy Dave (David) Letterman's style and give you the top ten reasons why you, too, should take the time and the effort to study this book and learn the language that, like the Jews who speak it, has miraculously survived far longer than anyone dreamt imaginable.

10. Yiddish is the best way to understand the soul of the Jewish people.

9. Yiddish allows you to communicate with the past—the dead as well as the living.

8. Keeping Yiddish alive is one of the most powerful ways we have to defeat Hitler's goal of "the Final Solution"—to eradicate every last vestige of the Jewish people.

7. Yiddish is the way to enter the doors of a magnificent literature and culture.

6. Yiddish brings sacred concepts and beautiful traditions down to earth and makes them comprehensible.

5. Yiddish has profound insights and wisdom that lose a great deal of their power in translation.

4. Yiddish teaches an optimistic vision that allows us to view the world with joy and with hope.

3. Yiddish teaches us how to laugh more loudly and how to weep with more feeling.

2. To know Yiddish is to become an artist with words and a master at describing the foibles, the quirks, and the strengths of human character.

1. And the No. 1 reason for learning Yiddish? It's the same inimitable two words that serve as the answer to every other question: Why not?

Besides, you already bought the book, so it would be a *shande* (shame) to waste the money. Trust me. Your own mother would tell you: Read. Study. Talk a little Yiddish. And enjoy, enjoy!

The Least You Need to Know

➤ In this century, Yiddish has gone through a remarkable cycle, from a Golden Age to serious threats to its survival to a contemporary resurgence of significant strength.

➤ Yiddish previously was spoken by more than eleven million people who used it as a creative expression for literature, journalism, and poetry, as well as highly popular dramas and comedies offered by theater productions around the world.

➤ Yiddish continues to maintain a strong hold on modern Jews for its link with centuries of Jewish history, its unique insights and wisdom, and its distinctive evolution as an expression of the soul of the Jewish people.

➤ There are at least ten reasons to study Yiddish.

Chapter 2

So Where Does Yiddish Come From?

In This Chapter

➤ Where and when Yiddish was born

➤ Why Jews created another language for themselves

➤ The differences between Hebrew and Yiddish

➤ All the different languages in Yiddish

➤ The different accents and Standard Yiddish

A classic story of Eastern European Jewry has a little boy wondering: Since God is certainly Jewish and since his favorite language must be Yiddish, why in the world did he write the Bible in Hebrew? In the course of centuries, Yiddish became so identified with Jews and Judaism that it became almost unthinkable to consider any one of this group of three in isolation from the other two. To be a descendant of Abraham, Isaac, and Jacob; to accept the teachings of the Bible and the laws of Moses; and to share a common language with Jews living in many foreign lands came to be regarded as an inseparable partnership.

The truth, of course, is that the ancient ancestors of the Jewish people never spoke the language we today call "Jewish," or Yiddish. The holiest texts of the Jewish religion were also not written in "Jewish." The Torah (the five books of Moses), as well as the later books of the Bible were all recorded in Hebrew. The Talmud, the major clarification of Jewish law and commentary on the Bible, was authored by Jews in Babylonia in their native tongue of Aramaic.

So where did Yiddish come from? How did it get to be so identified with Jews and Judaism? Why does it look just like Hebrew and yet sound so different? Read on and I'll tell you.

What's in a Name?

The Yiddish word for "Jew" is *Yid*. Like so many other Yiddish words, it comes from German, *Jude*. The *–ish* is an add-on that suggests compatibility, just like places that make you feel at home are called *heymish* in Yiddish (the *heym*, of course, being Yiddish for "home").

What the word *Yiddish* fails to acknowledge, unless you realize its Germanic origin, is that it is only identified with its Jewish speakers of a particular region. Jews who lived in medieval lands influenced by Germanic dialects created this Jewish version of their neighbors' language. Medieval rabbis, who believed that after the flood one of Noah's great grandsons, named Ashkenaz, settled in Germany, gave rise to the term *Ashkenazim* for Jews of Germany and France as well as adjacent areas of Western Europe. Later exile and emigration brought these Yiddish-speaking *Ashkenazim* to Poland and Russia.

Jews of Spain, Portugal, North Africa, and Arab lands of the Middle East were all the while developing their own culture, their own traditions, and even their own special "Jewish" language. Called *Sephardim* (from the Hebrew word *sephard*, cited in the Bible as a place where Jews exiled from Jerusalem found refuge in a soon-to-be ancient Spain), Sephardic Jews in fact dominated Jewish creativity and influence until the expulsion of the Jews from Spain in 1492 C.E. Among those exiled were physicians, philosophers, poets, advisers to royalty, and rabbinic leaders of the stature of Rabbi Moses Ben Maimon (twelfth century), more commonly known as Maimonides, of whom it was commonly said, "From Moses to Moses there was none like Moses."

Khap a Nash

The letters A.D. used after a year stand for *Anno Domini* (in the year of our Lord). Because Jews do not believe in the divinity of Jesus, the preferred abbreviation is C.E., which stands for Common Era.

Sephardic Jews were among the first to immigrate to the New World and build the earliest American synagogues. To this day, different customs separate Sephardic Jews from the *Ashkenazim*. Many people don't realize that in addition to distinct rituals and differing liturgy, the "Jewish" language used in daily conversation other than Hebrew is totally different as well.

What Yiddish is to Ashkenazic Jews, Ladino is to *Sephardim*. Based on fifteenth-century Castilian Spanish—and mixed with biblical Hebrew, Talmudic Aramaic, Arabic, Turkish, and Greek words and phrases—Ladino is also called *Judaeo-Spanish*. Señor Moshe and Señorita Sarah also found ways to give their conversations a special Jewish flavor. The word they chose to describe their language, however, doesn't have the Spanish for "Jew" in it, but rather means "familiar with several languages."

Ladino is almost certainly as beloved by Sephardic Jews as Yiddish is by *Ashkenazim*. Unfortunately for this alternative to Yiddish, *Ashkenazim* outnumber *Sephardim* worldwide by about 20 to 1. In other words, Yiddish has had far greater opportunity to gain followers, produce its own literature, and have an impact on many other foreign cultures. That's also why you're reading a *Complete Idiot's Guide to Yiddish*, and not to Ladino.

Yiddish Is Older Than You Think

Scholars tell us that modern English dates from approximately the latter portion of the fifteenth century. Modern German is considered to have begun with Martin Luther's translation of the Bible in the sixteenth century. Yiddish has a right to consider these languages youngsters compared to the time of its birth.

Almost ten centuries ago, Jews from areas that would later become Italy and France began to settle in towns along the middle Rhine Valley, where people spoke various medieval German dialects. Mixing their own Romance languages with the vernacular of their neighbors, these Jewish settlers created a uniquely Jewish tongue, different enough so that often their gentile neighbors wouldn't be able to understand them. That was no accident, of course. Jews didn't *want* their conversations to be accessible to a world that more often than not seemed bent on their destruction. Language became a unifier for those who shared it while powerfully separating and guarding its users from a hostile world of "outsiders."

Khap a Nash

While *Sephardim* have long been outnumbered by Ashkenazic Jews around the globe, Israel today is witnessing a remarkable population shift. With the large families common for those of Middle Eastern background, *Sephardim* are now just about numerically equal to *Ashkenazim* and may well surpass them in the years to come. The implications for Israel, as well as for world Jewry, remain to be seen.

Wise Sayings

"To call Yiddish an offshoot of Middle High German with an admixture of Hebrew and Slavic is entirely misleading; the tone and spirit of Yiddish are as remote from German as the poetry of Burns is from the prose of Milton."

—Maurice Samuel, Russian novelist and essayist (1895–1972)

Yiddish became the equivalent of slang created by minority groups to give themselves a greater sense of identification with each other as well as a sense of superiority over those not privileged to share in its secrets. As the persecution of the crusaders and exile forced the Jews to constantly wander from country to country, maintaining their collective ties through the use of a common language proved to be an incredible blessing. It also turned out to have an extremely important fringe benefit: Unlike other merchants, Jews could do business almost everywhere because they knew the language—at least of their Jewish kin.

Jewish history during the Middle Ages most often followed the path of west to east. Anti-Semitism proved strongest in western Europe, and for several centuries Ashkenazic Jews found havens deep in the Slavic territory, settling in Poland, Lithuania, and the Ukraine. They brought with them few belongings, great talent, and a special Jewish dialect of German that they proudly called their own and, no matter where they lived, that they continued to embrace as their mother tongue.

Wise Sayings

"Yiddish is the Robin Hood of languages. It steals from the linguistically rich to give to the fledgling poor."

—Leo Rosten, American writer (1908–1997)

Why Not Hebrew?

You must be wondering, though, why Jews needed to create yet another language if they already had one that was uniquely theirs. Jewish children were always taught the Bible in its original language, Hebrew. Usually from as early as the age of three or four, youngsters were instructed to pray in Hebrew, which was always referred to as "the holy tongue."

No matter what the language of their surroundings, Jews had to be bilingual if they were to be true to their faith and their religious teachings. Hebrew made them feel Jewish, set them apart from their neighbors, and served as a common bond and a way to communicate without their neighbors' comprehension. Why, then, did Jews need to create yet another Jewish language?

Simply put, because "the holy tongue" was meant to remain holy. The language of the Bible and of prayer couldn't possibly be debased by being used in the marketplace. Imagine speaking to God in prayer with the very words someone would subsequently use to yell at his neighbor! As a matter of fact, Hebrew doesn't even have in it a single obscenity. If you want to curse, you just have to go elsewhere. Hebrew is *shul* (synagogue) talk; Yiddish is street talk. Hebrew is for saints; Yiddish is even for sinners. And saints and sinners don't even have to be two different people—they can be one and the same person but at different times.

Mame-loshen—*A Language Spoken by Mothers*

Yiddish is also known as *Mame-loshen*, literally, "language used by mothers." A classic Yiddish joke has it that Yiddish was given the name *Mame-loshen* because fathers rarely ever get a chance to speak it in the presence of the dominating figure of the household. The real reason is even less flattering to male behavior. In the patriarchal society of old, Jewish women weren't taught Hebrew because it was considered too difficult and too holy for them. *Mame* was allowed (and able) to speak only Yiddish—hence, it was *Mame-loshen* to differentiate it from *loshen-ha-kodesh*, "the sacred language."

What ended up happening, of course, was that mother's language became as precious and as nourishing as mother's milk. By becoming identified with every child's first object of love, Yiddish found its way into Jewish hearts, very often in even greater measure than the words later learned for service of God. So, because mothers had the first word, they ironically enough had the last word as well.

What a *Mishmash!*

Yiddish, as we saw, began with Middle High German. Next came Hebrew words and phrases. After all, it would have been very difficult to find just the right Germanic expressions to ask, "Where is my *yarmulke*? I have to go to *shul* for *Yom Kippur*." Scholars estimate that between 15 and 20 percent of the vocabulary of Yiddish comes directly from Hebrew, with some slight alterations of the Yiddish accent. Then come the French, Polish, Russian, Rumanian, Ukrainian, and other borrowings, which serve as vivid reminders of our places of dispersion and our willingness to retain something of value even from places that cruelly mistreated us. The end result? A perhaps zany but delightful *mishmash*,

Oy Vey

Please be careful! Don't mispronounce *mishmash* the way a congressman once did on Groucho Marx's show, *You Bet Your Life*. Pronouncing the second half, *mash*, as if it rhymed with cash, he caused Groucho to sternly lecture him that, "You'll never get votes in the Bronx if you ever say it again that way." That was truly making a *mishmash*, a real fouled-up state of things, of the word *mishmash*.

A Gut Vort

Yom Kippur is the Hebrew name for the holiest day of the Jewish year, the Day of Atonement. Biblical law asks Jews to fast for a full night and day. A **yarmulke** is the head cloth covering worn by traditional Jews to express the idea that they believe there is always someone above them. A **shul** is the common name used for a synagogue.

Wise Sayings

The contemporary Yiddish journalist Charles Rappaport once boasted: "I speak ten languages—all of them in Yiddish."

With a Shmaykhel

A tourist in Hawaii goes over to a native and asks: "For years I've been wondering how to pronounce the name of your state. Is it Hawaii or Ha–vaii?" "It's Ha–vaii," the native answers. "Thank you so very much for the information," the tourist says gratefully. "You're velcome," responds the Jewish native.

a hodgepodge and hopeless mix-up that proves that the whole is greater than the sum of its parts.

Leo Rosten, the great popularizer of Yiddish words in the last century, showed how he could improve on the famous saying that Yiddish is the only tongue in the world in which you can speak three languages with three words, "Good *shabbes*, Madame." Rosten proved capable of making it five languages in five words: "*Guten erev shabbes*, Madame Chairman"—in order: German, Hebrew, Yiddish, French, and English. Altogether, the phrase expresses best wishes for a good eve of the Sabbath to a worthy lady.

One more thing about Yiddish's willingness to borrow from other languages: Like the Bible itself, it is very democratic. Yiddish will take words from anywhere. It is a highly pragmatic language. So, even English words have often been welcomed into the fold, although they had to pay the price either of slight alteration (a kind of verbal circumcision) or different pronunciation. The classic story of all times that illustrates this best is the one about the old lady anxiously asking passersby if they could speak Yiddish. When finally someone responded positively, with a great sigh of relief she asked the question she felt she could at last have answered: "Mister, *vot* time is it?"

No doubt, the fact that native Yiddish speakers have trouble with the pronunciation of certain letters leads to some interesting—and often hilarious—misunderstandings. Yiddish doesn't have a "W" sound as in "window," so, of course, you have to open a *vinde*. Then, there's no equivalent to the "th" sound, as pronounced in "the," for example. So, a request for fresh air must now include two changes, as we ask someone to open *de vinde*.

Finally, if word sequence is transferred as well, we'd probably end up with this: "*De vinde*—should be open, no?"

Yiddish likes to get to the point first: "What I want to talk about is the window. Let me then express my Messianic vision for it: It certainly should be open. But Jews love to disagree, and I realize that you may want to turn this into a discussion about the merits of fresh air as opposed to the dangers of catching a cold from the outside. So, I preface your anticipated response with a question, 'No?', almost daring you to reject my request."

Now *that's* a Yiddish sentence even though literally the words may appear to be English.

My Yiddish, Your Yiddish

With so many new words added and Yiddishized throughout the centuries in the different lands of Jewish dispersion, Yiddish obviously took on different forms and dialects. Historians give us the following chronology:

Initial Yiddish:	1000–1250 C.E.
Old Yiddish:	1250–1500 C.E.
Medieval Yiddish:	1500–1750 C.E.
Modern Yiddish:	1750–present

This breakdown, of course, is somewhat arbitrary. It marks major turning points in approximate stages. However, it does help us realize that languages develop over the course of time and reflect their eras in significant ways based on the cultures and geographic locations of their users. The most proficient English speaker would have trouble deciphering the works of Chaucer in the original. So, too, Yiddish slowly grew over one thousand years into its modern form.

I Don't Understand You

Even modern Yiddish, the last of the four major eras of Yiddish growth, didn't remain static or uniformly spoken. The course of time saw the emergence of four main dialects of Yiddish:

1. "Lithuanian," or *Northeastern Yiddish* spoken in Lithuania, White Russia, and Northeastern Poland. Anyone speaking this dialect is called a *Litvak*.

2. "Ukrainian," or *Southeastern Yiddish* spoken in the Ukraine, Eastern Galicia, Romania, and Southeastern Poland.

3. "Polish," or *Central Yiddish* spoken in the area between the German-Polish frontier of 1939 and the Rivers Vistula and San. This includes Central and Western Galicia. Anyone speaking the dialect of Galicia is called a *Galitsyaner*.

4. *Western Yiddish*, formerly spoken westward of the German-Polish frontier of 1939 (not to be mistaken with Hollywood Western Yiddish, where "stick 'em up" becomes "hold up *de hends*—please!").

Guess what: Even these four gave birth to many differences of dialect depending on exactly where Jews lived. That shouldn't surprise anyone. A Southern drawl is different from a Boston twang, and the United States enjoys countless different dialects that add to the melting pot flavor. Yet, somehow a standard American speech has evolved. For example, when in Brooklyn, a native may pronounce "these" or "those" as "dese" and "dose." A desire for greater respectability and acceptance, however, will modify Brooklyn-ese speech patterns to conform with more common standards. So, too, scholars have established a Standard Yiddish, bridging the various dialects into some semblance of universally accepted forms.

Do all Jews agree on standard Yiddish? Does the sun rise in the West and set in the East? Of course, Jews will continue to speak Yiddish, their *Mame-loshen*, the way Mama spoke it to them. The main beneficiary of Standard Yiddish is Yiddish literature, which can employ some common guidelines. But when you speak to Jews for whom Yiddish is their native tongue, be prepared to hear a host of variant dialects. Don't worry, though. With practice, you'll learn to ignore the Yiddish equivalent of a Southern drawl. I promise you that's the *emes*—the truth. For the purpose of this book, though, you'll be guided by majority usage and we'll stick to Standard Yiddish.

Hold the Back Page

Don't get scared now, but there's one last thing I have to tell you about Yiddish that makes it much more difficult to handle. Yiddish doesn't use English letters. Even though based mainly on German, Jews refused to write with the Latin alphabet. Latin belonged to Christians, the people who persecuted them. Latin letters were used by the church for their edicts. Thus, Jews decided to stick with the Hebrew alphabet they were so accustomed to from their religious studies. German words were adapted and then written out phonetically. The twenty-two letters of Hebrew that have no vowel sounds had to replace the twenty-six Latin characters, and vowel sounds were created by judiciously placing consonants together.

With a Shmaykhel

Maybe it never really happened, but who can resist retelling the story of the reporter for the Jewish newspaper who got the scoop of his life. With uncontrollable excitement, he called his editor and demanded: "I've got the story of the century. This time I insist: Hold the back page!"

Most important of all, though, was that Jews continued to write their daily language as they had always written Hebrew—from right to left. Jews open the back of the book first not because they want to get to the ending immediately, but because, as a wit once put it, "where others say they're finished we first begin."

Isn't it hard to learn a whole new alphabet and get used to switching directions as you read? Jews have done it for centuries. Maybe that's even one of the reasons that Jews have for so long been known for their wisdom. Doing something that's difficult is a challenge. Mastering it not only gives you a great sense of satisfaction, but it also helps to make you smarter. And please, just because this book is about Yiddish, don't turn to the back; since most of it is written in English, we decided to print it from left to right.

The Least You Need to Know

➤ Yiddish was created about 1,000 years ago by Ashkenazic Jewry, Jews primarily from Germanic regions.

➤ Sephardic Jews, Jews of Spain and Arab countries, concurrently created a variant of Spanish that is called Ladino.

➤ Yiddish is a conglomeration of many languages, including German, Hebrew, and at least a half dozen other languages.

➤ Yiddish fulfilled an important function as the vehicle for secular everyday conversation, for which Jews felt Hebrew was too holy.

➤ Yiddish has many different dialects based on geographic location.

➤ A Standard Yiddish has in the main been accepted as the most proper usage.

➤ Yiddish makes use of the Hebrew letters of the alphabet and is written from right to left.

Chapter 3

So Who Says You Don't Know Yiddish Already?

In This Chapter

➤ The Yiddish you already speak

➤ When Yiddish meets English and turns into *Yinglish*

➤ How Yiddish grammar crept into American speech

➤ Becoming cognizant of cognates

➤ The Yiddish expressions everyone knows in English

Just in case you are getting a bit nervous as you contemplate the awesome task of beginning to learn a new language, I have some great news for you: You are not really going to start a foreign tongue. Yiddish is already part of your native language.

Aha, I detect maybe a note of disbelief? From you maybe I'm getting a response of *feh*, like a disgusted rejection of such a heartfelt statement? You think maybe I'm chopped liver and don't feel pained by such callous mistreatment? What I'm getting at is that you hopefully recognize how the distinctly Jewish flavor of these last few sentences has had such a profound impact on American English, both written and spoken. Yiddish has entered speech patterns of non-Jews through grammar, specifically Yiddish prefixes and suffixes and, most commonly, through hundreds of Yiddish words so frequently used that they've been accepted into the dictionary.

Let me show you a sample of the Yiddish you already know but may not have realized you knew.

Some of My Best Friends Are Yiddish

Don't expect any translation for these words even though they're pure Yiddish. If you don't know what they mean, you should be ashamed yourself (a dramatic statement ignores the word *of*)—and get yourself a good dictionary:

bagel	*blintse*	*drek*	*farfel*
gefilte fish	*golem*	*heymish*	*khutspe*
kibutsnik	*kibits*	*kibitser*	*kishke*
klotz	*knaidel*	*knish*	*kreplakh*
kugel	*kvel*	*kvetsh*	*latke*
lekakh	*lokshen*	*loks*	*luftmentsh*
makher	*matse*	*mentsh*	*meshuge*
mezuma	*narishkeyt*	*nebish*	*nit*
nu	*nudnik*	*oy*	*pastrami*
plats	*pots*	*reb*	*rebetsin*
shlemiel	*shlep*	*shlepper*	*shlemazel*
shlokh	*shlob*	*shmalts*	*schmatte*
shmek	*shmeer*	*shmuz*	*shmuts*
shnoook	*shnorer*	*shadkhen*	*shiker*
shidukh	*shikse*	*shtetl*	*shtik*
shul	*tsutske*	*tsatske*	*tsores*
tumler	*tzimes*	*yortsayt*	*yarmulke*
yente	*yikhus*	*Yidishkeyt*	*yok*
yom tov	*zaftig*		

Believe me, that was just a *nash*, a little taste, like a small piece of pickled herring before the main. Hopefully though, it will make you realize that it's not only Yiddish that borrowed from other languages. English is also just as big a *ganef* (thief).

And Then There's *Yinglish*

Sometimes, only a part of a Yiddish word made it into English as a sort of carry-on, like a *yarmulke* worn by a gentile. Take the Yiddish suffix *nik*, as in *nudnik*, that identifies an ardent devotee of something. It wasn't hard for Jewish immigrants to decide that someone deserves to be called an "alrightnik," but it surely says a great deal about the incursion of Yiddish into contemporary speech when society's rebels happily identify themselves as "beatniks" (please understand that I don't mean to imply that they are also no-goodniks).

Another word ending that's strictly Yiddish is *–el* (sometimes *–le*). This is a diminutive that makes everything just a little bit smaller. A *bokher* is a young boy, but a *bokherel*—well, you get the point.

Just to clarify a little bit, let me remind you of this classic story: A little old lady scrounges around the pickle barrel and finally comes up with a suitable candidate. She asks, "How much is this pickle?" The deli man tells her, "It's a nickel." Upset by this exorbitant price, she flings it back, pulls out another which in her eyes is microscopically smaller, and demands, "And how much for this *pickele*?" To which the storekeeper firmly replies, "A *nickele*."

To make a word Yinglish, you can also add a typically Yiddish prefix. The "sh" sound is a good example. A Cadillac is just a car, and the best put-down for a *nouveaux riche* friend who thinks ownership now makes him better than you, is to remind him that, "Cadillac, *shmadillac*, it still only has four wheels and stays on the ground." So remember, it's okay to be fancy, but to take it to an excess always reduces to "fancy-*shmancy*."

Yinglish is also what happens when those for whom Yiddish is their native tongue try somewhat unsuccessfully late in life to cope with the strange phonetics of English. Why is it, someone once asked me, that one word, pronounced exactly the same, should have so many different meanings.

For example, the word *bet* (bed) is something you sleep on, a way to wash yourself (bath), something not good (bad), a stick used by baseball players (bat), and a wager (bet). With a Yiddish accent making all these words sound alike, imagine how peculiar it must seem to learn that they are all spelled so differently. When a subway becomes a *sobvay* and a streetcar a *stritt cah*, the descriptives may probably deserve being referred to as Yinglish rather than English.

Oy Vey

Some words you won't find in this list because they shouldn't be used in polite company. For example, I decided against including the pejorative that begins with "shm" and rhymes with "luck." Although the term is frequently used, it's another word for the male organ. Remarkably enough, its original source in German isn't at all derogatory or dirty. It means "jewelry" and has the same relationship to its modern usage as a man's "crown jewels" has to the word *testicles*.

Oy Vey

Be very careful of **shmaltsl**. In food, too much chicken fat could be a killer. In conversation, books, or movies, if it's too *schmaltzy*, it may be emotional, but it won't be believable.

And Don't Forget the Grammar

Yiddish sentences also have a beat of their own. It's not just the lyrics that count; it's also the music. That special Yiddish style is apparent even when a Yiddish speaker talks in English. You've also been influenced by Yiddish, perhaps on a subconscious level, if you've absorbed some of these basic Jewish rules of grammar:

➤ Phrase statements as questions. Instead of telling Ida that she looks gorgeous, ask her, "How stunning do you have to look?"

➤ Instead of answering questions definitely, answer with another question. When someone asks how you feel, answer, "How should I feel?"

➤ Whenever possible, end questions with "or what?" This allows the other person to interject another question: "Has she grown up, or what?" "Can you remember when she was just a baby, or what?" (About now a spontaneous rendition of "Sunrise, Sunset" from *Fiddler on the Roof* should be expected.)

➤ Begin questions with "what," as in "What, my *blintzes* are not good enough for you?"

➤ Drop the last word in a sentence, which is typically a direct or indirect object: "What, do you want to get killed going alone? Ira will go with." (Drop "you.")

➤ Move the subject to the end of sentences: "Is *she* getting heavy, that Esther?"

➤ Use "that" as a modifier to infer contempt: "Is Esther still dating that Norman fellow?"

➤ Use words such as "lovely" to describe actions taken by someone else that the listener should have done, too: "We got a lovely note from the Rabinowitzes for inviting them to our *seder*." Translation: "How come we never heard from you?"

➤ Ignore the word "of" if a really important word, especially the name of a food item or drink, is standing in the wings waiting to be mentioned. For example, "You want a plate pastrami?" or "How about a cup coffee?"

With a Shmaykhel

Ginsberg tells his friend: "It wasn't easy for me at first living out in the country. I used to be depressed until I got myself a paramour. It's made a tremendous difference in my life." Cohen is shocked: "A paramour? Does your wife know?" "Of course," Ginsberg answers. "And she doesn't mind?" Cohen wonders. "Why should she?" Ginsberg answers. "She doesn't care *how* I cut the grass."

Speaking Yiddish-style identifies you as a member of the Club of Jewish literati, a true *luftmentsh*, and permits you to practice proper speech patterns even when you're not actually speaking Yiddish.

Almost Identical Twins

Here's an amazing fact about many languages: Even if a tongue is totally foreign to you, you will understand quite a few words because they're so similar to their counterparts in your own language. Linguists have a word to describe these almost identical twins: They call them cognates. A perfect cognate is a Yiddish word such as *lip*. Almost as clear—what I would call a fraternal twin—are the Yiddish words *hant* or *harts*. It's almost impossible to miss the hand and the heart connection.

A Gut Vort

A **noz** is just a plain nose, but a **shnoz** or **shnozzola** is a super gift given by God to only a blessed few. Jimmy Durante proved worthy even though he was an Italian and a Catholic, proving that olfactory greatness is not restricted to the chosen people.

To give you some feeling for how many of these old friends in disguise there are, glance over this list:

dos blut (the blood)	*di lung* (the lung)
der zinger (the singer)	*der kapitan* (the captain)
der ofitsir (the officer)	*der inzhinir* (the engineer)
der aktyor (the actor)	*di aktrese* (the actress)
der fraynd (the friend)	*der kolir* (color)
gold (gold)	*zilber* (silver)
grin (green)	*vays* (white)
der numer (number)	*dos bukh* (the book)
dos postkartel (the postcard)	*der fish* (the fish)
dos ayz (the ice)	*der hunger* (the hunger)
di konferents (the conference)	*der kontrakt* (the contract)
di kopye (the copy)	*dos dokument* (the document)
di muzik (the music)	*dos konsert* (the concert)
dos papir (the paper)	*der epel* (the apple)

A dank Got (and for sure you know I mean "Thank God"), sometimes learning another language is really easy.

Oy Vey

Note that even when Yiddish and English words are identical, the word for "the" changes for Yiddish, depending on whether the word is considered masculine or feminine. But don't worry about sex now—we'll clarify all that later.

Khap a Nash

Linguists discovered that the word for "mother" in almost every language, begins with an "m" sound: Mama, *muter, mère,* and so on. That's probably because we make the sound the same way that we move our lips to nurse as an infant. Words never allow us to forget the source of our very first nourishment.

So How Come?

Proper English demands that the right way to phrase a question is, "How is it that you …?" In Yiddish, the way to say it is, "*Vi kumt es …?*" (How come?) If you say, "How come you didn't show up?" it's obviously because you're familiar with Yiddish. The "how come" phrase is one of a list of expressions that are taken directly from a Yiddish source and that are commonly used by people who don't have a clue that they're speaking the language of Jewish immigrants.

Here are some other famous examples:

➤ **Go know**—From the Yiddish, *Gey veys*. How did this colloquialism slip into common English usage? Go know.

➤ **Go talk to the wall**—From the Yiddish, *Gey red tsu der vant*. You know you don't have a chance in the world to convince someone really stubborn who will listen to you just as much as if you were talking to, well, a wall.

➤ **If you keep trying anyway, you must have a hole in the head**—From the Yiddish, *lokh in kop*. When Arnold Shulman wrote a play using this phrase as a title, *A Hole in the Head*, and Frank Sinatra starred in the movie version, a Yiddish expression made it big-time—even though we needed it like a hole in the head.

➤ **To know from nothing**—From the Yiddish *veis fun gornisht*. English really needed this Yiddishism. Just think how much more powerful it is to declare, "I know from nothing," than to simply say, "I don't know."

➤ **How's by you?**—From the Yiddish *Vi geyts bay dir*? Who can ever forget the great Yinglish version of the French nursery song, "Frère Jacques," created by Alan Sherman:

Sarah Jackman, Sarah Jackman
How's by you, how's by you?

Replace the line with, "How are you feeling?" and see how it sounds!

➤ **I could bust from ...** *(fill in the missing word)*—Assumes you really wanted to use the Yiddish word *plats* the way it appears in the original version. Yiddish exuberance demands a word such as *plats* for super emotion, and Yinglish is pleased if at least you maintain a reference to the word by saying, "I could bust."

➤ **Look who's talking**—From the Yiddish *Kuk nor ver síret!* This doesn't really want to have you see who's speaking. It's the Yiddish (now English) way of making clear that the speaker is totally unqualified to make that statement. Even if the speaker *is* qualified, what a nerve to say it, considering .... Without saying, "What a hypocrite," the point is made perhaps even in a blunter manner.

➤ **Kosher**—From the Hebrew for "suitable, proper" (from a religious perspective). Today, however, the term serves even Americans of Irish descent to identify the real McCoy. That's why the CIA won't pass on secrets to anyone unless they're approved as *kosher* recipients.

With a Shmaykhel

A worried Jew rushed to his Rabbi with a question: "What if Arafat discovers the power of praying to God at the Western Wall and goes there to ask for victory for his people over the Jews?" "Don't worry," answered the Rabbi. "He'll only be talking to the wall."

With a Shmaykhel

Seen on a bumper sticker: "If it tastes good, it's probably not kosher."

So Now You Can *Kvel*

To *kvel* is to glow with pleasure, to gush with pride, to burst with joy, usually from the achievements of your children or grandchildren. When Sadie met Sarah wheeling a baby carriage with her two little boys in it, she asked, "How old are they?" The mother *kveled* (past tense of *kvel*), "The doctor is eight months; the lawyer is two."

Don't be surprised, though, if I tell you that you're even allowed to *kvel* over your own accomplishments. So now that you know how much Yiddish is already part of your vocabulary and how familiar you are with its cadences, word sequences, and even grammar, you have a right to *kvel* just a little and be prepared to accept the challenge of the rest of this book: *Zay nisht foyl* (Don't be lazy), and turn to Part II where we finally begin to get into the heavy stuff.

The Least You Need to Know

➤ Many Yiddish words are included in standard English dictionaries.

➤ *Yinglish* is a mix between English and Yiddish.

➤ Yiddish cognates are very helpful in deciphering words from other languages.

➤ Many popular English phrases are almost literal translations from their original Yiddish sources.

Part 2

So Let's Get Started Already

You learn to swim by jumping into the water. So, too, you'll learn to speak Yiddish by jumping right in, even if at first you feel like you're sinking. Part 2 will get you started with the basics. You'll become familiar with the letters and words you'll need in the most common everyday situations.

Once you learn the sounds and the accent, you'll be introduced to a little grammar—not enough to discourage you, but just enough to get you going with pronouns, definite and indefinite articles, and the like. Before you know it, you'll master the most frequently used words and expressions, as well as the key phrases for engaging in conversations and social repartee. You'll even learn some wise idioms—so that people don't think you're an idiot.

Before long, you'll realize that people no longer think of you as an amorets, an ignoramus. With all the Yiddish you know, they'll have to acknowledge that you're a Talmid khokhom—a real scholar.

Chapter 4

It's as Easy as ABC—That's Easy?

In This Chapter

➤ What the Yiddish letters look like

➤ How to pronounce consonants and vowels

➤ The letters with different sounds and double forms

➤ Great expressions with which to surprise your friends

Letters are the building blocks of words, words become sentences, and sentences have the ability to express the most profound thoughts of humankind. There's no way you're going to learn to speak the language without having at least a passing familiarity with the individual bricks that go into the building of linguistic castles.

Unfortunately, Yiddish uses the letters of the Hebrew alphabet rather than the characters we're familiar with in English. So, learning the language is not quite "as easy as ABC." To complicate matters even further, Yiddish letters have both a printed as well as a written script version. However, for you to learn and to speak Yiddish as quickly as possible, I'll transliterate Yiddish words for you so that you can readily read them. As you become more proficient, you can then add the skill of reading Yiddish in the original. If you think about it, that's the way every child learns its native tongue—speaking first, and only later learning to read and write.

A Gut Vort

A *mitzvah,* literally a commandment, describes any good deed. The Talmud is the major work of Judaism after the Bible, with explanations of laws, biblical commentaries, and insights of the Rabbis who lived in the first five centuries of the Common Era.

Khap a Nash

As the Promised Land, Israel is referred to in the Bible as the land flowing with "milk and honey." Milk gives us life as an infant. The sweetness of honey is what makes life worth living. The child who has been nursed by his mother with her milk is then given the sweetness of honey by acquiring knowledge of the letters that will make life worthwhile.

Study this chapter to become familiar with the names of the letters, the way to pronounce them, and their special features. Keep the alphabet chart handy so that when you feel that you can move on to a higher level, you'll be able to turn the transliterations back to their original form. It's time now to meet the bit players who together form the beautiful ensemble of language.

Try It with Honey

Here's an amazing fact about Jewish history: When approximately 90 percent of humankind was illiterate, every Jewish boy above the age of 6 was taught to read and to write. Illiteracy couldn't be tolerated because it would prevent fulfillment of the major *mitzvah* of Judaism: "The study of Torah is more important than everything else" (Talmud).

And how is it possible, you ask, to get children that young to absorb knowledge that seemed beyond the reach of their adult neighbors? Modern educators should take note of the system developed over the course of centuries to teach Jewish youngsters the Hebrew alphabet.

When a young boy first entered Hebrew school, his teacher would draw an *aleph,* the first letter of the alphabet, on a tray, using honey. "Look carefully," the teacher would instruct the youngster, "how there is a slanted line, how on either side there are these little feet, one going up and one going down. Now trace the form of the letter with your tongue and lick up the honey. Taste how sweet the letter feels. Remember that its sweetness is what becomes the sweetness of Torah, and never forget what you've studied today. You have absorbed it with the honey and it is now a part of you."

You've got to admit, that was a sweet deal. Smile if you will at its simplicity, but remember that it worked!

You're free to replicate the same method with or without honey (just don't do it on the book itself—it'll get too messy). Look carefully at the following chart, moving from right to left, one line following the other:

G / Giml ג	V / Veyz בּ	B / Beyz ב	A / Alef א
Z / Zayen ז	U / Vov ו	H / Hey ה	D / Daled ד
K / Kof כּ	I / Yud י	T / Tes ט	Kh / Khes ח
M / Mem מ	L / Lamed ל	Kh / Langer Khof ך	Kh / Khof כ
S / Samekh ס	N / Langer Nun ן	N / Nun נ	M / Shlos Mem ם
F / Langer Fey ף	F / Fey פֿ	P / Pey פּ	E / Ayen ע
R / Reysh ר	K / Kuf ק	Ts / Langer Tsadik ץ	Tz / Tsadik צ
S / Sof ת	T / Tof תּ	S / Sin שׂ	SH / Shin שׁ

Every letter also has its own story. The mystics even derive a message from the size of the letters. The smallest letter in the alphabet? It's the *yud*. The largest letter? The *lamed*. So call it coincidence, but the Rabbis note that the word *Yisroel* (Israelite) begins with the smallest letter and ends with the largest because the Jewish people will start as the smallest of all nations and in the end be acknowledged as the greatest.

A Gut Vort

Kabbalah is the esoteric tradition passed on among Jewish mystics beginning in Roman times and continuing in diverse forms through the Middle Ages into the modern era.

Khap a Nash

The Torah, the five books of Moses, begins with the letter *beyz*. Wouldn't it be more appropriate, ask the Rabbis, if it started with the first letter of the alphabet rather than the second? No, they answered, *beyz* deserves the honor because it means "house"—without the home and its influence, there can be no Torah!

Every letter of the alphabet also represents a number. *Aleph* is one, *beyz* is two, and so on. In that way, words also have a numerical value that afford us deeper meanings and sometimes even prophecies. For examples of this fascinating approach, you have to get hold of books on the Kabbalah. This information is meant to be off-limits to anyone under the age of forty—and, dear reader, I don't know how old you are.

A Picture Is Worth a Thousand Words

As an ancient language, Hebrew letters have a lot in common with hieroglyphics. They began as pictorial representations of things people recognized from their surroundings. For example, look at the second letter in the previous chart, the letter *beyz*. Also called *bet* in Hebrew (which is short for the word for "house"), the letter was meant to suggest a dwelling with a roof, wall, and floor, as well as an open door as a sign of welcome for strangers.

For another example, look at the second letter on the sixth line in the chart, the letter *pey*, which in Hebrew means the word "mouth." Do you see the cute little face now, with the pug nose as well as the open mouth? Or how about the letter right before it, the *ayen*, which is Hebrew for "eye"? Do you see the two eyes almost glaring out at you at the top of the letter?

Be creative. Don't just use other people's explanations. Go over each of the letters, and see if you can create a mental picture of something the form reminds you of. Be bold. Make it dramatic. Let your mind wander, and imagine a story unfolding from the lines before you. Then keep repeating the name of the letter to yourself. Cover the letter and draw it in your own mind. Say the name of the letter aloud as you think of it. As Professor Higgins said to his "fair lady," "There, I think you've got it."

The Sound of Music

Now that you know what the letters look like, let's work a little bit on their pronunciation. Before you look at the next chart, two points deserve special attention. First, as strange as it seems, there is a letter—the *aleph*—that has no sound. A silent letter may not make any sense to you now. Eventually, you'll see how it serves a purpose as a resting place for a vowel underneath it. Just accept the fact that the very first letter of the Hebrew alphabet is wise enough to realize that even as there is a time for speech, there is also a time to be silent.

Wise Sayings

"Any Jew can sing better than the *chazen*—only at this very moment he happens to have a cold."

—Yiddish folk saying

The second point to stress is that three of the letters—the *khes*, the *khof*, and the *langer khof*—all share a sound that has no equivalent in English. Admittedly, the sound isn't pretty. I wouldn't be surprised if you'd be moved to say, "YECHHHH!" when you heard it. If you did it right, the way the Mad Comics creators intended, you'd have the sound I'm talking about. If you still don't get it, think of the old movies where Germans would yell out, "*Ach.*" Or, imagine yourself trying to clear your throat if you swallowed a bone. Yes, I know it's not pretty, but then again, I've learned to live with it, especially since my name is Blech.

Spelling a letter in English that doesn't have a sound in the language presents an interesting problem. The approved answer given by Yiddish scholars is to use the combination "kh." That makes a cantor a *khazen* and the Festival of Lights *Khanukah*. Very often, though, you'll see *chazen* and *Chanuka* as preferred options (or sometimes even *Hanuka*, ignoring the "ch" sound because it will usually not be heard anyway).

The problem arises for words that aren't as familiar as these, and a "ch" at the beginning of a word can be taken for the same sound as the first syllable for the word "church." A foolish consistency, as Ralph Waldo Emerson pointed out, "is the hobgoblin of little minds, adored by little statesmen and philosophers and divines." It's tempting to stick with one rule for every case, but there are times when transliterations will go with the "kh" and other times when the "ch" is somehow more appropriate. Don't worry—you'll know when you have to make the "chhhh" sound as clearly as if a strange object were really stuck in your throat.

Here's a handy list of Yiddish letters and sounds. As you can see, every letter has a name as well as a sound I give you in transliteration as well as an English equivalent. For now, just acquaint yourself with the letters by reading their names aloud. You'll have plenty of opportunities to become more familiar with all of them as you read Yiddish selections later in the book.

LIST OF YIDDISH LETTERS AND SOUNDS

PRINTED LETTER	YIDDISH NAME	TRANSLITERATION OF SOUND	ENGLISH EQUIVALENT
א	Shtumer Alef	Silent, therefore not shown	silent
אַ	Pasekh Alef	a	no exact equivalent, close to A in **Ma**.
אָ	Komets Alef	o	no exact equivalent, close to O in **Fo**rt
ב	Beyz	b	B
בֿ	Veyz	v	V
ג	Giml	g	G
ד	Daled	d	D
ה	Hey	h	H
ו	Vov	u	OO as in **Hoo**d
וּ	Melupm Vov	u	OO [used when ו appears next to וו. The dot distinguishes ו from וו.]
וו	Tsvey Vovn	v	V
וי	Vov Yud	oy	OY
ז	Zayin	z	Z
ח	Khes	kh	KH as in **Kh**an

PRINTED LETTER	YIDDISH NAME	TRANSLITERATION OF SOUND	ENGLISH EQUIVALENT
ט	Tes	t	T
י	Yud	i or y	EE or consonant Y
יִ	Khirek Yud	i	EE [used when stressed vowel precedes another vowel to show that י is in a different syllable.]
יי	Tsvey Yudn	ey	AY as in **Say**
ײַ	Pasekh Tsvey Yudn	ay	Y as in Dr**y**
כ	Kof	k	K
כ	Khof	kh	KH as in Ba**ch**
ך	Lange[r] Khof	kh	KH as in Ba**ch** only at the end of a word.
ל	Lamed	l	L
מ	Mem	m	M
ם	Shlos-Mem	m	M, only at the end of a word.
נ	Nun	n	N
ן	Lange[r] Nun	n	N, only at the end of a word.
ס	Samekh	s	S
ע	Ayin	e	short E as in B**e**t
פ	Pey	p	P

continues

continued

LIST OF YIDDISH LETTERS AND SOUNDS

PRINTED LETTER	YIDDISH NAME	TRANSLITERATION OF SOUND	ENGLISH EQUIVALENT
פֿ	Fey	f	F
ף	Lange[r] Fey	f	F, only at the end of a word.
צ	Tsadek	ts	TS
ץ	Lange[r] Tsadek	ts	TS, only at the end of a word.
ק	Kuf	k	K
ר	Reysh	r	R
שׁ	Shin	sh	SH
שׂ	Sin	s	S
תּ	Tof	t	T
ת	Sof	s	S
דז	Daled Zayin	dz	DZ as in towa**rds**
זש	Zayin Shin	zh	ZH as in **Zh**ivago.
דזש	Daled Zayin Shin	dzh	J
טש	Tes Shin	tsh	CH as in **Ch**arles

Show Me You're Finished

Here's one more peculiarity about Hebrew/Yiddish letters. (I promise you, this is the last surprise.) Five of the letters of the alphabet have a slightly different form when they appear at the end of a word. These are called final letters, or, in Yiddish, *lange* (larger) because they are written as larger letters than their equivalents when they have the honor of closing a word. As you can see from both charts, they are the *lange khof*, the *shlos mem* (this is the only one of the final letters that is not written larger, hence its name *shlos*, meaning "closing," or "final"), the *lange nun*, the *lange fey*, and the *lange tsadik*.

Ask me why these five letters require a different look when they close a word, and all I can tell you is this: We don't really know. There are some ingenious suggestions and explanations. One possibility suggests that it may have been a great solution to prevent run-on words and sentences before commas and periods came in use. Let's leave these theories to linguists and accept the fact that we have to know five more letters.

Here's How to Say It

The Yiddish Scientific Institute, known far better by its acronym YIVO (*Yidisher Visenshaftlikhe Institut*), established rules for standard transliteration. With slight exceptions, these guidelines are almost always followed. All consonants are pronounced close to the way they're pronounced in English. Vowels are pronounced as follows:

> *a* as in *father*
>
> *ay* as in *my*
>
> *e* as in *bed*; never silent, pronounced even when it is the final letter in a word
>
> *ey* as in *day*
>
> *i* as in *bid*, or in *bee*
>
> *o* as between *aw* in *dawn* and *O* in *done*
>
> *oy* as in *boy*
>
> *u* as in *rule*

And don't forget that the "kh" is that clear-the-throat sound, as in "Yechhhhhh," and the "zh" stands for the sound of the "s" in *pleasure*.

Khap a Nash

According to biblical law, cursing parents carries a more severe punishment than physically assaulting them. Physical pain goes away, but a hurt caused by speech can survive for a lifetime.

With a Shmaykhel

The *shadkhen* (matchmaker) assures the prospective groom that the girl he wants to introduce to him is just a shade over 20 years old. "Is that really true?" asks the young man looking at an obviously older woman. "Well," answers the *shadkhen*, "it was."

Try Speaking a *Bisel* (Little)

The best way to learn how to swim is to jump right in. So don't worry about not understanding the words yet. Just let your mouth get used to speaking full Yiddish sentences. What follows is a list of wise sayings. See if you can find a situation where the thought is appropriate, and surprise a Yiddish speaker with your brilliant insight. Call your grandparents, if you're lucky enough to have them, and see if they understand *mame-loshen*. Above all, *shem sikh nisht*—don't be embarrassed. There is a law of the universe that teaches us that God Himself will come to the aid of anyone who attempts to speak Yiddish. So get started:

➤ *A klap fargeyt, a vort bashteyt.*

(A blow passes on, a spoken word lingers on.)

➤ *A kluger farshteyt fun eyn vort tsvey.*

(A wise man hears one word and understands two.)

➤ *A ligner darf hoben a guten zikoren.*

(A liar must have a good memory.)

➤ *A mentsh iz a mol shtarker fun ayzen un a mol shvakher fun a flieg.*

(Man is sometimes stronger than iron and at other times weaker than a fly.)

➤ *Az di velt zogt, zol men gloiben.*

(If everybody says so, there's some truth to it.)

➤ *Az me hot nit tsu entfern, muz men farshvaygen.*

(If one has nothing to answer, it is best to shut up.)

➤ *Az me leygt arayn, nemt men arois.*

(If you put something in, you can take something out.)

➤ *A mentsh trakht un Got lakht.*

(Man plans and God laughs.)

➤ *Az me muz, ken men.*

(When one must, one can.)

➤ *Az me redt zikh arop fun hartsen, vert gringer.*

(When one pours out his heart, he feels lighter.)

Your assignment at the end of this chapter is to memorize at least three of the sayings you loved the most from the ones listed here. Then tell them to at least three friends. If they don't understand Yiddish, condescendingly tell them that you're amazed how someone couldn't know these basic words. Then admit that you've just started to learn Yiddish, show them this book, and convince them to buy it. (My mother says I deserve that this book becomes a bestseller.)

The Least You Need to Know

➤ Little children used to learn Hebrew/Yiddish letters by licking their images drawn in honey.

➤ Hebrew/Yiddish letters can best be memorized by connecting them with mental images of familiar objects.

➤ Some of the Hebrew/Yiddish letters have sounds that have no English equivalents.

➤ YIVO has established guidelines for a commonly accepted system of transliteration.

➤ A good way to begin studying Yiddish is to keep repeating some popular phrases and proverbs.

Chapter 5

The Basic Words

In This Chapter

➤ Ten exclamations you can't do without

➤ Learn to say "the" the right way

➤ Know how to ask questions

➤ Talking about people

➤ Little words you can't do without

A classic cartoon has a voluptuous young maiden telling her confused-looking boy-friend, "What part of *NO* don't you understand?" The word *no* is just about as clear and concise as you can get. In fact, there are a lot of other words like it. These are the nuts and bolts of any language. When used correctly, they can accomplish in seconds what lengthy sentences often are unable to convey. That's why we're going to start your Yiddish vocabulary with the one-word-says-it-all variety.

You'll find that some of these words can stand alone. With just a word, you'll sound like a scholar. Some can be added to English and *voilà*—people are sure you're bilingual. Finally, some words are so frequently used that you can't really say anything unless you know them. By now you ought to be saying, *Nu*, so let's get started.

The Ten Most Popular Words in Yiddish

I don't have statistics to back this up, but I'm willing to bet that the first ten words I'm going to teach you here are the ten most popular words in Yiddish. These words are exclamations, interjections, laments, protests, and cries that enable you to express a wide range of ideas and emotions. You'll get the hang of when to use these terms as you begin to speak the language. Before you know it, you will be able to use these words almost automatically without having to think about them. Start sprinkling these words into your everyday use of English, and they'll add a Yiddish touch to almost everything you're saying.

Make sure you memorize every single one of the following words:

1. *Nu* (sometimes also *nu-nu*)—*Nu*, what can I tell you about *nu*? Valley girls say "like" and "you know." Jews say *nu*. As a crutch word, it means "well." Depending upon the intonation, it can be a sigh, a grin, a grunt, a reproach, or a demand. It can also be an answer: "Why didn't you show up for your appointment?" "*Nu!*" It can be a question: "You know I lent you the money, so *nu*?" And if you ask me, "How can one word mean so many different things?", all I can say is, "*Nu-nu*" (translation: "Well, what are you going to do? That's the way it is.")

With a Shmaykhel

Mr. Cohen was amazed as the Chinese waiter in the *kosher* restaurant took his order in perfect Yiddish. At the end of the meal, he went over to the owner and asked him: "How did you ever get a Chinaman so dedicated to his job that he was willing to learn Yiddish?" "*Sha!*," answers the boss, "he thinks we're teaching him English."

2. *Oy*—Oy, it has been said, isn't a word—it's a vocabulary. Within it resides all the pain of the past, the discomfort of the present, and the fear of the future. *Oy* is the short form of *Oy vey iz mir* (oh, woe is to me). It can be used to react to simple frustration (*oy*, it's you!), minor tragedy (look at the way they sent me back this dress from the laundry), and true grief (*oy*, my son didn't get into medical school). The word itself doesn't make clear the level of pain. That's reserved for the intonation and the facial gestures that accompany it.

3. *Aha!*—At last I got it. Now I see. It's finally clear. The reason I couldn't find my glasses? *Aha*, I knew it, they're on my nose. The mail came and his check isn't there: *Aha*, I knew he wasn't telling me the truth. *Aha*, of course she had a boy. What else could it be, a girl?

4. *Halevai*—This is not to be confused with *halava*, a delectable treat made of honey and ground sesame seeds. *Halevai* (literally, "would that") is attached to almost every wish, desire, or blessing to make sure that the evil eye doesn't get there first to negate it. From the moment a mother welcomes her daughter to this earth she begins the litany of, "*Halevai*, she should meet a nice boy, get married, and have children." "*Halevai*, every good friend should live to 120, every enemy only to 119 so that their lives should be cut short in the middle." "*Halevai*, the sick should get better, the poor should become rich." "*Halevai*, all our prayers should be answered."

Khap a Nash

A common blessing is, "You should live to 120." That's how long Moses lived, and since he was the greatest Jew, we can't imagine anyone surpassing his life span.

5. *Epes*—Here's another real multipurpose word: I need *epes* (something). *Epes*, I can't eat: Somehow, for some reason, I have no appetite. Who has *epes*? A suggestion, anything, no matter how small, will do. I am *epes* trying to explain it to you well— somehow, some way—but I'm not 100 percent sure that you're *epes* understanding it. Still, if an impoverished person begs you, "gib *epes*," don't be cruel, and please give him something more than just a little.

A Gut Vort

Fe probably comes from the German *pfui*. English, by way of Yiddish, turned it into *phooey*. No matter how you say it, it's disgusting.

6. *Fe*—You're not going to tell me you don't understand that word! Like the Supreme Court ruled about the definition of pornography, you know *fe* when you see it. *Fe* is the correct verbal response for the ugly, the malicious, the immoral, the unspeakable. How could he walk out on his wife? *Fe*. How could they make a movie like that? *Fe*. How could he get up and give a speech like that? *Fe*. Linguists have noted the strongest words of distaste in a language usually begin with the "F" sound.

7. *Gotenyu!*—The Yiddish use this exclamation for, "Oh, my God," and it can indicate joy or despair. Referring to the Almighty adds passion to either explanation. "*Gotenyu*, he graduated!" and "*Gotenyu*, we're ruined!" are equally valid. The language of Tevye, who spent his days constantly talking to God in *Fiddler on the Roof*, clearly makes frequent use of this interjection.

8. *Efshar*—*Efshar* (maybe) you want to go out? *Efshar* (maybe) you want to make a contribution to the United Jewish Appeal? Life is full of possibilities. A major teaching of Judaism is that human beings are endowed with free will. So, the word *efshar* can often be heard to introduce a host of choices. So tell me, *efshar* you're going to study this book carefully and become a real Yiddish *mayven*?

With a Shmaykhel

A countess is lying in the magnificent Louis XIV bedroom of her imposing mansion awaiting the birth of her child. The count, her husband, is in the drawing room playing cards with the doctor. "*Mon Dieu,*" the mother-to-be cries from the bedroom. "Not yet," says the doctor to the anxious husband. "Help me," comes a second cry. The doctor continues to shuffle the cards. Finally comes a scream: "*Gotenyu!*" Says the doctor, "Now it's time."

9. *Nokh*—Any one of these three translations is correct: more, another, yet. The poor boy is hungry, give him *nokh a bisel* (literally, "more a little"). You didn't give him the full change, give him *nokh* a dollar. And the most popular usage, the use of irony and sarcasm: I should give a compliment, *nokh*? He should be glad I didn't boo him off the stage.

10. *Sha!*—Sure, you can just have somebody shut up by saying "shh." But that's not the same as using the Yiddish word for quiet: *sha*. *Sha* is about as explicit as you can get when you demand silence. One of my most vivid memories as a child is hearing the Rabbi (he was my father) having to repeatedly walk up to the pulpit and yell "*Sha!*" to quiet noisy congregants. (Why the Shah of Iran was blessed with that title is beyond me.)

The Sexy Words

Now just because I mentioned sex, please don't tell me *sha!* Nouns in Yiddish, as in many other languages (including German), have a gender. Words are masculine or feminine, even if they're inanimate, like table and chair. The definite article, the word for "the," must agree with the gender of the item you're talking about.

There are three ways to say "the" in Yiddish:

1. *Der* is used for *the* **masculine** nouns. For example, *der ta-te* (the father), *der man* (the man).

2. *Di* is used for **feminine** nouns. For example, *di mame* (the mother), *di hant* (the hand).

3. *Dos* is used for **neuter** nouns, words not characterized as either masculine or feminine. For example, *dos bukh* (the book), *dos lid* (the song).

Plural nouns always get the word *di* for "the," even if they are masculine. For example, *di ta-tes* (the fathers), *di mames*, (the mothers).

How can you tell whether a word is considered masculine, feminine, or neuter? Most often, you can't. There are some rules that at this point would only confuse you. For now, just remember that *der, di,* and *dos* all mean "the," and every plural always gets the same Yiddish definite article, *di*, as feminine words.

Oy Vey

Don't be so sure that a word is masculine or feminine just because of its meaning. The word for "beard" in Yiddish, *bord*, believe it or not, is feminine, and we say *di bord*. A girl in Yiddish is a *dos* word, *dos maydel*, and considered neuter. Go figure!

Asking Questions in Yiddish

Smart people ask questions. How else do you think they get to be so smart? It's only fools who really believe they know all the answers. As a budding Yiddish scholar, you're going to need a lot of question words. Just don't be a *noodsh* (a real pest), and try not to use them all at once. Study the following table carefully for the key words you need to have your questions answered.

Question Words in Yiddish

Word	Meaning	Example	Translation
Far vos?	Why?	*Far vos shlofst du?*	Why are you sleeping?
Ven?	When?	*Ven kumst du aheim?*	When are you coming home?
Vi azoy?	How?	*Vi azoy tust du dos?*	How do you do that?
Vi vayt?	How far?	*Vi vayt forst du?*	How far are you going?
Vi lang?	How long?	*Vi lang vardst du?*	How long are you waiting?
Ver?	Who?	*Ver kumt?*	Who's coming?
Vos?	What?	*Vos iz dos?*	What is this?

Getting Personal in Yiddish

Next on the agenda are the personal pronouns. Once you know them, it won't take you long to be able to speak in full sentences:

I is *ikh*

You (singular) is *du*

He is *er*

She is *zi*

Now let's add a verb to every one of these pronouns and see how it's conjugated:

I learn	*ikh lern*
You learn	*du lernst*
He learns	*er lernt*
She learns	*zi lernt*

Now do the same with *zogn*, which is Yiddish for "to say":

I say	*Ikh zog*
You say	_____
He says	_____
She says	_____

Try to continue the series with these verbs:

I sing	*Ikh zing*
You sing	_____
He sings	_____
She sings	_____
I live	*Ikh leb* ·
You live	_____
He lives	_____
She lives	_____

Now let's move on to plurals:

We learn	*Mir lernen*
You are learning	*Ir lernt*
They are learning	*Zey lernen*

Do the same with *zogn* and *zingen*:

We say	_____
You are saying	_____
They are saying	_____
We sing	_____
You are singing	_____
They are singing	_____

Here's Looking at You

The word for "you," *du*, is very concerned with respect. *Du* is *you* if you're a friend, a peer, and someone of the same social standing. For anyone who is not in an intimate relationship with you, the more respectful second-person plural, *ir*, is used. For example, when talking to your child, you would say, "*Vi filst du zikh?*" (How are you feeling?). By contrast, when speaking to your teacher, your Rabbi, or a prominent stranger, you would ask, "*Vi filt ir zikh?*"

Khap a Nash

Amazingly enough, the form of address used when speaking to God is *du*. The intimacy of the relationship is obviously more significant than the difference of status between humankind and God. We have known each other for so long that God wants us to address Him as *du*.

Let's Be Objective

One last thing about personal pronouns. You know that there is a big difference between *he* and *him*. One is the subject, and the other is the object: He does; please hand it to him. Note how Yiddish speakers use *me*, *you*, *him*, and *her* with a verb such as *give*:

Give it to me	*Gib mir*
Give it to you	*Gib dir*
Give it to him	*Gib im*
Give it to her	*Gib ir*

Now for the plurals:

Give it to us	*Gib unz*
Give it to you	*Gib aykh*
Give it to them	*Gib zey*

For practice, try to ask for help in Yiddish, using the word *help*:

Help me	<u>*Help mir*</u>
Help him	_____
Help us	_____
Help them	_____

Did you get them all right? Grade yourself 100.

Short and Sweet

Sometimes it's not a picture that's worth a thousand words; it's possible for a word to be worth a thousand pictures. They're short and sweet and leave no doubt about your intent. Our conversations are peppered with them, and we'd probably be struck dumb if we didn't have them. The following table provides a list of basic words you'll need to know. Look them over often and try to use them whenever you can so that they become part of your basic vocabulary.

Words You Can't Do Without

English	Yiddish	Example	English
yes	yo	Yo, ikh kum.	Yes, I'm coming.
no	neyn	Neyn, ikh vil nit	No, I don't want ....
thanks	dank	A Dank far di Matone.	Thanks for the gift.
here	do	Ikh voyn do.	I live here.
there	dorten	Dorten iz kalt.	There it's cold.
to	tsu	tsu zen mayn khaver	to see my friend
from	fun	Fun vanet kumt ir?	Where are you from?
with	mit	kave mit milkh	coffee with milk
without	on	on a dayge	without a problem
in	in	in a shif	in a boat

English	Yiddish	Example	English
on	oyf	oyf a trep	on a step
near	noent	noent tsu mir	near to me
far	vayt	vayt avek	far away
in front of	far	far mayn hoyz	in front of my house
behind	hinter	hinter der tir	behind the door
inside	in erveynik	In erveynik iz varm.	Inside it's warm.
outside	in droysen	In droysen iz finster.	Outside it's dark.
nothing	gornit	Es iz gornit mit gornit.	It's nothing with nothing.
many	sakh	a sakh tsores	many problems
few	veynik	veynik kroyvim	few relatives
enough	genug	Genug iz ge'nug.	Enough is enough.
too much	tsu fil	Ikh veg tsu fil.	I weigh too much.
good	gut	Dos essen iz gut.	The food is good.
better	beser	Es ken zayn beser.	It could be better.
best	best	Vos iz best?	What's best?
bad	shlekht	Zayn hunt iz shlekht.	His dog is bad.
worse	erger	Es ken zayn erger.	It could be worse.
again	vider	Es regent vider.	It's raining again.
also	oykh	Er vil oykh kumen.	He also wants to come.
now	itst	Itst iz tsayt.	Now is the time.
immediately	teykef	Ikh kum teykef.	I'm coming immediately.
soon	bald	Bald iz sumer.	Soon it's summer.
as soon as possible	vos gikher	Vos gikher, als beser	The sooner, the better
later	shpeter	Shpeter iz tsu shpet.	Later is too late.
slowly	pamelekh	Er geyt tsu pamelekh.	He's going too slowly.
quickly	gikh	Kum gikh.	Come quickly.
look out	hit zikh	Hit zikh farn ayz.	Watch out for the ice.
listen	hert	Hert vos ikh zog.	Hear what I say.
stop	oyfheren	Amol muz men oyfheren.	Sometimes you've got to stop.

With a Shmaykhel

The volunteer nurse from the United States in the Israeli hospital thought she was familiar with all the medical terms doctors used to memorize the condition of patients on the chart attached to their beds. She was stumped, though, when she saw the diagnosis: *gimel mem gimel*—three Hebrew letters with a period after each one. When she saw the attending doctor, he explained: "For this hypochondriac, I just write the acronym for *gornit mit gornit*—nothing with nothing."

Time for Some Exercise

Some of the words in these proverbs you already know. See if you can figure out the meaning of the entire sentence:

> *A gut vort iz beser fun a nedove.*
>
> *A guter soine eyder a shlekhter fraynt.*
>
> *Di zun shaynt likhtiger nokh a regen.*
>
> *Dos harts iz a halber novi.*
>
> *Got iz a foter; dos mazel iz a shtif-foter.*

And here's what they mean, in order:

> A good word is better than a donation.
>
> Better is a good enemy than a bad friend.
>
> The sun shines brighter after a shower.
>
> The heart is half a prophet.
>
> God is a father; luck is a stepfather.

To make it all stick, reread this chapter one more time and then take a well-deserved rest. You've come *zer vayt* (very far). And just think, you've only finished five chapters!

The Least You Need to Know

➤ Words such as *oy, nu,* and *fe* are essential for almost any conversation in Yiddish.

➤ The word for "the" depends on whether the noun is masculine, feminine, neuter, or plural.

➤ Without the right question words, we'll never get the answers.

➤ Pronouns identify us, and they differ when they are used as subjects or objects.

➤ Short words are really important ideas in little packages, and we need to know them all.

Chapter 6

Meeting People and Making Friends

In This Chapter

➤ Learning how to greet people

➤ Asking polite questions

➤ Giving the right answers

➤ A little grammar about infinitives and conjugations

➤ Knowing how to say goodbye

God put Adam into a place called Paradise, but Adam wasn't happy there. The surroundings may have been beautiful, but there was one thing missing that made his life miserable. Adam had nobody to talk to. Loneliness, as the Yiddish proverb puts it, is worse than death. People *do* need people, and life that isn't shared with others is no less than a living hell.

Scholars have pointed out that the Yiddish (and Hebrew) word for "life" is *khayim*. Grammatically, that makes it a plural. The reason? A life that's lived in the singular, for yourself alone, has no meaning. As Voltaire said, friendship "is the marriage of the soul." The Bible says it most succinctly: "It is not good for a person to be alone."

Years ago, Dale Carnegie made a fortune writing a book called *How To Make Friends and Influence People*. Prepare yourself for the Yiddish version as this chapter gets you started reaching out to others, knowing just what to say, and becoming familiar with the words that will make you a good conversationalist. More important, you'll also become a wonderful friend.

Saying Hello

Greetings in Yiddish are more than simple hellos. They represent a ritual that takes into account the person and the time, offers a prayer, and calls for a special response. Note the different possibilities for each of these greetings:

Khap a Nash

Sholem Aleykhem is the name of a beautiful song sung by observant Jews upon their return from synagogues on Friday night before beginning the Sabbath meal. It welcomes the angels who, according to tradition, make their appearance for this festive occasion and bless the family.

Oy Vey

Be sure to say *gezuntheit* when somebody sneezes. Tradition has it that in biblical times, people died with a sneeze, a soul departing through the nose as it had entered with the creation of Adam. In almost all cultures, there is a comparable blessing, just as in English we say, "God bless you."

➤ *Sholem Aleykhem*—The literal translation is "peace be upon you." The word *Sholem* is also another name for God. The greeting, therefore, also contains a request for divine protection. The proper response to *Sholem Aleykhem* is *Aleykhem Sholem*: "What you wish for me, I immediately return to you" (emphasizing the "upon you" first, as if to say that you deserve it more than I do).

➤ *Gut morgen*—"Good morning." The response to *Gut morgen* is *gut yohr*, a good year: What you wish for me, I multiply hundreds of times over.

➤ *Guten ovent*—"Good evening." The response is "*guten ovent.*"

➤ *A gute nakht*—"Good night." This is said upon leaving or going to bed. The proper responses can be: *A gute nakht tsu dir* ("Goodnight to you"); *Shlof gezunt* ("Sleep well," familiar); *Shloft gezunt* ("Sleep well," formal); and *Zise khaloymos* ("Sweet dreams").

➤ *Gut Shabes*—"A good Sabbath." Wishing someone a good Sabbath is appropriate all day Friday or even earlier if you won't see the person again before Friday night when the Sabbath begins. It's similar to the secular, "Have a good weekend." On the entire Sabbath day, *Gut Shabes* is the appropriate greeting instead of allusions to morning, afternoon, or night.

➤ *Gut Vokh*—"A good week." The week begins on Saturday night after the *Havdalah* service separating the holiness of the Sabbath from the days that follow. The division between sacred and profane outweighs the traditional "good evening" of the other six nights of the week.

➤ *Gut Yontef*—"Good holiday." *Yontef* is a Yiddish distortion of the Hebrew *yom tov*, good day or holiday. Pronouncing *yom tov* rapidly somehow turned the words into *yontef*. (There is no historic validity to the claim that a Jew met the Pope on Passover and told him *Gut yontef*, Pontiff.) The proper response to *Gut yontef* is *Gut yor*, fulfilling once more the ideal of giving even more than getting.

➤ *L'shonoa toyva tikosevu*—"May you be inscribed for a good year." On *Rosh Hashanah*, when Jewish tradition teaches that God decides on people's fate for the coming year and writes down His decree in the heavenly Book of Life, it's appropriate to offer a prayer instead of the standard greeting. Traditional Jews switch to these words an entire month before the High Holy Day season. The proper response is either a repetition of the same words or *gam atem*—"you, too."

➤ *Halo*—Yes, you guessed it, that's the Yiddish for "hello." It's *ha*, like when you laugh (ha ha ha), followed by *lo*, as in law. Yinglish won out and adopted the word with its somewhat altered pronunciation. Remarkably enough, though, it's almost universally understood that this greeting is valid in Yiddish only for answering the telephone. (The psychology behind that is probably worthy of a Ph.D. study.)

A Gut Vort

Havdalah is the religious ritual bringing the Sabbath to an end. It is recited over a cup of wine, together with spices and a candle, emphasizing the *Havdalah*—the separation—between the holy and the profane.

Oy Vey

What do you do if **yontef,** a Jewish holiday, coincides with the Sabbath? Which greeting comes first? The Rabbis reply, because Sabbath comes more frequently than any other holiday, it is holier and should therefore be acknowledged first. The right way is: *Gut Shabes, Gut Yontef.*

Opening Questions

A bore, it has been said, is someone whose only interest in any meeting is "me." A good conversationalist is interested in the other person. The following table lists some of the most basic opening questions on meeting a friend or upon greeting a stranger.

I'd Like to Ask You ...

English	Yiddish
How are you? (familiar)	*Vos makhstu?*
How are you? (formal)	*Vos makht ir?*
What's new?	*Vos hert zikh?*
So what's new?	*Vos hert zikh epes?*
What's the good news?	*Vos hert zikh epes guts?*
How are you doing?	*Vos makht a Yid?* (Literally, "How is a Jew?")
What's your name? (familiar)	*Vi heistu?*
What's your name? (formal)	*Vi heist ir?*
Where do you come from? (familiar)	*Fun vanet kumstu?*
Where do you come from? (formal)	*Fun vanet kumt ir?*
Where do you come from, neighbor? (familiar)	*Fun vanet bistu a landsman?*
Where do you come from, neighbor? (formal)	*Fun vanet zeit ir a landsman?*
From where does a Jew come? (if the person you're speaking to is Jewish)	*Fun vanet kumt a Yid?*

A Little More About "You"

The most popular greeting of all, *vos makhstu?* (how are you?), illustrates an interesting rule of grammar about the word "you" when it appears in a contraction.

Let's backtrack a little first and review the conjugation of a word such as *makh*, which is very similar to the English "make" and means "make" or "do." The forms with the different pronouns are as follows:

Ikh makh	I make, I do
du makhst	you make, you do
er makht	he makes, he does
zi makht	she makes, she does
mir makhen	we make, we do
ir makht	you (plural) make, you do
zei makhen	they make, they do

Now here's the rule: If the subject of a sentence is *du* (you) and it comes after the verb, then the verb fuses with the *du* to form one combination word. For example, *makhst du* becomes *makhstu* (pronounced with the t, not the d, sound). It's a simple contraction, and it works only for the familiar, singular form of you. No other personal pronouns can be merged with the verb in this manner.

Giving the Right Answers

If the other person went first and started the conversation with the familiar "How are you?", you have a number of options for your response:

➤ If things are fine with you or that's what you want the person to believe (or even if you just don't want to go into detail), you can use any of these replies:

> *Borukh hashem*—Blessed be God
>
> *Got tsu danken*—Thank God
>
> *A dank*—Thank you (the implication is "fine")

➤ If you don't want to go overboard with a positive response because you just lost your job, your wife ran off with her lover, or your daughter just charged an extra thousand dollars on your credit card, you might prefer one of these alternatives:

> *Gants gut*—Pretty good
>
> *Nish-koshe*—Not too bad
>
> *A-zoy*—So-so (this word is always accompanied by face and hand gestures—you know what I mean)

S'ken alemol zayn beser.—It could always be better.

S'ken alemol zayn erger.—It could always be worse.

➤ Or, if you want to really give it a Yiddish twist, it's perfectly okay to answer the question with a question, like so:

> *Vos zol ikh makhen?*—How should I be doing?
>
> *Vos makhstu?*—How are *you* doing? (familiar; emphasize the final *du*)
>
> *Vos makht ir?*—How are *you* doing? (formal)

If you're hoarse and you can't really speak, Yiddish lets you act out an answer with your hands, facial expressions, or a shrug, all of which are also perfectly acceptable.

Oy Vey

Be careful never to pronounce the name of God as written in the Bible. That would be taking His name in vain. Instead, use the word **Hashem,** which is Hebrew for "the name," as an alternative. Its meaning is obvious to every Jew.

Wise Sayings

"A pessimist is a mis-fortune teller."

—Anonymous

Infinitives and Introductions

You should know by now that a verb in its infinitive form (the form that names the action, for example, to sing, to speak, to listen) always ends in *–en* or *–n*. For example, *reden* is the Yiddish for "to speak."

Here are some infinitives with their *–n* endings:

> *kenen* (to know)
>
> *voynen* (to reside, to live)
>
> *zingen* (to sing)
>
> *esen* (to eat)
>
> *kuken* (to see)
>
> *heysen* (to call)

Oy Vey

Be careful: **Voynen** and **leben** mean different kinds of living. *Voynen* is where you live—your home, your dwelling place. *Leben* is living as in being alive. *Ikh voyn in New York* (I live in New York). *Ikh leb, barukh Hashem, in gezunt* (I live, thank God, in good health).

Let's take *heysen* and conjugate it in all its forms so that we can make proper introductions. Fill in the names of your friends and family, and create the sentences that will identify everyone:

Ikh heys _____.	My name is _____ (literally, I am called).
Du heyst _____.	Your name is _____.
Er heyst _____.	His name is _____.
Zi heyst _____.	Her name is _____.
Mir heysen _____.	Our names are _____.
Ir heyst _____.	Your names are _____.
Zey heysen _____.	Their names are _____.

Now you can be a social butterfly, a master of ceremonies, or even the Rabbi who greets all the guests at the door of the synagogue.

Did You Notice?

Go back to the form for the first-person singular of *heysen*. Now look at the other cases. Do you notice the similarity? The conjugation for the third-person singular (he and she) is the same as the second-person plural, always: *Er heyst, zi heyst, ir heyst.*

Can you spot one more pair where the forms are the same? The first-person plural, *mir* (we), and the third-person plural, *zey* (they), are also always conjugated the same way: *Mir heysen* and *zey heysen.* That makes it at least a little bit easier, doesn't it?

Now try this for fun: Conjugate *kenen*, which means "to know," and remember that at long, long last when you write the words *Ikh ken Yiddish*, you're finally telling the truth! Here goes:

Ikh _____

du _____

er _____

zi _____

mir _____

ir _____

zey _____

Be Polite

There's a special phrase for proper etiquette in Yiddish. It's called *derekh eretz*. A famous proverb has it that *derekh erets geit afilu far Tora*: Etiquette (or proper behavior) precedes even the laws of the Torah. The following table lists some polite phrases that you should commit to memory.

Polite Phrases You Should Know

Yiddish	English
Tzi ken ikh eikh forshtelen ____?	May I introduce ____?
Es frayt mikh eikh tsu kenen.	I am happy to make your acquaintance.
Vos makht ayer mishpokhe?	How's your family?
Zetst zikh avek zayt azoy gut.	Sit down, please.
Ikh hob zeyr gut farbrakht.	I enjoyed myself very much.
Ikh hof az mir velen zikh bald vider zen.	I hope to see you again soon.
Git mir ayer adres.	Give me your address.
Git mir ayer telefon numer.	Give me your telephone number.
A grus ayer mishpokhe.	My regards to your family.
Mazel tov.	Congratulations.
Mazel tov tzum geboyrentog.	Happy birthday.

Asking a Question

There are three ways to ask a simple question in Yiddish. The easiest way is just to change your intonation. *Du bist Goldberg* (You are Goldberg) can go from statement to question just from the tone of your voice. *Du bist Goldberg?*—I can't believe it!

Alternatively, you can also reverse the word order: *Bist du Goldberg?* The implication is that the questioner is somewhat more incredulous that you, of all people, are really Goldberg.

A Gut Vort

Mazel tov literally means "a good constellation." While Jews don't believe that the stars determine your fate—Judaism stresses free will as a central religious belief—it doesn't hurt to hope that the configuration of the planets are also in your favor.

Finally, you can preface the question with the word *tzi*: *Tzi bist du Goldberg?* The word *tzi* has no English translation. It's often added to indicate that a question is on the way, especially a question that bears on a very important issue. In this case, you're saying that Goldberg has been missing for years. Is it indeed possible that this person is the one you've been looking for? The phrase *"Iz er a gut kind?"* (Is he a good child?) is a simple question that can be asked of his teacher. By contrast, *"Tzi iz er a guter man?"* is a question properly put to a matchmaker who suggests that this person is worthy of your daughter.

Parting Is Such Sweet Sorrow

Yes, it's already time to say goodbye. So let's conclude this chapter with some typical expressions suitable for parting:

➤ *A gutn*—A good one (obviously, the forerunner of "Have a nice day")

➤ *Zay gezunt*—Be well

➤ *A grus in der heym*—Regards home

To which I hope you will have the decency to respond: *Ir oych* (Same to you).

The Least You Need to Know

➤ Most ways of saying "hello" in Yiddish take into account the time of day or the special nature of the occasion.

➤ Etiquette, *derekh erets*, is extremely important.

➤ There are many standard forms of address and aspects of polite conversation.

➤ Infinitives and conjugations are fairly easy to remember and a must for learning Yiddish.

The Days of Our Lives

Jews are always in a hurry, perhaps because their survival has so often been threatened. Not surprisingly, time is very important, and there is an almost obsessive concern with its passage. For example, it is not uncommon for a Jewish mother to ask her teenage daughter or son, "So when already will you find a nice doctor or lawyer to settle down with?" or "So when already are you going to make plans to enter medical school?"

More significantly, time defines the moments of meeting with God. Holidays and holy days are the focus of the entire year. Every week has as its goal the seventh day, the *Shabes*. From Sunday through Friday, Jews had to work for a living. It was the *Shabes*, though, which gave them life itself and a reason for living. In this chapter, you'll learn how to identify the days, the months, and the seasons, as well as how to tell time and count the numbers that summarize the years of our lives.

Is It *Shabes* Yet?

If you've ever gone on a very long car trip with your children, you must have learned two things: 1. Don't ever do it again; 2. The most frequently asked question, beginning in the suburbs of Manhattan as you are on the way to Los Angeles, is "Are we there yet?"

The Jewish equivalent to the question children ask when they travel is the way days are identified. Since ancient times, days have no independent name but are simply referred to as "the first day to *Shabes*," "the second day to *Shabes*," and so on. The real importance of the secular day rests only in its proximity to the holy Sabbath. Jews long for the day devoted to the life of the spirit, and all the days of the work they merely want to know, "Are we there yet?"

That probably explains why the Yiddish names for the days of the week, having no Hebrew sources available, became almost exact duplicates of the German words for them:

Sunday	*Zuntik*
Monday	*Montik*
Tuesday	*Dinstik*
Wednesday	*Mitvokh*
Thursday	*Donershtik*
Friday	*Fraytik*

Khap a Nash

For many centuries, words in the Hebrew language had been pronounced in the Ashkenazic manner used for prayer. The word *Shabbos* for Sephardim turns the final "s" sound into a "t" and alters the "o" to an "a." Hence, *Shabbos* becomes *Shabbat*. Modern Hebrew has adopted the Sephardic pronunciation, so an Israeli will always say *Shabbat Shalom*. Those who continue to prefer Yiddish even in Israel will wish you a *Gut Shabes*.

Only the seventh day, *Shabes*, shares no connection with the original German. Instead, it refers to its Hebrew origin, *Shabbos*, for its name.

The Months and the Seasons

In the Bible, months, just like days, were identified solely by number. It was only during the years of exile that Jews adopted names for their months, like their Babylonian and Persian neighbors. These months, in accordance with the Jewish calendar, are lunar months of 29 or 30 days, with a leap month added 7 out of every 19 years to reconcile the year with the solar passage of time. Jewish months, therefore, only roughly but never exactly correspond to English counterparts.

That's why the Yiddish names for the months of the secular calendar are identical—with just a little adjustment for Yiddish pronunciation—to the way in which we know them:

January	*Yanuar*	July	*Yuli*
February	*Feber*	August	*Oygust*
March	*Merts*	September	*September*
April	*April*	October	*October*
May	*Mey*	November	*November*
June	*Yuni*	December	*Detsember*

The four seasons are these:

Spring	der friling	Autumn	der harbst
Summer	der zumer	Winter	der vinter

Side by Side

You may very often find months referred to by their Hebrew names. Remember that they do *not* refer to a specific equivalent English month. However, they usually overlap, as shown in the following table.

The Months of the Year

Hebrew Month	English Month
Tishrei	September/October
Cheshvan	October/November
Kislev	November/December
Tevet	December/January
Shvat	January/February
Adar	February/March
Adar Sheni (second *Adar*)	(the leap month, 7 years out of 19) February/March
Nissan	March/April
Iyar	April/May
Sivan	May/June
Tammuz	June/July
Av	July/August
Elul	August/September

An Ode to Potatoes

An old folk song gives expression to the day-in, day-out sameness of the week, with its one-dish menu, and the longing for *Shabes* with its new dish of yet again the same food prepared in a different style. The lyrics of this song are a great way to review the days of the week and also to add a few more words to your vocabulary:

Hebrew	English
Bulbes	Potatoes
Zuntik—bulbes,	Sunday—potatoes,
Montik—bulbes,	Monday—potatoes,
Dinstik un mitvokh—bulbes,	Tuesday and Wednesday—potatoes,
Donershtik un fraytik—bulbes,	Thursday and Friday—potatoes,
Shabes in a novene—a bulbe-kugele,	Saturday for a change—potato pudding,
Zuntik—vayter bulbes!	Sunday—again potatoes!
Broyt mit bulbes,	Bread with potatoes,
Fleysh mit bulbes,	Meat with potatoes,
Varemes un vetshere—bulbes,	Lunch and supper—potatoes,
Ober un vider—bulbes.	Again and again—potatoes.
Eyn mol in a novene—a bulbe-kugele,	Once for a change—a potato pudding,
Zuntik—vayter bulbes!	Sunday—again potatoes!
Ober—bulbes	Again—potatoes,
Vider—bulbes	Again and again—potatoes,
Ober un vider—bulbes	Time and again—potatoes,
Vider un ober—bulbes	Again and again—potatoes
Shabes nokhn tsholnt—a bulbe-kugele,	Saturday after the *tsholnt*—a potato pudding,
Zuntik—vayter bulbes!	Sunday again—potatoes!

Khap a Nash

Tsholnt is an ideal dish for the Shabes midday meal, because cooking is prohibited on this day. *Tsholnt* is cooked before Shabes and kept warm on the stove the entire day.

At least on *Shabes* they also had *tsholnt*, a delicious stew of meat, beans, onions, carrots, and, you guessed it, potatoes. That's probably why Jews never said TGIF (Thank God it's Friday). For them, it was always TGIS—Thank God it's *Shabes*.

Units of Time

For Einstein time may be relative, but for the rest of us when we schedule a family reunion, we much prefer that our relatives be on time. If there's one thing time teaches us, it's precision. Every second counts, and our timepieces remind us of the exactitude of its passage. The words that define the moments of time are equally precise. It's crucial for you to know them so that if you say, "Wait a minute," you won't come back in an hour.

Use the following table to identify the time periods, from a second (there is no word for a nanosecond in Yiddish) to a millennium:

Time Periods

English	Yiddish (Singular)	Yiddish (Plural)
second	*di sekunde*	*di sekundes*
minute	*di minut*	*di minutin*
hour	*di sho*	*di sho-en*
day	*der tog*	*di teg*
24-hour day	*der me-es l'es*	*di mislesn*
week	*di vokh*	*di vokhen*
month	*der khodesh*	*di khadoshim*
year	*dos yor*	*di yoren*
decade	*der yortsendlik*	*di yortsendliker*
century	*der yorhundert*	*di yorhunderter*
millennium	*der yortoyzent*	*di yortoyzenter*

Note that although the words for minute, hour, and year have plural forms, they are nonetheless expressed in the singular when combined with a specific number. For example, "wait 10 minutes" translates into *vart tzen minut*, not *minutin*. If it's a conceptual time unit with no specific number—such as, the years fly—then you'd say *di yoren fliyen*.

Timely Words and Expressions

We may not realize how much of our lives is determined by time until we notice how many common words and expressions revolve around it.

Khap a Nash

The very first commandment given to the Jews by God, preceding even the Ten Commandments, was to establish a calendar. To a people about to be freed from slavery, God taught that freedom allowed former slaves the opportunity to be in control of their own time.

Time and Time Again

English	Yiddish
today	*haynt*
tomorrow	*morgen*
yesterday	*nekhten*
the day before yesterday	*eyernekhten*
the day after tomorrow	*ibermorgen*
a week ago	*farakhtogen* (literally, eight days ago)
daily	*teglekh*
day to day	*togteglekh*
weekly	*vokhntlekh*
this year	*hayntiks yor*
year in, year out	*yorayn, yoroys*
next year	*iberayor*
last year	*farayorn*
the coming (Sunday, Monday, and so on)	*kumendiken (Zundik, Montik)*
What's today's date?	*Der vifelter iz haynt?*
just a second	*a sekunde,* or *a minutkle*
just one moment	*a moment*
a little while	*a vaylinke*
quite a while	*a hipshe vayl*
now	*itzter*
then (at that time)	*demolt*
before	*far*
after	*nokh*
during	*beshas*
at the same time	*tzu der zelbiker tzeit*

Wise Idioms

Some Yiddish expressions take for granted a basic knowledge of Jewish history, the Bible, the holidays, and even folk tales and legends. Using them identifies you as a real *talmid khokhom*, an obvious scholar. Memorize the expressions in the following table with special care, and watch the stunned response you get when you use them.

Say It in Yiddish

English	Yiddish	Comment
a long, long time ago	*fun khmelnitskis tsayten* (literally, "from Chmeilnitski's times")	Refers to the terrible period of massacres of Jews in the Ukraine in 1648 and 1649 led by the murderous Bogdan Chmeilnitski. Considered the most horrible of persecutions until the Holocaust, it was vividly remembered for centuries and served as a time marker to ensure that we never forget.
seldom	*ayn mol in a shmitah* (literally, "once in a sabbatical")	Refers to the biblical law that slaves had to be freed after six years of servitude. The seventh year, corresponding to the holiness of the seventh day, the Sabbath, was "the sabbatical year," which brought freedom to all.
very seldom	*ayn mol in a yoyvel* (literally, "once in a Jubilee")	Refers to the Jubilee Year, which occurred in 50-year intervals. Slaves who refused to go free in the seventh sabbatical year could opt for continued servitude, although the Bible was not pleased with their decision. The ear of the slave who chose to remain had to be pierced, symbolically expressing the fact that he didn't hear the message of the first commandment identifying God as the one who took us out of the bondage of Egypt. The choice of additional servitude had its limits, though. The Jubilee Year proclaimed "liberty throughout the land unto all the inhabitants thereof." (Leviticus 25:10)
very long	*lang vi der golus* (literally, "long as the Diaspora")	Equates length with the 2,000-year-long Jewish expulsion from the Holy Land.
a very short time	*fun tayanis Ester biz Purim* (literally, "from the fast of Esther to Purim")	Refers to the time between two consecutive days. In the briefest of moments, Jews went from weeping to rejoicing as the decree of wicked Haman was overturned and Jews were permitted to defend themselves. Sometimes the passage of but a moment can accomplish a miracle!
until a ripe old age	*biz Metushelakh's yoren* (literally, "until Methuselah's years")	Takes for granted that you remember that Methuselah, who according to the Book of Genesis lived 969 years, holds the biblical Guinness record for longevity.

The biblical verse proclaiming the ideal of freedom for all became the text inscribed on the Liberty Bell prominently displayed in Philadelphia, Pennsylvania. Its association with the Bible made it a rallying cry for the colonists who sought to break away from servitude to Great Britain. The significance of the Jubilee being in the 50th year is that the number 50 comes after the square of the holy number of 7. The seventh day, the Sabbath, multiplied by itself, 7 times 7, is 49. The Jews received the Torah on the 50th day after leaving Egypt. Every 50th year is an especially holy one as well.

So How Old Are You?

Yes, it's true, as Tevye sings in *Fiddler on the Roof*, "Sunrise, sunset, quickly flow the years." But tell me, *Vi alt zent ir?* (How old are you?) Or, if we're a little more familiar, *Vi alt bist du?* The answer, of course, depends on whether you are a man or a woman. For a woman, the correct response is *Freg nisht*—Don't ask. For a man—or for a woman who doesn't care if others know her real age—the response begins with the words *Ikh bin* followed by the correct number, *alt*. You'll need these cardinal numbers for many other purposes aside from divulging your age, so it is imperative that you become familiar with them:

one	*eynts*	eleven	*elf*
two	*tsvey*	twelve	*tzvelf*
three	*dray*	thirteen	*draytzen*
four	*fir*	fourteen	*fertzen*
five	*finf*	fifteen	*fuftzen*
six	*zeks*	sixteen	*zekhtzen*
seven	*zibn*	seventeen	*zibetzen*
eight	*akht*	eighteen	*akhtzen*
nine	*nayn*	nineteen	*nayntzen*
ten	*tzen*	twenty	*tzvontzik*
thirty	*dreisik*	eighty	*akhtzik*
forty	*fertzik*	ninety	*neintzik*
fifty	*fuftzik*	hundred	*hundert*
sixty	*zekhtzik*	thousand	*toyznt*
seventy	*zibetzik*	million	*milyon*

Combining Numbers

When it comes to compound numbers, Yiddish is not that different from English or other Indo-Germanic languages. Once you get beyond 20 in English, you simply say,

21, 22, and so on until you get to 30. In Yiddish, we do the same with one minor difference: Place the smaller unit first and add the word *un* (and)—22 is *tsvey un tzvontzik*; 23 is *dray un tzvontzik,* and so on.

You'll notice that I skipped the number 21. That's because where one (1) is used in combination, it changes from *eynts* to the shorter *eyn.* So, 21 is *eyn un tzvontzik*; 31 is *eyn un draysik;* and so on.

Now try to say your age in Yiddish. Follow up with the age of your wife (if she'll let you), the ages of your children (if you remember them), and the winning numbers for next week's lottery. (Then e-mail them to me immediately so that I can check them for accuracy.)

One last point to remember: So far I've done double-digit combinations and remembered to put the smaller number first. For example, in Yiddish, 48 is 8 and 40; 71 is 1 and 70. In the multiple digit combinations, however, where you're into the hundreds, thousands, and millions, the largest number goes first. Thus, the prayer that you live until 120 is *biz hundert un tzvontzik.* For the extended wish that you live until 121—because I wouldn't want you to die suddenly—the number is *hundert un ayn un tzvontzik.* Got it?

Try 365 for the days in the year. If you said *dray hundert un finf un zekhtzik,* you got it right! How about 5,271? The correct answer is *finf toyzent tsvey hundert un ein un zibetzik.* That one makes you the grand prize winner! (The grand prize allows you to buy another copy of this book.)

What Time Is It?

If you can tell your age, you can also tell the time. Yiddish has already allowed for the phrase *Vat* time *iz* it? to be accepted. However, far more correct as a question is *Vifil iz der zeyger?* (literally, "How much is the clock?")

If it's one o'clock, the answer by the hour is *es iz* (or the contraction *s'iz) eynts azeyger.* If it's ten minutes after one, say *s'iz tzen minut nokh eyntz.* If it's twenty-four minutes after one and you want to be *that* exact, say, *s'iz fir un tsvontzik minut nokh eyntz.* If you're coming at two o'clock, say *ich kum tsvey azeyger.* You don't need the preposition "at"; you just get right to the point. Hours and minutes are given consecutively without using the word for hours. If it's 8:30, say *s'iz akht ur draysig.*

With a Shmaykhel

Abie is chasing Jake. "Why are you running?" Abie's friend asks after stopping him. "Because," Abie sputters, "he had the nerve to tell me that at *halb tzen,* I should kiss his behind." "So why are you running?" Abie's friend asks him. "You still have half an hour!"

However, half hours allow for two alternatives of expressing the time. For example, instead of saying *s'iz akht ur draysik*, the far more common form in Yiddish, as in English, is to say *halb nokh akht* (half past eight). As in German, you can also say *halb nayn*—half before the following hour (in this case, nine o'clock).

Oy Vey

As the man said to the lost tourist who wanted to know how to get to Carnegie Hall: "Practice, practice, practice." To make the contents of this chapter stick, you must practice as well. Tell your friends what time it is in Yiddish, and make sure you do it for several hours so that you can keep changing all the numbers. Remember, a broken clock is right only twice a day, and you want to be correct every time.

Note that quarter hours also have English equivalents in Yiddish:

a quarter to	*a fertel tsu*
a quarter past	*a fertel nokh*

The final thing you want to do when you tell people *vat* time it *iz* is to indicate whether it's nine o'clock A.M. or P.M. In Yiddish, you have several options to clarify the time of day:

➤ Before daylight—*far tog;* for example, 3:00 A.M. is the same as *dray fartog.*

➤ Morning (before noon)—*in der fri;* for example, 11:00 A.M. is the equivalent of *elf in der fri.*

➤ Early afternoon until dark—*nokh mitog;* for example, 4:00 P.M. translates into *fir nokh mitog.*

➤ After dark—*bay nakht;* for example, 10:00 P.M. can be expressed as *tzen bay nakht.*

One last thing before we finish this chapter. Tell me, in Yiddish, how long did it take you to read and absorb this chapter?

The Least You Need to Know

➤ The Yiddish names of the days of the week and the months are very similar to English.

➤ The words for the units of time include some beautiful idiomatic expressions with allusions to the Bible and Jewish culture.

➤ We count on numbers—and numbers count.

➤ Telling time is a round-the-clock activity.

Part 3

Home, Sweet *Heym*

Home is not just where the heart is. It's where our most precious memories are created. It's where we share our formative years with our family. It's where the world gains its meaning from the values we imbibe from our parents. Not even the word paradise *is more powerful in Jewish tradition than the word* heym *(home).*

Part 3 concentrates on the people, the places, the activities, and some of the most important items to be found in the locus of the most important domain of our lives.

Here you'll meet the whole mishpakha—*the entire family. You'll tour the rooms and have a chance not only to be impressed by the furniture (sofas covered with see-through plastic, of course), but also to peek into the closets. You'll also be asked to sit down and eat—and then eat some more until you, God forbid,* plotz. *(If you can't wait until you get to that word, it means* explode.*) Finish this section, and you'll never again feel nervous about accepting an invitation to a Yiddish-speaking household. You'll feel so confident about your ability to carry on a conversation that you'll gladly accept with an enthusiastic "Es vet zayn mayn fargnigen" ("It will be my pleasure").*

Chapter 8

All in the Family

In This Chapter

➤ Learning all about a Yiddish mother

➤ Identifying the members of the family

➤ Some Yiddish songs that moved previous generations

➤ Describing family and friends

➤ How to turn adjectives into nouns

When asked about the secret of Jewish survival, William Safire, the brilliant author and columnist for *The New York Times*, once said: "Jewishness ain't chicken soup or Israeli politics or affection for guilt. Jewish identity is rooted in a distinctive old religion that builds individual character and group loyalty through close family life. That is how the Jewish people have survived through five millennia, and that is the light the Jews—whatever the number—must continue to offer the world."

The word for "family" both in Hebrew and in Yiddish is *mishpokhe*. In this chapter, you'll get a chance to meet *di gantse mishpokhe* (the whole family). These are the real stars of Jewish life. More than the priests and the rabbis, the papas and the mamas have served as preachers and teachers, mentors and guides, and sources of inspiration and traditional Jewish guilt for thousands of years. Make fun all you want of family life that's restricted, consumed with the fate of its members, and overly intrusive. The family is still the single most powerful institution to ensure the future for a people so often selected for destruction throughout all of history.

With a Shmaykhel

A Jewish man goes to see a psychiatrist and complains: "Everyone I see reminds me of my mother. My wife, the women I meet, even your secretary reminds me of her. I'm so obsessed that I go to sleep and I dream about my mother. I keep waking up, can't get back to sleep, and have to go downstairs and have a glass of tea and a piece of toast." The psychiatrist says, "What? Just one piece of toast for a big boy like you?"

The Mamas and the Papas

The Yiddish word for "old" is *alt*. "Older" translates as *elter*. *Eltern*, literally "elders," usually refers to parents. If you want to talk about your parents, you say *mayne eltern*. The best place to start talking about the family is with the matriarch and the patriarch. After all, without the mamas and the papas, where would we all be?

A Yiddish Mama

Okay, Jewish mothers definitely are unequalled as subjects for satire. *Nu*, after all, isn't that what mothers are for? So go ahead and laugh at mama because she's overprotective. At least you'll remember to put on your sweater so you don't "*ketsh* a *kolt;*" and if you're laughing at *her*, she'll feel good, knowing that laughter is good for *you*.

Mama gives you two ties for your birthday, and when she meets you wearing one of them, she says with a sigh, "What's the matter? The other one you don't like?" Of course, you'll never get the best of a Jewish mother. The flip side is that because of her, you'll always get the best out of yourself. That's why these proverbs about Yiddish mothers are almost universally repeated to this day:

S'iz nishtdo a shlekhte mame un s'iz nishtdo a guter toit.
(There is no bad mother, and there is no good death.)

Di beste gopel iz der mame's hant.
(The best fork is mother's hand.)

A mame hot oygen fun gloz.
(A mother has glass eyes [meaning, she can't see her children's faults].)

Mames farshteyen vos kinder zogen nisht.
(Mothers understand what children do not say.)

Eyn mame ken ton mer fun hundert lerer.
(One mother can do more than a hundred teachers.)

Got hot nish gekent zayn iberal, hot er bashafen mames.
(God couldn't be everywhere, so He created mothers.)

Eyn mame, tzen kinder iz laykht; tzen kinder, eyn mame iz shver.
(One mother, ten children is easy; ten children, one mother is difficult [mean-ing, a mother easily takes care of ten of her own. When she needs to be taken care of, ten children find it difficult to take care of her].)

Judaism recognizes a mother's unique role in the following statement: "The life of a mother takes priority over the unborn child." That is the decision of Jewish law if, while giving birth, a mother's life is in danger. A mother can have more children. Children can never have another mother.

A Lid far der Mamen

Non-Jews came to appreciate the reverence Jews have for mothers when singer Sophie Tucker popularized the *leed* (song), "My Yiddishe Mame." The lyrics, by Jack Yellen (1892–1991), captured a great deal of the reason why Jewish mothers earned such devotion:

> I long to hold her hands once more
> As in days gone by
> And ask her to forgive me for
> Things I did that made her cry.
> How few were her pleasures
> She never cared for fashion styles.
> Her jewels and treasures
> She found them in her baby's smiles.
> Oh I know that I owe what I am today
> To that dear little lady so old and gray,
> To that wonderful Yiddish *mame*,
> *Mame* mine.

So you want to be sarcastic and remind me of the famous Jewish mother joke: How many Jewish mothers does it take to change a light bulb? None—it's all right, why should you bother? I'd rather sit in the dark! Laugh, if you will, at their self-sacrifice, but remember that they always choose to sit in the dark so that *you* can have light.

Khap a Nash

Mame can turn into *mamenyu*. The *yu* at the end of a word expresses special fondness. It's also a diminutive that changes the word into "little momma." So *mamenyu* could be a special word of endearment for one's own mother—*oy, mamenyu*, you have no idea how much I miss you—or it could be applied to the next generation, the sweet little daughter cradled in your arms whom you already address as *mamenyu* because of her future crucial role in her own family.

Der Tate: The Father

Some years ago, a study of American culture pointed out a remarkable phenomenon: Hundreds of songs are dedicated to mothers. Only one song had tribute to a father as its theme. The words were, "Oh dad, you were like a mother to me."

The same is very much true in Jewish tradition. It's taken for granted that mothers are more special than fathers. The fifth commandment reads, "Honor Your Father and Your Mother." In Yiddish, the admonition was often repeated: *"Gib koved tsu dayn tate un tsu der mamen."*

When the rabbis of the Talmud wondered why the father came first in the biblical verse, they answered: "The Torah stresses what we need to be taught, not what is obvious. A child loves the mother more. That's why the Bible has to try to undo the imbalance and emphasize that you must honor your father just as much."

However, for all the short shrift that fathers have been getting in proverbs and familiar expressions, they have certainly been compensated by a common Yiddish expression. *Tate in himel*—Father in heaven—of course refers to none other than God. The cry *Tate*, when shouted skyward, is an appeal for divine assistance. Why the one who helps us from above should be labeled a male when our greatest caregiver in the world is female is a linguistic paradox I will leave to others to solve.

It's interesting that Hebrew doesn't make the same mistake. In Hebrew, God has two names, one of which is commonly translated God and the other as Lord. According to the rules of grammar and the interpretation of mystics, one name considers God masculine and the other feminine. Of course, the words don't refer to gender as defined by physical characteristics. Yet, God has a "male" and a "female" component, suggesting a divine duality duplicated on earth by father and mother. In that sense, one could just as appropriately pray to our Mother in heaven.

A Gut Vort

Although Hebrew by origin, the word **khosen** snuck into English as another word you'll readily recognize. The "kh" of Hebrew is "ch" in English, so a *khosen*, of course, is your "chosen," the one decreed from above to be your mate.

The Members of the Wedding

To have the *mishpokhe* increase, we've got to have a *khasene*—a wedding. (And, please God, you should be invited to every wedding because that's a real *simkhe*, a joyous occasion.)

When invited to a *khasene*, you'll want to know how to identify the most important people at this momentous occasion: the groom, the bride, and the in-laws. *Khosen* is the Hebrew word for "groom." A *bokher* is a boy or a young man. To indicate that someone is of marriageable age, he's referred to as a *khosen bokher*. In the world of the *shtetl*, in Poland and Russia, that would be as early as age 13. If you're already the age of *bar mitzvah* and responsible for your actions before God, you might just as well be responsible for your actions to a wife!

An eligible young maiden is called a *kale moid* (a bride girl), and the bride proper is known as *di kale*. The word *kale* is part of many popular proverbs. If someone complains about something that is really positive—"But the house has five bedrooms and seven bathrooms"—the correct response is a rhetorical question: A *khasoren di kale iz tzu shen*?!—A failing that the bride is *too* beautiful? You should also remember the proverb: *Yede kale iz shein* (Every bride is beautiful).

The father-in-law and the mother-in-law are referred to as *der shver* and *di shviger*, respectively. The *shver* somehow gets away almost scot free in Yiddish expressions. But pity the poor *shviger* (rhymes with "trigger" and is just as dangerous). Psychologists will tell you at great length why mothers-in-law are universally the targets of so much humor. Yiddish probably is most outspoken about this family figure. After all, if Jewish mothers are domineering and interfering, just imagine the self-imposed mission of a mother-in-law!

Oy Vey

Religious law demands that you compliment a bride on her wedding day and tell her that she is beautiful. But what if she's ugly? Are you permitted to lie? Does making the bride happy override the ethical transgression of lying? The rabbis debate the issue and conclude that even if she is as ugly as sin, you are permitted—or, shall I say commanded—to tell her that she looks like Sharon Stone.

Sholom Aleichem, the great Yiddish humorist, called Adam the luckiest man who ever lived. After all, he said, Adam was the only person who never had a *shviger*. Then who is the unluckiest person in the world? Here's a funny verse that tells us:

> *Toyzent vayber hot gehat*
> *Shloyme hamelekh der kliger.*
> *Fargest nisht az tsu yeden vayb*
> *Hot er oykh gekrogen a shviger!*

> (A thousand wives were had by king
> Solomon the wise.
> But don't forget
> That with every wife he also
> Acquired a mother-in-law!)

Other members of the family include these:

The son-in-law	*der eydem*
The daughter-in-law	*di shnur*
The brother-in-law	*der shvoger*
The sister-in-law	*di shvegerin*

Guess what? There is no English word for the parents of your son-in-law or daughter-in-law, but there is one in Yiddish: *di makhetonim*.

Does English refuse to acknowledge any special relationship with people who just happen to be the parents of your child's spouse, while Yiddish recognizes them because, after all, we have to discuss the financial arrangements for the wedding? Just something to think about!

It's a *Zun*

Of course it's not politically correct. Granted, when you think about it, it's really a *shande*, a terrible shame. Truth be told, though, the world was sexually prejudiced for the longest time, and the birth of a boy was greeted with greater joy than that of a daughter.

To declare, "*S'iz a zun* (it's a son)," was to announce a child whose importance is the same as the sun. The boy was *der zun* and the sun of the parents' life. Another word for the little boy is *yingel*, and you may still very hear often the good news reported, "*mazel tov, s'iz a yingel*." Add the affectionate "e" to the word to express special feeling, and you get *yingele*.

In the late 1800s, the song *Mayn Yingele*, by Morris Rosenfeld, the best-known of the "sweatshop poets" (chroniclers of the horrible working conditions in the sweat shops that employed the newly arrived immigrants) enjoyed overwhelming popularity. With great pathos, it merges the themes of great love for a child with the depressing labor conditions that prevented fathers from spending time with their beloved. See how many of the words you can make out in the Yiddish, and then match the lines of the English translation with the original:

Mayn Yingele	*My Little Boy*
Ikh hob a kleynem yingele,	I have a little boy,
A zunele gor fayn!	A sonny quite fine!
Ven ikh derze im, dakht zikh mir,	Whenever I see him, it seems to me
Di gantse velt iz mayn.	The whole world is mine.
Nor zeltn, zeltn ze ikh im,	But seldom, seldom do I see him
Mayn sheynem, ven er vakht;	My pretty, when he's awake;
Ikh tref im imer shlofndik,	I come upon him always when he's sleeping,
Ikh ze im nor bay nakht.	I see him only at night.

Di arbet traybt mikh fri aroys,	Work drives me out early,
Un lozt mikh shpet tsurik;	And lets me back late;
O, fremd iz mir mayn eygn layb,	O, strange to me is my own flesh,
O, fremd mayn kinds a blik!	O, strange to me my child's gaze!
Ikh kum tseklemterheyt aheym,	I come home tense,
In fintsternish gehilt—	Enveloped in darkness—
Mayn bleykhe froy dertseylt mir bald,	My pale wife tells me right away,
Vi fayn dos kind zikh shpilt.	How fine the child plays.
Vi zis es redt, vi klug es fregt:	How sweet it talks, how cleverly it asks:
"O mame, gute ma,	"O, mama, good ma,
Ven kumt un brengt a peni mir,	When comes and brings me a penny,
Mayn guter, guter pa?"	My good, good pa?"
Ikh shtey bay zayn gelegerl	I stand at his little bed,
Un ze, un her, un sha!	I see and hear and—hush!
A troym bavegt di lipelekh:	A dream moves his lips:
"O, vu iz, vi iz pa?"	"O, where, O, where is pa?"
Ikh kush di bloye eygelekh;	I kiss his blue eyes;
Zeh efenen zikh: "o, kind!"	They open: "O, child!"
Zey ze'en mikh, zey ze'en mikh	They see me, they see me
Un shlisn zikh geshvind.	And close quickly.
"Do shteyt dayn papa, tayerer,	"Here stands your papa, dear one,
A penile dir na!"	A little penny for you, here!"
A troym bavegt di lipelekh:	A dream moves his lips:
"O vu iz, vu is pa?"	"O, where, O, where is pa?"
Ikh blayb tseveytikt un tseklemt,	I stay, hurt and anguished,
Farbitert, un ikh kler:	Embittered, and I think:
Ven du dervakhst a mol, mayn kind,	When you awaken some time, my child,
Gefinstu mikh nit mer.	You'll find me no more.

Imagine how moving the song must have been with a haunting melody added to these dramatic words.

The Rest of the *Mishpokhe*

Now let's imagine that it's time for a huge family dinner. You're standing by the door greeting everyone. Don't forget their names as well as their relationships. Study the following table so that you won't commit a *faux pas* that is nothing less than an *aveyre*, a sin.

Getting to Know the Family

English	Yiddish	English	Yiddish
mother	*di mame*	mother-in-law	*di shviger*
father	*der tate*	father-in-law	*der shver*
son	*der zun*	son-in-law	*der eydem*
daughter	*di tokhter*	daughter-in-law	*di shnur*
brother	*der bruder*	brother-in-law	*der shvoger*
sister	*di shvester*	sister-in-law	*di shvegerin*
uncle	*der feter*	aunt	*di mime*
niece	*di plimenitse*	nephew	*der plimenik*
grandchild	*dos eynikel*	cousin (male or female)	*dos shvesterkind*
cousin (male)	*der kuzin*	cousin (female)	*di kuzine*
grandfather	*der zeyde*	grandmother	*di bobe*

Khap a Nash

A **bobe meyse** is a tall tale, an unbelievable story. Probably, it means a homespun story told by a grandmother. Some scholars insist, however, that the expression is based on a famous book published in Yiddish in Italy in 1507 by Elia Levita, the *Bobe Bukh*, recounting the famous adventures of Prince Bobe.

Welcoming the "Green" Cousin

A newcomer to the United States used to be called a *griner*. Many Yiddish stories, novels, and plays dealt with the fate of these *griners,* the immigrants who arrived in the New World with dreams of streets paved with gold, only to find the harsh realities of *makhen a leben* (making a living). One of the most famous songs describing the conflict between expectation and American life in the early part of the twentieth century is the song *Di Grine Kuzine* (lyrics by Hyman Prizant). Ask your Yiddish-speaking *bobe* or *zeyde*, and I can almost guarantee they'll be able to sing it to you:

Di Grine Kuzine	The Green Cousin
Tsu mir iz gekumen a kuzine,	To me came a cousin,
Sheyn vi gold iz zi geven, "di grine,"	Pretty as gold was she, the "green one,"
Bekelekh vi royte pomerantsn,	Little cheeks like red oranges,
Fiselekh vos betn zikh tsum tantsn.	Little feet that beg to dance.
Herelekh, goldene, gelokte,	Little hairs, golden, curled,
Tseyndelekh vi perelekh, getokte,	Little teeth, like pearls, polished,
Eygelekh vi taybelekh—a tsviling,	Little eyes like little doves—a twin,
Lipelekh vi karshelekh in friling.	Little lips, like little cherries in spring.
Nit gegangen iz zi—nor geshprungen,	She didn't walk—she jumped,
Nit geredt hot zi—nor gezungen;	She didn't talk—but sang;
Freylekh, lustik iz geven ir mine,	Happy, cheerful was her mien,
Ot aza geven iz mayn kuzine.	Such a one was my cousin.
Ikh bin arayn tsu mayn "nekst-dorke,"	I went into my "next-door-ke,"
Vos zi hot a "milineri-storke,"	The one who has a "millinery-store,"
A "dzhab" gekrogn hob ikh far mayn kuzine,	A "job" I got for my cousin,
A lebn zol di goldene medine!	Long live the golden land!
Avek zaynen fun demolt on shoyn yorn,	Many years passed since then,
Fun mayn kuzine iz a tel gevorn;	My cousin became a wreck;
"Peydes" yorn lang hot zi geklibn,	"Paydays" she gathered for many years,
Biz fun ir aleyn iz nisht geblibn.	'Til of herself, nothing was left.
Unter ire bloye sheyne oygn,	Under her blue pretty eyes,
Shvartse pasn hobn zikh fartsoygn;	Black stripes were drawn out;
Di bekelekh, di royte pomerantsn,	Her cheeks, the red oranges,
Hobn sikh shoyn oysgegrint "in gantsn."	Became thoroughly "greened out."
Haynt, as ikh bagegn mayn kuzine,	Today, when I meet my cousin,
Un ikh freg zi: Vo zhe makhstu, grine?	And I ask her: How are you, green one?
Entfert zi mir mit a krumer mine:	She answers with an ugly mien:
"Brenen zol Kolombuses medine!"	"May it burn, Columbus' land!"

Thankfully, the despair of the last line was soon transformed by the positive experiences of the next generation. The proverb that would replace the curse on Columbus' land soon became a beacon of light to Jews throughout the world: *Amerika iz a goldene medine*.

So What Are They Like?

It takes all kinds to make a world. I'll bet your family is no different than anyone else's—you have the good and the bad, the normal ones and the characters, the saints and the sinners. Sure, you shouldn't talk about them behind their backs, but it wouldn't hurt to know how to describe them when the occasion calls for it.

The following table lists important adjectives, descriptives, and personal comments that will come in very handy—and not just for your family, but for all the people you know.

Adjectives and Descriptives

English	Yiddish
a bad person	*a shlekhter mentsh*
a one and only	*an eyn un eyntsiger*
a strong person	*a shtarker*
a pig	*a khazer*
absent-minded	*tsetrogen*
an angry person	*a kasnik*
anxious	*fardayget*
an ass	*a khamor*
an attractive girl	*a sheynhayt*
an authority	*a meyven*
an average person	*a mitelmesiger*
an awkward person	*a klots*
bashful	*shemevdik*
a bashful person	*a shemevdiker*
a bastard	*a mamzer*
a quiet person	*a shtiler*
befuddled	*farmisht*
big shot	*groyser knaker*
a braggart	*a shvitser*
brave	*heldish, mutik*
brazen	*khutspedik*

Adjectives and Descriptives

English	Yiddish
bright	*khokhem*
buffoon	*shmegege*
bum	*trombenik*
burglar, thief	*ganef*
buxom	*zaftig*
chattering	*yatatata*
cheap (price)	*bilig*
cheap (person)	*karger*
coarse	*grob, prost*
complainer	*kvetsher*
compulsive eater	*freser*
friend	*khaver*
conceited	*ongeblozen, balgayve*
confused	*tsetumelt*
conniver	*dreykopf*
corny	*shmaltsy*
cross-eyed	*kasoke*
crude	*grob*
dirty	*shmutsik*
drab	*nebish*
drunk	*shiker*
emaciated	*oysgedart*
erudite person	*lamden*
excited	*tsekokht*
exhausted	*farmutshet*
faker	*zhulik*
fat	*fet*
feeble-minded	*tamevate*
fighter	*kempfer*
fine (upstanding)	*balebatish*
fool	*nar*
senile	*oyver botel*
hanger-on	*nokhshleper*
happy	*freylekh*
heavy	*shver*

continues

Adjectives and Descriptives (continued)

English	Yiddish
highly connected person	*yakhsen*
honored	*bekovedik*
idler	*leydikgayer*
know-it-all	*a gantser kener*
large	*groys*
liar	*ligner*
lively person	*lebediker*
loudmouth	*pisk*
married man	*bavaybter*
meek person	*lemeshke*
miracle worker	*a balness*
moaner	*a krekhtser*
moocher	*shnorer*
moral	*opgehiten*
naive	*tam*
neighbor (from old country)	*landsman*
newlywed	*yungermantshik*
nutty	*tsedreyt*
outcast	*oysvurf*
pauper	*kabtsen*
proud person	*shtolts*
righteous person	*tsadik*
shrew	*marshas*
sick person	*kranker*
slowpoke	*koym vos er krikht*
spinster	*alte moyd*
stranger	*fremder*
sweetheart	*neshomeleh, ziskayt*
swindler	*shvindler*
ugly	*mis*
ugly person	*a miskayt*
unkempt	*shlumpi*
very, very wealthy	*ongeshtopt*
witch	*makhesheyfe*
worthless	*gornit vert*
youngest child infamily	*mezinikl*

Time for Some Exercise

Now how would you describe:

1. Your least favorite relation: _____

2. Your most favorite relation: _____

3. Your best friend: _____

4. Your worst enemy: _____

5. Your next-door neighbor: _____

6. Your favorite teacher: _____

7. Your worst teacher: _____

8. Your wife/husband: _____

9. Your son (if applicable): _____

10. Your daughter (if applicable): _____

11. Your boss (if applicable and printable): _____

12. Your ex-boyfriend/girlfriend (if applicable): _____

13. Your favorite actor: _____

14. Your favorite actress: _____

15. The President (of the United States, your synagogue, your organization): _____

There are no correct or incorrect answers. After all, only you can be the judge of the people you know. If you care to, however, you might want to share your evaluation with the people involved (if your opinion of them is positive), and let them learn the Yiddish word that best describes them.

Turning Adjectives into People

You may have noticed an interesting rule as you look over the lengthy list of adjectives and descriptions. I call it the "to *er* is human" law: You turn an adjective into a person who possesses that trait by adding the suffix –"*er*" to the word. For example:

Shtark is strong.

A *shtarker* is a strong person.

Shemevdik is bashful.

A *shemevdiker* is a bashful person.

Opgelozen is careless.

An *opgelozener* is a careless person.

Why not try it by yourself:

1. *Opgehiten* is chaste; a chaste person is an _____.
2. *Grob* is coarse; a coarse person is a _____.
3. *Shmutsik* is dirty; a dirty person is a _____.
4. *Freylekh* is happy; a happy person is a _____.
5. *Groys* is large; a large person is a _____.

Congratulations. You can now talk about everyone. That's why when it comes to being *klug* (smart), you are really a *kluger*.

The Least You Need to Know

➤ The Jewish mother is featured in many Yiddish proverbs.

➤ Every member of the family has a Yiddish name, including even some for whom there is no English equivalent.

➤ There is a lengthy list of Yiddish adjectives for every kind of person.

➤ The suffix "*–er*" when added to an adjective indicates a person who possesses that attribute.

Chapter 9

Kum Areyn— Come in, Please

> ### In This Chapter
>
> ➤ Learn to identify the rooms of a Yiddish home
>
> ➤ Dare to look into drawers, closets, and cabinets
>
> ➤ Learn some "colorful" language
>
> ➤ Discover the secrets of the Yiddish kitchen
>
> ➤ Become a master chef with new recipes

It's hard to believe that Benjamin Franklin was familiar with Yiddish. Yet, a well-known saying often attributed to him—"Fish and visitors start smelling after three days"—has its origin in this ancient Yiddish saying: *"A fish und a gast nokh dray teg— shtinken beyde."* The guest that stinks, of course, is the guest who overstays his welcome.

In general, however, taking in strangers is more than a courtesy for Jews—it's a *mitzvah,* a divine commandment rooted in the Bible. Hospitality goes back to Abraham, who sat at the door of his tent looking for strangers whom he could invite into his home. If Abraham spoke Yiddish, he, too, would have used the phrase so often repeated by Jews today as they try to induce friends to step into their homes for just a few moments: *"Kum areyn* (Come in), let me show you around; have a glass of tea, and let's talk for a while." So be nice, dear reader, *loyf nisht* (don't run), and spend *a por minut mit mir* (a few minutes with me) as I take you on a tour of a typical Jewish home.

Such Nice Rooms!

If you're lucky, you have a *hoiz* (a house). If you're really lucky, it's a *grois hoiz* (a big house). And if you're wealthy, or perhaps just exaggerating to friends who haven't seen your house yet, you have a *palatz* (a palace). Of course, the purpose of telling others that you have a *palatz* is that they should *platz*, a powerful Yiddish word that means to burst or to explode, usually from anger or envy.

Not everyone, however, can *afoder* (an accepted Yiddish corruption for the English word *afford*) such spacious dwellings. Some people must do with a *dira*, otherwise known even in Yiddish as an *apartement*. An *apartement* can be *tsen tsimer neben Riverside Drive* (ten rooms near Riverside Drive) or *a lokh in der vant* (a hole in the wall) *vos past nisht afilu far a bhema* (that isn't suitable even for an animal).

Still, regardless of what your dwelling looks like, there's no place like home. Come join me for a stroll through the most important rooms in a *Yiddishe heim*.

➤ *dos voyntsimer* **(the living room)**—The living room is a museum area meant only for guests and it's usually off limits to the family. Its main purpose is to stand in waiting for the day when the parents of a child's prospective mate come to visit. Until then, *di meibel* (the furniture) must be covered, usually with see-through plastic, so that the living room not be—God forbid—contaminated by living.

➤ *dos estsimer* **(the dining room)**—Here is where *di gantse mishpokhe* gets together every *Shabes* and *yontif* for a festive meal and good conversation. *Di keylim* (the dishes) are brought *tsum tish* (the table). Everyone sits on his or her *shtul* (chair). It is the role of the Jewish mother to repeat this refrain, almost as a religious mantra, to all those gorging themselves at their seats: *"Farvos est du nisht? Nem nokh a bisel!"* ("Why aren't you eating? Take a little more.")

➤ *di kikh* **(the kitchen)**—The place of preparation for the magical food items that seem to stream almost endlessly to the appreciative diners is *di kikh* (the kitchen). Here *di kekhin* (the cook) performs her (or his) wonders stepping back and forth between *dem oyven* (the oven) and *dem frijalider* (the refrigerator), preparing food items and handling *di tep* (the pots) and *di fendlekh* (the pans). The secret ingredient of the Jewish culinary expert, of course, transcends ingredients and recipes. Sholem Aleichem said what made every dish prepared by his mother so special was the love she put into it that he tasted with every bite.

➤ *dos shloftsimer* **(the bedroom)**—*Vos tut men in shloftsimer? Men shloft. Un nokh epes. Ober red nisht hoykh—di kinder heren.* (What do you do in the bedroom? You sleep. And one more thing. But don't speak loudly—the children might hear.) *Dos shloftsimer* (the bedroom) is for making love. According to Jewish tradition, that also is a *mitzvah*, another truly divine commandment.

If parents didn't want their children to listen in to their conversations, they either spoke privately to each other in the bedroom, or, when in front of their children, they said it in Yiddish. From that parental attempt to hide things from their offspring by speaking in a foreign tongue came the new generation's love for understanding Yiddish. That may very well be your motivation in studying this book—so that you can finally understand what your parents were saying.

With a Shmaykhel

The times they are a–changing. A sign in a modern bakery: "Cake, like Mother used to buy."

➤ *dos vanetsimer* (**the bathroom**)—A *vane* is a bath, and Yiddish uses the same euphemism as English for the room you frequent when nature calls. Modern American usage, however, makes *toylet* the more common word used in Yiddish today. Propriety prevents me from giving you the Yiddish words for the natural functions performed in the toilet. Yet, one of these is so well known that I'll give it to you by way of a true story I just heard recently.

My friend's father, who speaks only Yiddish, was in the hospital confined to total bed rest. When the son came to visit in the morning, the nurse told him that she couldn't understand why this seemingly rational gentleman kept telling her all night that he wanted to go fishing. My friend knew that his father had never fished his entire life and didn't understand what could possibly have happened. It didn't take him long, however, to discover that what the nurse understood as "fishin'" was really a very similar word in Yiddish that begins with a "p" instead of an "f." Poor Dad only wanted to urinate, and his non-Jewish nurse didn't have an inkling (or should I say tinkling?) of what he meant!

Looking All Around You

Now that you know the names of the various rooms, why not take some time to look around. Here's a handy list of items you'll find in the various rooms that you'll surely want to identify by their Yiddish names:

Yiddish	English	Yiddish	English
dos bet	the bed	*di koldre*	the blanket
di komod	the bureau	*der tepekh*	the carpet
di stelye	the ceiling	*der keyler*	the cellar
der forhang	the curtain	*di tir*	the door

continues

continued

Yiddish	English	Yiddish	English
di podloge	the floor	*der koridor*	the hall
der lomp	the lamp	*di vesh*	the linen
der matrats	the mattress	*der shpigel*	the mirror
di shpayzkamer	the pantry	*der kishen*	the pillow
di perene	the quilt	*der dakh*	the roof
dos beshtek	the silverware	*dos fentster*	the window
der tshaynik	the teakettle		

Help Me Find It

Let's see how well you remember the names of the rooms of the house. Alongside each of the items listed, fill in the place where you'd probably find it:

Khap a Nash

The most powerful retort to a bore is the famous Yiddish saying *"Hak mir nit kayn tshaynik"* ("Don't knock me a teapot"). What is the source of this strange saying? Have you ever heard a child take a spoon and bang it endlessly against a teapot? It could drive you crazy—just like somebody who yaks and yaks and yaks (note the similarity to "hack") without making any sense. It even works in the short version: "Don't *hak* me!"

1. *Di vesh (the linen) iz in* _____.
2. *Der shpigel (the mirror) iz in* _____.
3. *Dos fendel (the saucepan) iz in* _____.
4. *Der kavenik (the coffeepot) iz in* _____.
5. *Di koldre (the blanket) iz in* _____.
6. *Men est (one eats) in* _____.
7. *Men shloft (one sleeps) in* _____.
8. *Men kukt oyf televizye (one watches television) in* _____.
9. *Men vasht di hent (one washes one's hands) in* _____.
10. *Men zitst bakvem (one sits comfortably) in* _____.

And here are the answers:

1. *der kikh*
2. *dem voyntsimer*
3. *der kikh*
4. *der kikh*
5. *dem shloftsimer*

6. *dem estsimer*

7. *dem shloftsimer*

8. *dem voyntsimer*

9. *dem vanetsimer*

10. *dem voyntsimer*

When "Men" Are Not "Men"

It's time for a little more grammar. You may have noticed the word "men" in some previous sentences. Note how this is used in the following examples:

> *Men est in estsimer.*

> *Men shloft in shloftsimer.*

> *Men kokht in kikh.*

"Men" is an impersonal pronoun that means one, or people, in the general sense: One eats in the dining room; one sleeps in the bedroom; or one cooks in the kitchen.

A proverb or rumor is often introduced with the words *men zogt* ("people say"). For example, *men zogt az a kluger mentsh veyst vos er zogt; a nar zogt alls vos er veyst.* (A wise person knows what he says; a fool says what he knows.) See, sometimes "men" aren't so stupid after all. Another proverb has it: *Az men zogt, ken men gloyben*—If men (people) commonly say it, you can believe it.

Note that *men* can also be shortened to *me*, as in *me geyt in gahs* (people walk in the street) or *me zingt in der vane* (people sing in the bathtub). Both *me* and *men* view people as a singular collective identity, which means that you use only the third-person singular form of the verb in conjunction with either *me* or *men*; there is no plural form.

Oy Vey

Don't pronounce *me* as the English word "me." It's *me* as in *fe*. To explain why you won't go on the roller coaster, state very clearly that *me ken geharget veren* (somebody can get killed), and I don't just mean me: I mean *me*—any person besides a *shlemazel* like me.

Wear It in Good Health

As long as we're touring the house, let's take a look in the closets. Clothing is very important for Jewish people. According to religious law, every Jew needs two sets of clothes: one for weekdays, and one for Sabbaths and holidays. That's probably why Jewish women consider shopping such a religious experience.

Here's a handy list for the Yiddish words to describe some of the most common garments:

Yiddish	English	Yiddish	English
a kleyd	a dress	*a hemd*	a shirt
a dzup	a skirt	*a por hoyzen*	a pair of slacks
an unter-kleydel	a slip	*a sporthemd*	a sport shirt
a por zoken	a pair of stockings	*a sveter*	a sweater
an unterhemd	an undershirt	*untervesh*	underwear
a vest	a vest	*a por shleykes*	a pair of suspenders
a por shtek-shikh	a pair of slippers	*a por shikh*	a pair of shoes
a por unter-hoyzen	a pair of shorts	*a shal*	a scarf
a por sandalen	a pair of sandals	*a mantel*	a coat
a regenmantel	a raincoat	*a khalat*	a robe
a por heyzlekh	a pair of panties	*a bluze*	a blouse
a stanik	a brassiere	*a por shponkes*	a pair of cuff links
a por hentsh-kes	a pair of gloves	*noztikhele*	handkerchiefs
a hut	a hat	*a shnips*	a tie
a nakhthemd	a nightgown	*a mantel*	an overcoat
a fartekh	an apron	*a bodkostyum*	a bathing suit
a korset	a girdle	*vindelekh*	diapers

As you go through the clothes closet, you're bound to find a garment you can only call a *shmate*. What's a *shmate*? *Shmate* is a disparaging word for an inferior piece of clothing, dress, or material. You can use it to describe any of the following:

➤ The dress worn by your ex-husband's new wife.

➤ The dress you couldn't afford that's now worn by somebody else.

➤ The item you desperately want to buy, but only for a much lower price, as in, "How much do you want for that *shmate*?"

Such Beautiful Colors

So what color is your new dress? And how did you paint the new room? Did you notice how everything matched so beautifully? Have a look at the Yiddish words for the most popular colors, and then see if you can use them in sentences in combination with some of the other words you've just learned:

Yiddish	English	Yiddish	English
royt	red	*bloy*	blue
gel	yellow	*grin*	green
orandj	orange	*lila*	purple
shvarts	black	*vays*	white
roz	pink	*groy*	gray
tunkel	dark	*broyn*	brown
krem	cream		

Now try saying these sentences in Yiddish:

1. *Di kaleh hot getrogen nor _____.*
   (The bride wore only white.)

2. *Dos shloftsimer iz geven _____.*
   (The bedroom was blue.)

3. *Ikh hob lib a kleyd mit a bisel _____.*
   (I love a dress with a little yellow.)

4. *Der forhang makht dos tsimmer _____.*
   (The curtains make the room dark.)

5. *Di mebel zayhen shvarts un _____.*
   (The furniture is black and gray.)

If you missed any of these, *vert mir shvarts far di oygen*—it's getting dark before my eyes (self-understood in this popular expression is that it's because I'm so upset).

Khap a Nash

Did you know that Jews make a blessing whenever they put on a new garment, thanking God for the joy of this moment? However, a Jew would never pronounce a blessing for a garment made out of leather. Why? Because an animal had to die for us to acquire it, so our joy can't be complete. Jewish law allows its use, yet still commands we maintain our sensitivity. What is allowed is not necessarily the ideal!

With a Shmaykhel

Shmate is also the ideal word to use for all your outfits if you want an excuse to go on a shopping spree: "I haven't got a thing to wear except for all these *shmates*!"

Try the House "Specials"

Are you getting a little tired from your lengthy tour of the house? Are you maybe feeling some hunger pains as you think of a Yiddish home filled with the sweet scents of all the delicious *makholim* (foods) prepared by the typical *mame*? No description of a Jewish household could be complete without mention of some of the culinary "specials" that make *di kikh* so memorable and the *estsimer* so inviting for family and guests.

Every *baleboste* (the female head of the house), of course, has her own favorite recipes. Asking, "Whose *gefilte fish* (stuffed fish) is better?" is a profound question so difficult to answer that it remains to be resolved only by God Himself in the world to come. But I, like every good Jewish husband, know for sure that there is nobody in the whole world who cooks and bakes like my wife.

So, as an added bonus to you, dear reader, instead of just teaching you the Yiddish words you need to know for the whole subject of food preparation, I'm going to share with you three wonderful recipes. This way, you'll be able to enjoy the true "taste" of Yiddish as you follow the simple directions that will let you create foods with a veritable *tam Gan Eden*, a flavor of the Garden of Eden.

Baked Stuffed Gefilte Fish—a la Ita

Yes, Ita is my wife's Yiddish name (in English, Elaine). Try this recipe once as a *forshpayz* (an appetizer), and I guarantee you'll become a life-long devotee of this dish favored by Jews for centuries.

Before you get started, here's a list of ingredients that you'll need. The Yiddish appears alongside the English. Practice the words by reading every line aloud at least three times—and then salivating.

Gefilte Fish	Stuffed Fish
Eyn fish fun 2½ funt	1 fish, weighing about 2½ lbs.
6 matsos	6 matzos
4 eslefel petrishke	4 tbsp. parsley
2 eslefel tseribene tsibeles	2 tbsp. grated onion
1 tsibele tsehakt oyf kleyne shtiklekh	1 onion, minced
1 teylefel thyme	1 tsp. thyme
¼ teylefel royten fefer	¼ tsp. red pepper
¼ teylefel shvartsen fefer	¼ tsp. black pepper
2½ teylefele zalts	2½ tsp. salt
5 eslefel mardjerin	5 tbsp. margarine
2 kopes vaser	2 cups water

Gefilte Fish	Stuffed Fish
2 kopes tomeytozaft	2 cups tomato juice
½ eslefel Vustershir sos	½ tbsp. Worcestershire sauce
2 eslefel grinem feffer	2 tbsp. green pepper
1 eslefel kartofel mel	1 tbsp. potato flour
1 shtikel knobel (oyb ir vilt)	1 piece garlic, if desired

Now here's what you do: Read the Yiddish. Then, to make sure you understand, read the English translation. When you're sure you know what it means, follow the instructions carefully:

1. *Nemt arunter di liskes un reynigt di fish un bashprinkelt mit zalts fun inveynig un fun droysen.*

1. Scale and clean fish, and sprinkle with salt inside and outside.

2. *Vaykt di matsos in vaser biz zey zaynen vaykh, dan drikt oys azoy truken vi meglikh.*

2. Soak matzos in water until soft, then squeeze as dry as possible.

3. *Git tsu 2 eslefel petrishke, tseribene tsibeles, thaym, a helft fun di shvartse un royte feffer un 1½ teylefel zalts.*

3. Add 2 tbsp. parsley, grated onion, thyme, half of the black and red pepper, and 1½ tsp. salt.

4. *Filt on di fish mit dem un farshpilet mit tutpiks 1½ intshes eyns fun di andere, un vikelt a shtrikel arum di tut-piks.*

4. Stuff fish with this and pin the edges of the fish together by inserting toothpicks in holes pierced about 1½ inches apart and then lacing a string around the toothpicks.

5. *Bashprinkelt di fish mit matsomel, zalts, fefer, un legt aroyf 5 es-lefel mardjerin.*

5. Dredge fish with matzo meal, salt, and pepper, and put 5 tbsp. margarine on top.

6. *Legt aroyf oyf a "fish-rek" bashmirt mit fets, oder oyf a shtikel leyvend vos iz oyf'n d'no fun a bakfendel, kdey ir zolt kenen laykht aroysnemen di fish.*

6. Place on a greased fish rack or on a strip of cloth laid in the bottom of a baking pan to facilitate the removal of the fish.

7. *Shtelt avek in oyven oyfgedekterheyt (der oyven darf zayn ongevarmt tsu a temperatur fun 450°) far 30 minut.*

7. Place uncovered in oven with heat at 450° for 30 minutes.

8. *Verent es smolyet, misht tsuzamen kartofelmehl, vaser, tomeytozaft, Vustershir sos, tsehakte green fefer un tsibele, knobel un 2 eslefel petrishke, 1 teylefel zalts, un di ibergeblibene royte un shvartse fefer.*

8. While searing, mix together potato flour, water, tomato juice, Worcestershire sauce, minced green pepper and onion, garlic, 2 tbsp. parsley, 1 tsp. salt, and remainder of the red and black pepper.

9. *Bagist di fish mit der sos nokh dem vee es hot gesmolyet 30 minut, farklenert di temperatur biz 300° un bakt vayter, 15 minut far yeden funt, biz es vert fartig.*

9. Pour the sauce over the fish after it has been seared for 30 minutes, reduce heat to 300°, and continue to bake fish, 15 minutes for each pound, until done.

10. *Bashtrayet oft mit der sos nemt aroys dem gantsen fish un servirt di sos fun a "greyvi bowl."*

10. Baste frequently with the sauce. Remove fish whole, and serve sauce from gravy bowl.

Khap a Nash

Fish is traditionally served on Friday nights in Jewish homes because it is a symbol of fertility and because Friday night is reserved for the *mitzvah* of marital relations. Christians may say "never on Sunday," but Jews say, "always on *Shabes*," and hope that good sex will produce good offspring. Can you figure out why Jews prefer to serve the fish "stuffed?"

With a Shmaykhel

Legend has it that Marilyn Monroe was so overwhelmed by her first taste of *matza* balls that she innocently asked the chef, "Tell me, do Jews use any other parts of the *matzah* animals for food?"

Only one thing left to do now. Enjoy—and listen to the compliments from your guests and family.

Light-as-a-Feather Matza Balls

Once you've gotten such raves on the appetizer, you'll want to solidify your reputation with *matza* balls, the likes of which you've never tasted. Add them to chicken soup, and you have a combination that can't be beat: The soup is like medicine that brings immediate relief, and the *matza* balls will stay in the stomach for a long time as a physical reminder of an unparalleled feasting experience.

Here are the ingredients you'll need for this delicacy:

Matza Balls	Matza Balls
1 kope tshiken fets	1 cup chicken fat
3 eyer (gut oyfgeshlogen)	3 eggs, well beaten
1/3 kope heyse tshiken brot	1/3 cup hot chicken broth
1 lefele zalts	1 tsp. salt
1 lefele nutmeg (oder ingber)	1 tsp. nutmeg (or ginger, if preferred)
2 kopes matsomeal	Matzo meal (about 2 cups)

We're doing this not just for the sake of learning the recipe, but also for becoming familiar with the Yiddish words, so use this as an exercise and recite aloud every line first in Yiddish and then in English. Try to associate the Yiddish words with their English counterparts, and become familiar with the measurements as well as the ingredients (and be prepared for a little review quiz when we get finished):

Kilt op di kope shmalts fun a gedempten hun biz es vert taylvayz kil.
Cool a cupful of fat from a stewed chicken until it becomes lukewarm (partly cool).

Shlogt es gut oyf.
Beat well.

Git tsu di andere shtofen, dan makht kneydlekh in der groys fun a velshener nus.
Add other ingredients, then roll the balls about the size of a walnut.

Badekt zey mit a dinem tukh, un shtelt zey avek in a kilen plats far 1 biz 24 shtunden.
Cover them with a thin cloth and set aside in a cool place from 1 to 24 hours.

Ven ir vilt zey gebroykhen, kokht oyf di zup nokhdem vi ir nemt aroys dos hun.
When ready to use them, boil the remaining soup after you have removed the chicken.

Dan leygt arayn di kneydlakh in der zeedendigter zup un lost es kokhen 18 minut.
Then drop the balls into boiling soup, cover, and boil for 18 minutes.

Fun der resipee vet ir hoben arum 42 kneydlekh.
From this recipe you will have about 42 matza balls.

Okay, how many people will you be able to serve with 42 matza balls? If your answer was 42 people, or 21, you obviously don't know the first thing about how delicious these matza balls are. Figure 10 people at the most, and you'll be lucky.

What's a Meal Without Cake?

It makes no difference what your main dish is: Guests will always remember the dessert. The last item served is like your signature at the end of a letter. It identifies you even as it serves as your final words. Put your best foot forward, therefore, when you prepare this part of the menu. And since your guests have been sponging off you the entire meal, why not close with a classic sponge cake that will leave them licking their lips and begging for more.

Here's what you need for this final *pièce de resistance*:

Leykekh	Sponge Cake
12 eyer	12 eggs
2 kopes tsuker	2 cups sugar
1 limene (tseribene sholekhts un zaft)	1 lemon, juice and grated rind
1 kope keyk-mehl	1 cup cake meal
1 lefele kartofel-mehl	1 tsp. potato flour

101

You've done so much work until now that you might at this point want to involve your family. Why don't you read the ingredients to them and see if they understand them well enough to bring them to you. Warn them that if they mess up, you'll use whatever they bring, whether it's called for in the recipe or not. (That should really prove interesting.) Now listen carefully as I tell you what to do with the foods you've prepared:

> *Shlogt oyf tsuzamen di geylekhlekh fun di eyer mit tsuker far 30 minut.*
> Beat egg yolks and sugar together for 30 minutes.
>
> *Vikelt ayn di gedikht-oyfgeshlogene vayslikh fun di eyer.*
> Fold in stiffly beaten egg whites.
>
> *Git tsu limene zaft un tseribene sholekhts.*
> Add lemon juice and grated rind.
>
> *Misht oys di matsokeykmel un kartofel mel un vikelt ayn, bislekhvays.*
> Sift together cake meal and potato flour and fold in, a little at a time.
>
> *Bakt in a mesigen oyven (325°) far a shtunde.*
> Bake in a moderate oven (325°) about one hour.
>
> *Ir kent tsugeben 2 kopes tseribene nis, oyb ir vilt.*
> You may add 2 cups chopped nuts, if you desire.

If you have any left over (which I sincerely doubt possible), please mail to Alpha Books, c/o my attention.

Your Handy Cooking and Baking Guide

You've had so many different words introduced to you that it might be getting just a little bit confusing. To help you out, here's a handy chart listing the most common words you'll need to know in planning future meals:

Mosen	**Measurements**
eslefel	tablespoon
teylefel	teaspoon
a halb teylefele	½ teaspoon
a fertel tey-lefele	¼ teaspoon
kope(s)	cup(s)
shtikel	piece

Inhalt	Ingredients
puter	butter
petrishke	parsley
tsibele	onion
fefer	pepper
zalts	salt
vaser	water
zaft	juice
kartofel	potato
mel	flour
knobel	garlic
eyer	eggs
tsuker	sugar
fets	fat

Onvayzingen	Instructions
kilt	cool
shlogt	beat
badekt	cover
kokht	cook
misht	mix
bakt	bake
git tsu	add
kokht oyf	boil
bashprenkelt	sprinkle
filt on	stuff
bashmir	smear
farklenert di temperatur	lower the temperature
makht hekher di temperatur	increase the temperature
bagist	pour

After you finish all that, remember the most important instruction of all: *Es, es, mayn kind* (eat, eat, my child)—and enjoy.

The Least You Need to Know

➤ Yiddish identifies rooms by their primary purpose, with the addition of the word *tsimer*.

➤ *Men* and its abbreviated form, *me*, are very common and important words to remember.

➤ Many of the words for colors in Yiddish are almost identical to their English equivalents.

➤ Cooking and baking have their own "language" for measurements, ingredients, and instructions.

Chapter 10

Let's Eat— Esen, Esen, Esen

Did you ever hear of the Jewish cruise ship? It was called the S.S. *Mayn Kind*. Okay, I know you're never supposed to explain a joke, but just in case you don't get it, *Es, es, mayn kind* ("Eat, eat, my child") is one of the classic lines of every Jewish mother.

For a people persecuted throughout the centuries, an overemphasis on food is a fairly obvious reaction. Eat now—who knows if we'll have any food later. Eat now—we may have to flee for our lives, and it may be your last full meal. Eat now—you'll need every last ounce of energy the food will give you in our difficult struggle to survive.

A Yiddish proverb has it that *azoy vi di meysim esen, aza—ponim hobben zey*—the way the dead eat, that's how they'll look. So often on the verge of death itself, Jews didn't have the luxury of worrying about dieting for most of their history. *Es* became almost a Yiddish mantra. Eat, so that you live. Eat, it's a *mitzvah*, a divine commandment to take care of yourself. Eat, because on every *Shabes* and *yontef* we are obligated to worship God by way of consuming special foods. In this chapter, you'll learn the most important food-related words and expressions.

Don't Forget Breakfast

How many meals a day are there? If you answered three, you're clearly not Jewish. For a Jew, the correct answer is either one or four. One is the ideal because you should start eating as early as possible in the morning and keep going straight through until the night. Four is to accept the traditional division of breakfast, lunch, and supper, and to add the most important meal of all—the *nash*, which takes place at intermittent and personally chosen moments throughout the day. Let's give each of these meals their well-deserved attention:

➤ **Breakfast**—Eaten in *der fri* (the early morning), breakfast goes most often by the name of *frishtik*. Some people also refer to it as *iberbaysen*. To *khap a bays* is to grab a bite, and it's very possible for someone just to make do with a bagel and a *glayzel kave* (a cup or glass of coffee). So what's so bad about that? What did you expect? Bacon and eggs?

➤ **Lunch**—There was a time when the midday meal was the most important and elaborate meal of the day. Guess the ancients knew that it wasn't a very good idea to go to sleep on a full stomach. When lunch is plentiful and lavish, it's called *der mitog*. If it's just fast food or a sandwich on the run, it's called—surprise—*der lontsh*, obviously in honor of its American origin.

With a Shmaykhel

A spaceship lands near a Jewish bakery. The Martian enters the store and sees a bagel. "What are these wheels for?" he asks. "They're not wheels, they're food," the baker answers. "Why not try one?" The Martian tastes this exotic new delicacy, thinks for a moment, and with the wisdom of a superior civilization, declares, "Good, but I think these would really go great with cream cheese and lox."

If the menu features dairy, it's called *milkhig* (note the similarity to the word "milk"). That's when you're too far from a deli and don't have the possibility of a pastrami on rye. A meat meal is *fleyshig*, or *fleyshedik* (note the similarity to the word *flesh*). Jewish law forbids the eating of meat and milk products together. Hence, a cheeseburger is for a religiously observant Jew just as much of a culinary no-no as Dr. Seuss's proverbial ham and eggs.

➤ **Dinner**—If you're eating the main meal in the evening, it's *dos onbaysen*, or *dos vareme*. If it's simply supper, it's *di vetshere*. When dinner is served on Friday night, the traditional *Shabes* meal, or on a holiday, it deserves a new name. It's not just a meal, it's a *se'udah*. The root of this Yiddish word is no longer German, but Hebrew. It takes us back to olden times with visions of banquets with innumerable courses, choices of wines, and incredible desserts. A dinner is just a dinner, but a *sude* is a *tam fun gan eden* (a taste of the Garden of Eden).

➤ *Nash*—The *nash* is the all-purpose "meal" eaten whenever the spirit moves you. By tradition, a *nash* may not include lettuce, celery, or any other healthy foods. Usually, it consists of a piece of cake, a bowl of ice cream, a piece (or two) of candy—all right, maybe one more, but not more than five or six. After all, it's not a meal—I'm just having a *nash*!

When Do We Eat?

Ready for a little more grammar? We've saved the future tense until now so that you can attach it to something pleasant and then reward yourself with some refreshment after you've mastered it.

What you need to know at the outset is that the future comes in two different shapes and forms: There is the immediate future followed by the more distant future. Both make use of the infinitive—in this case, *esen* (to eat). What's different is the word preceding it that needs to be conjugated. For what you intend to do immediately, you use the various forms of the word *geyn* (to go). For example, I am going to eat breakfast, you are going to eat lunch, he is going to eat supper, and so on. For a delayed action future, the word preceding *esen* is *vel* (will or shall), followed by the infinitive: "Yes, mama, don't keep nagging me, I will eat supper—but not just now."

Expressing yourself using the future tense probably sounds harder than it is, so let's illustrate it with all the pronouns. Remember that the same rule applies for almost all other verbs as well.

The I'll-Do-It-Now Words

Let's see what happens when people are ready to eat right now:

Yiddish	English
Ikh gey esen.	I'm going to eat.
Du geyst esen.	You are going to eat.
Ir geyt esen.	You (formal) are going to eat.
Er geyt esen.	He is going to eat.
Zi geyt esen.	She is going to eat.
Mir geyen esen.	We are going to eat.
Ir geyt esen.	You (plural) are going to eat.
Zey geyen esen.	They are going to eat.

If you hear a form of the word *gey* used by anyone with the infinite *esen*, you'd better get to the table quickly if you hope to find anything left. When people say *mir geyen esen*, they mean business, and they're ready to reach for the food *right now*.

The I'll-Do-It-Later Words

Sometimes you're just not in the mood to do something right this minute. However, you know that will change at a later point in time. To express this future intention, you'll switch from the *gey* word to the *vel* word. For example, you're in a karaoke bar and someone asks you to sing. However, you're not in the mood to do it right now, but you agree to do it in a little while; you're not declining, you're just postponing. The proper response would be: *Ikh vel zingen.*

These are the conjugations for the different pronouns:

Yiddish	English
Ikh vel zingen.	I will sing.
Du vest zingen.	You will sing.
Ir vet zingen.	You (formal) will sing.
Er vet zingen.	He will sing.
Zi vet zingen.	She will sing.
Mir velen zingen.	We will sing.
Ir vet zingen.	You (plural) will sing.
Zey velen zingen.	They will sing.

Now try to conjugate the immediate and not-so-immediate future using these verbs: *koyfen* (to buy), *reden* (to speak), and *zogen* (to say).

Immediate Future

Ikh _____ (koyfen/reden/zogen)

Du _____ (koyfen/reden/zogen)

Ir (formal)_____ (koyfen/reden/zogen)

Er _____ (koyfen/reden/zogen)

Zi _____ (koyfen/reden/zogen)

Mir _____ (koyfen/reden/zogen)

Ir (plural)_____ (koyfen/reden/zogen)

Zey _____ (koyfen/reden/zogen)

Postponed Future

Ikh _____ (koyfen/reden/zogen)

Du _____ (koyfen/reden/zogen)

Ir (formal)_____ (koyfen/reden/zogen)

Er _____ (koyfen/reden/zogen)

Zi _____ (koyfen/reden/zogen)

Mir _____ (koyfen/reden/zogen)

Ir (plural)_____ (koyfen/reden/zogen)

Zey _____ (koyfen/reden/zogen)

Practice the immediate future and the postponed future for as many action words you can think of. Just remember, if you're going to do it immediately, *go* for it. If you're going to put it off for a while, *vel* ... what are you going to do?

So What's for Dinner?

As we prepare for a verbal meal, it's important to remember that for Jews, food isn't just food. Here's the way Jane Kinderlehrer, the famous American nutritionist and cookbook author, puts it:

"Chopped liver with grated black radish, moistened with rendered chicken fat, and a whisper of chopped onion—pure ecstasy in the mouth. Fluffy kneydlech swimming in chicken soup flecked with gold; hot knishes, crisp and delicious with a spicy potato, kashe for cheese fillings; homentaschen bursting with poppy seeds or prunes; or honey-soaked teyglekh, or creamy kugels—pure bliss to bite into. Mushroom and barley soup to warm your bones; hearty kashe varnishkes with hot gravy; strudel with heavenly fruit and nut fillings. You don't need a "fiddler on the roof" to tell you that these foods spell tradition. Their very names evoke blissful memories of small kibitzers crowding around the big black stove, and a lovely warm feeling that mama's in the kitchen and all's right with the world."

With a Shmaykhel

Want to know the best definition of a **kibitser?** He's the one who read a sign on the doctor's door:

Doctor Ben Goldberg, Brain Surgery

Doctor Sam Cohen, Psychiatry

Doctor Charles Gordon, Proctology

He couldn't resist, so underneath he scrawled:

We specialize in Odds and Ends

So get ready to start drooling. Memorize all the words—you never know when you'll have a *tayve* (strong urge) for something, and nobody will know what to give you unless you're able to ask.

Khap a Nash

Every Friday night, **gefilte fish** is a must for a religious reason. Fish are a symbol of fertility. Eating them ensures the blessing of children. According to Jewish law, Friday night is the time when married couples should observe the joy of the Sabbath by enjoying sexual relations. Roman Catholics may have taught "never on Sunday," but Jews throughout the ages have lived by the maxim, "always on *Shabes*." The *gefilte fish* symbolizes pregnancy and is a delicate reminder of the activity the heads of the household look forward to at the end of the meal.

Start with an Appetizer

One thing you'll probably never have to ask for is *gefilte fish*. That's stuffed fish made either sweet or salty, depending on the tradition of the household. It's assumed, for some mystical reason, that you definitely want this course, and it will always be waiting for you—with a little horseradish on the side.

Here are some of the other things you might want to choose for an appetizer:

Yiddish	English
geraykherte fish	smoked fish (lox)
gehakte hering	chopped herring
marinirte hering	pickled herring
gehakte leber	chopped liver
melon	melon
ugerkes	pickles
zoyere ugerkes	sour pickles
zis un zoyere ugerkes	sweet and sour pickles
grikhisher salat	Greek salad
sardinkes	sardines
zoyere kroyt	sauerkraut

Well, did you work up an appetite? Good, because the soup is next.

Jewish Penicillin

Why in the world, Jews wonder, did they give the Nobel prize to Sir Arthur Fleming for his discovery of penicillin and not to the Jewish housewives who, centuries before him, figured out the curative powers of chicken soup?

In Yiddish, chicken soup is known as *yoykh*—and the *oy* in the middle is probably an exclamation of delight. Chicken soup with noodles is referred to as *yoykh mit lokshen*. Add *matzoh* balls, and it's known as *yoykh mit kneydlekh*. With the layer of fat on top, it's *yoykh mit kolesterol*. (Okay, the last one is only my addition to give you a little health warning.)

Jewish tradition has it that when God fed the Jews *manna* from heaven as they wandered for 40 years in the desert, the divinely dispensed miracle food had the magical ability to taste like whatever the person who consumed it wanted it to be. According to legend, the most requested flavor was *yoykh*, usually ordered "the way Mama makes it."

Obviously, you'll have to take a bowl of the chicken soup first. Nothing stops you, though, from ordering another *zup* as well just to make sure that you don't starve and that you have something warm in your *boykh*, your belly. Try a *borsht* (same in Yiddish and in English); a *perl groypen-zup*, a barley soup; a *shthav*, a shave soup; an *arbeszup*, a split pea soup; a *kartofel-zup*, a potato soup; or a *grinsen-zup*, a vegetable soup. That should hold you until we come to the main course.

Ready for the Entree?

For the main entree, you'll have to decide whether you want your meal *gekokht* (boiled) or *gebroten* (roasted). If *gebroten*, do you like it *roy* (rare), *farbrent* (well-done; literally, burned), or somewhere in the *miten* (middle)? *Yeder eyner hot lib vos er hot lib*—everyone likes what he (or she) likes. Here are some choices of different foods:

With a Shmaykhel

In the middle of a dramatic performance of *Hamlet*, the house lights dimmed and the stage manager stepped forward with a tragic announcement: "We regret to inform you that we must stop the play because the star just had a heart attack and died."

From the balcony came the scream of an elderly woman, "Give him chicken soup."

"Madam, I don't think you understand—he's dead. What good would chicken soup possibly do for him?"

"It *vudent hoyt*," came the reply of the chicken soup *meyven*.

Yiddish	English	Yiddish	English
rinderns	beef	*pekel-fleysh*	corned beef
bolonyer vursht	bologna	*holubtshes*	stuffed cabbage
kaphon	capon	*karp*	carp
hun	chicken	*gehakte hun*	chicken fricassee
kelberne kotleten	veal chops	*oyfshnit*	cold cuts
kishke	stuffed derma	*katshke*	duck
ayer mit salami	eggs with salami	*gepregelte fish*	fried fish
vurshtlekh	frankfurters	*gebakene beblekh*	baked beans
gandz	goose	*gulash*	goulash
shepsenfleysh	lamb	*kotleten*	chops, cutlets
leber	liver	*leber mit tsibeles*	liver and onions

continues

111

continued

Yiddish	English	Yiddish	English
lokshen-kugel	noodle pudding	*latkes*	pancakes
roselfleysh	pot roast	*shepsene riplekh*	rib steak
Tsung	tongue	*indik*	turkey

You're Entitled to Two Sides

You can't have a main course without a little something on the side. Here are a few suggestions:

Yiddish	English	Yiddish	English
fasolyes	beans	*burikes*	beets
meren	carrots	*kalifyor*	cauliflower
seleri	celery	*ugerkes*	cucumbers
salat	lettuce	*shvemlekh*	mushrooms
tsibeles	onions	*arbes*	peas
fefer	peppers	*bulbes*	potatoes
retekhlekh	radishes	*shpinat*	spinach
tomaten	tomatoes		

Khap a Nash

The word for carrots, **meren,** also means to make more, to increase. That's why Jews traditionally eat carrots on **Rosh Hashanah,** the Jewish New Year's Day—it's a sign that their good deeds and length of their days will hopefully increase during the coming year.

A Little Dessert?

You can't possibly be full yet. How do I know? Your eyes are still open, and you haven't collapsed. Every Jewish host and hostess will now insist that you top off the meal with a little dessert, the specialty of the house. You have your choice of fruits, nuts, pies, pastry, and sherbet:

Yiddish	English	Yiddish	English
epel	apple	*yagedes*	berries
kirshen	cherries	*oybst*	fruit
troyben	grapes	*fershkes*	peaches
barnes	pears	*ananasen*	pineapples
floymen	plums	*getrikente floymen*	prunes
rozhinkes	raisins	*mandlen*	almonds

Yiddish	English	Yiddish	English
nis	nuts	*erdnislekh*	peanuts
velishenis	walnuts	*pikanen*	pecans
gebakener epel	baked apple	*kukhen*	cake
kavekukhen	coffee cake	*honiglekekh*	honey cake
tort	sponge cake	*kikhlekh*	cookies
kompot	stewed fruit	*gebeks*	pastry
shtrudel	strudel	*frukhtayz*	sherbet

Don't you dare say you're finished yet. The meal isn't over until you wash everything down with a *gleyzel tey* (a glass of tea). As the classic Jewish story goes, "Why," wondered the hotel guest, "do I feel so bloated after having only several doubles of every course offered?" After a bit of reflection, he came to the only logical conclusion: *Dos gleyzel tey hot mikh avegeharget*—"The glass of tea killed me."

The Least You Need to Know

➤ For things you're doing right away, use the forms of the word *geyn* (to go), followed by the infinitive.

➤ For things you're going to do in the future, use the forms of *vel* (will), followed by the infinitive.

➤ Knowing the correct words for food items will allow you to order what you want to eat in Yiddish.

Part 4

On the Town

Tired of hanging out only around the house?

Part 4 will help you get out and really enjoy yourself. Of course, you'll need to know how to get wherever you're going—car, taxi, bus, or subway. Don't worry. Not only will your Yiddish get you there, but you'll have a great time whatever your destination. If it's a restaurant you're headed for, there's hardly a thing you won't know how to order (unless it's bacon and eggs, which you shouldn't say in Yiddish). The movies, the theater, sporting events—Yiddish can take you to all of them. And let's not forget the ultimate entertainment for a people committed to worship of the retailing concept known as wholesale—the art of shopping. If you work too hard studying this section, you'll be delighted to know that it closes with everything you always wanted to know about vacations but were afraid to ask.

As you embark upon Part 4, I offer you every Jewish mother's parting words as her child leaves the house: "Have a good time—and don't forget your sveter."

Chapter 11

How Should We Go?

In This Chapter

➤ Driving with confidence

➤ Taking public transportation

➤ Talking about things that happened in the past

A great *New Yorker* cartoon has two women standing behind Moses in the desert and complaining, "Forty years we've been wandering, lost in the desert, and just like a man he refuses to ask for directions." The ancient Israelites may have been slow to get to the Promised Land—but then again they didn't have the benefit of modern transportation. Today, we thankfully have many options for getting around quickly. A Yiddish conversationalist like yourself should be familiar with the words and the expressions needed to get around speedily and safely.

As a general rule, it's good to remember that modern inventions that came into being within the last century are generally identified by their English names, even in Yiddish. A car is a *kar*, a subway is a *subvey* (notice the "v" sound), and a taxi is a *teksi* (for some reason, Yiddish prefers the "e" sound to a broad "a"). But if you're going to use the modern means of transportation, you have to be prepared for a host of contingencies that require indigenously Yiddish expressions. This chapter will help you get out of the house and move around comfortably.

Let's Take the Car

Let me start by dispelling the rumor that, for years, Jews allegedly thought another word for car was *Kedillak*. That may have been the dream of every *shvitzer* (braggart or show-off, literally "someone who perspires" because he's so busy trying to impress you) or *plosher* (an even greater version of a blow-hard egotist who inflates and exaggerates his resources). In reality, however, most Jews had to settle for a *Karele*—the diminutive *le* not only communicates that the car they drove was smaller, but also considerably cheaper.

With a Shmaykhel

Cohen came into a lot of money late in life and didn't stop trying to impress his old friends with his newfound riches. You want to know what kind of **plosher** he was? After a trip to Rome, he claimed he had a personal audience with the Pope. His duly impressed friends couldn't help but gasp with awe and ask: "Well, what did you think of him?" "*He* was marvelous. *Her* I didn't care for," was the *plosher's* reply.

Here's a handy list of important phrases you'll need for your car trip. I strongly suggest that you look carefully at the first one and take care of it before doing any driving.

Travel Tips by Car

English	Yiddish
Where do I get a driver's license?	*Vu krig ikh a firlitsentz?*
How long does it take to learn to drive a car?	*Vi lang nemt dos zikh oys-lernen tsu traybin an auto?*
Where do you buy gas?	*Vu koyft men gazolin?*
Where is the gas station?	*Vu iz faran a gazolin stantsye?*
Where am I?	*Vu bin ikh?*
What town is this?	*Velkhe shtot iz dos?*
Can you show me the right way?	*Efshar kent ir mir vayzen dem rikhtigen veg?*
Is this a good road?	*Tzi iz dos a guter veg?*
Where does that road go?	*Voo-a'heen firt yener veg?*
Do you perhaps have a map?	*Tzi hot ir a karte?*
Can you show it to me on the map?	*Tzi kent ir mir es vayzen oyf der karte?*
How much is a gallon of gas?	*Vifil kost a galon gazolin?*
Give me ten gallons.	*Git mir tzen galon.*
Please change the oil.	*Zayt azoy gut, bayt oys di oyl.*

English	Yiddish
I use light oil.	*Ikh nuts laykhte oyl.*
I must have medium oil.	*Ikh muz hoben mitele oyl.*
My car needs heavy oil.	*Meyn auto darf hoben shvere oyl.*
I need water in the battery.	*Ikh darf vaser in der baterye.*
Can you wash my car soon?	*Tsi kent ir ovashen meyn auto bald?*

Oy Vey, I'm in Trouble

English	Yiddish
I have trouble with my brakes.	*Ikh hov tsores mit mayn tormoz.*
Do me a favor, check the tires.	*Tut mir a toyve, kent ir kontroliren di rayfen.*
Oh God, I have a flat.	*Oy ribono shel oylom, ikh hob a punktsher (a lokh in rayfen).*
Can you fix the flat tire?	*Tsi kent ir farrikhten dem geplatsten rayfen?*
Where can I find a mechanic?	*Vu ken ikh gefinen a mekaniker?*
I need air.	*Ikh darf luft.*
The _____ doesn't work.	*Di _____ arbet nit.*
What's wrong?	*Vos iz?*
There's a grinding.	*Es raybt zikh.*
There's a leak.	*Es rint.*
There's a noise.	*Es klopt.*
The engine overheated.	*Der motor hot zikh ibergehitst.*
Can I park here for a while?	*Tsi ken ikh do a vayle parken?*
I'm sorry to bother you.	*Zayt mokhel vos ikh bin aykh matriakh.*
My car has broken down.	*Mayn auto iz kalye gevoren.*
Can you pull me?	*Tsi kent ir mikh shlepen?*
Can you push me?	*Tsi kent ir mikh a shtup geben?*
Can you help me jack up the car?	*Tsi kent ir mir helfen unter-heyben dem auto?*
Can you drive me to a garage?	*Tsi kent ir mekh tsufiren biz a garadzh?*
My car is stuck in the mud.	*Mayn auto iz gebliben shteken in blote.*
My car is in the ditch.	*Mayn auto iz in groben.*
Officer, I didn't see the light.	*Ofitsir, ikh hob nish gezen di farkerlomp.*
Where is the traffic court?	*Vu iz des farker-gerikht?*
I don't deserve this summons.	*Der roof-tsetl kumt mir nisht.*

A Gut Vort

Shlemazel comes from the German **shlim** (bad) and the Hebrew **mazel** (luck). A **shlemazel** is somebody whom fate has designated as a born loser. He's so unlucky that his junk mail arrives "postage due." The **shlemiel** (clumsy neb) is, of course, the one who spills the soup, always making sure to get it all over the suit of the **shlemazel.**

A Gut Vort

Moshiakh is the Hebrew for *Messiah* and literally means "the anointed one." According to Jewish tradition, the Messiah (just like a king) would be initiated into his office by the sacramental pouring of oil on his head. The Latin for "the anointed one" is **Christus,** or Christ. And that's how Jesus got what most people erroneously think is his last name.

Now that you see the list of all the things that can go wrong, maybe you'll decide not to take the car after all!

Better by *Teksi* ...

If you prefer to take a taxi to get to your destination, you'll want to know these important phrases:

➤ *Zayt azoy gut, ruft mir a teksi.* (Please call me a taxi.)

In the old vaudeville routine, when someone asks his friend, "Call me a taxi," the friend replies, "Okay, you're a taxi." The construction of the sentence allows that peculiar interpretation because we don't say, "Call a taxi *for me.*" In Yiddish, we have the same margin for error. *Rooft mir* means call me, like in "Call me rabbi," or "Call for me a cab" or whatever else I need. It's when a Jewish mother says, "Call my son a doctor," that you're never really sure what she means. Is she boasting or pleading for medical assistance?

➤ *Vifil vet es kosten?* (How much will it cost?)

Take a cab in Israel, and invariably the driver will point to the meter and claim it doesn't work. Instead he'll quote you a price that depends totally upon whether he thinks you are a *shlemazel* or a native. Best to insist on the meter, but if that doesn't work, make sure you have a fixed price in advance.

➤ *Dos iz tsu fil.* (That's too much.)

This is one of the most important phrases you have to learn in Yiddish to survive. Just because it appears in the section on taxis doesn't take away its relevance for any other occasion where cost is a factor. Don't feel that you look like a cheapskate when you make this statement:

It's practically expected in almost every business transaction. If you accept the first offer, you're not only a fool, but you make the other person feel really bad. After all, he's going to say to himself, "This idiot would have paid anything I asked him—why did I start out so low?"

➤ *Zayt azoy gut, fort a bisel mer obgehiten.* (Please drive more carefully.)

The driver, of course, will respond to this perceived criticism with a question: *"Ir vilt az ikh zol varten far Moshiakh?"*—"Do you want me to wait for the Messiah? How slowly can I possibly drive? We all know that the Messiah will come riding on a donkey, and if I go any slower, he'll beat me to my destination."

➤ *Shtelt zikh do op.* (Stop here.)

The best thing to do to make sure you don't go past your stop is to make several announcements beforehand that you're getting close. For example, using the phrase *Mir halten shoyn noent* (we're already near) is a good choice for announcing your intentions to get off soon. When you are almost at the very spot, there's nothing more appropriate than a very rapid repetition of the word *ot*, as in *ot, ot, ot*. It's one of those untranslatable sounds that can be used in many situations implying, "That's it!"

➤ *Vart oyf mir.* (Wait for me.)

Here's another great phrase whose usage extends far beyond taxi passenger to driver. I can visualize almost a dozen scenes from the Yiddish theater where the young man or woman is forced by unavoidable circumstance to leave a loved one and pleads with a cry, *"Vart oyf mir,"* as the curtain closes to bring the first act to an end.

With a Shmaykhel

The rabbi stands in line in the other world waiting to be asked the questions that will determine whether he is worthy of entering heaven. With great fanfare, a rough-looking man is quickly ushered to the front of the line and given great respect. "Who is he", the rabbi wonders aloud, "to take precedence over scholars and religious leaders?" An angel overhears and responds, "He was a cab driver." "Why does that make him so special?", the rabbi persists. "You don't understand," the angel said. "You may have influenced a few people to turn to God, but whoever stepped into his cab immediately began to pray with total devotion."

Wise Sayings

"Poverty is no disgrace—which is the only good thing you can say about it."

—Folk saying

121

... or Public Transportation

You don't have to be a *kabtsen* to decide to take a bus or a subway. A *kabtsen* isn't just a poor person whose poverty makes him worthy of pity. To be a *kabtsen* is to be a cheapskate. When the rabbi asks people to make a pledge for a worthy charity and to give until it hurts, the *kabtsen* makes clear that the thought of giving alone causes him pain. Buses and subways are often not only a cheap, but also a preferable alternative.

Remember, it's perfectly good Yiddish to call a bus *a boss,* a streetcar *a streetkar,* and a subway *a subvey.* The driver of the bus is a *drayver,* and if you need to change for another bus you simply ask for a *trensfer.*

You may need just a little more Yiddish to express these ideas:

Yiddish	English
Tzi fort ir leben ____?	Do you go near ____?
Ikh vil aropgeyn baym kumendiken opshtel.	I want to get off at the next stop.
Velkhe numer bos zol ikh nemen?	What number bus do I take?

That should take care of most of your questions. Now get yourself a Jewish newspaper like the *Forward's* and enjoy the ride.

Did You Sing on the Trip?

Why do I ask if you sang while you traveled? Only because that's a great *segue* to another important bit of grammar we have to learn at this point. You studied the present tense in Chapter 6, "Meeting People and Making Friends." In Chapter 10, "Let's Eat—*Esen, Esen, Esen,*" you learned to conjugate verbs in the future tense. In the famous words of Santayana, "Those who do not remember the past are condemned to repeat it." So, let me show you how to express yourself in the past tense.

Living in the Past

Actually, the past tense in Yiddish is rather simple. In English, we can express the past in a number of ways. For example, you can say, I laughed, I did laugh, I was laughing, or I have laughed. In Yiddish, these are all expressed in one and the same way: *Ikh hob gelakht.*

To form a past tense, you need an auxiliary or helping verb which, in most cases, is the Yiddish word for the verb "to have": *hoben.* This word is conjugated and then added to the past participle of the infinitive. Don't let the descriptives confuse you. For the most part, a past participle is derived from the base of the verb in a simple way. The infinitive for the word *laugh* is *lakhen.* Ignore the suffix, which is there only to define it as an infinitive, and think of the root word, *lakh*. Always add the prefix *ge-* and the suffix *t-* and you have the past participle, *gelakht*. That word will remain constant in every form of the past tense as we conjugate the word "have" with every different pronoun. Here's an example:

English	Auxiliary Verb	Past Participle
I laughed	*Ikh hob*	*gelakht*
you laughed	*du host*	*gelakht*
you (formal) laughed	*ir hot*	*gelakht*
he laughed	*ir hot*	*gelakht*
she laughed	*zi hot*	*gelakht*
we laughed	*mir hoben*	*gelakht*
you (plural) laughed	*ir hot*	*gelakht*
they laughed	*zey hoben*	*gelakht*

Now that we're all in such a happy, laughing mood, why not try it yourself with these words? I'll give you the infinitive as well as the past participle to get you started.

English	Yiddish (infinitive)	Yiddish (past participle)
to work	*arbeten*	*gearbet*
to bring	*brengen*	*gebrengt*
to burn	*brenen*	*gebrent*
to hear	*heren*	*gehert*
to say	*zogen*	*gezogt*
to dance	*tantsen*	*getantst*
to think	*trakhten*	*getrakht*
to make	*makhen*	*gemakht*
to ask	*fregen*	*gefregt*
to know	*kenen*	*gekent*
to talk	*reden*	*geredt*

There's Always an Exception

Now that you have the hang of it, I have to break the bad news to you. Sometimes there is a different way to form the past participle. Occasionally, the suffix isn't the *-t* but rather an *-en*. When that happens, the shift in pronunciation causes a little change in the base word as well. Using the infinitive *zingen* (to sing) is a perfect example of this exception to the rule. Add the *ge-* to the beginning of the word, but don't drop the ending. Just change the pronunciation to *gezoongen*. Why? Don't ask me—it just sounds right.

Another example of a word in this series is the Yiddish for "to write," *shrayben*. The past participle is *geshriben*, and at this very moment, *Ikh hob geshriben* another chapter.

The following list provides some more examples of words ending in *-en* that maintain their suffix instead of getting a *-t* for the past participle:

English	Yiddish (infinitive)	Yiddish (past participle)
to give	*geben*	*gegeben*
to order	*haysen*	*gehaysen*
to see	*zen*	*gezen*
to do	*ton*	*geton*
to take	*nemen*	*genumen*
to eat	*esen*	*gegesen*

Now that you know every tense in Yiddish, you can stop being tense because you're almost a Jewish scholar.

The Least You Need to Know

➤ The past tense in Yiddish is formed by conjugating the word *hoben* (to have) and adding the past participle.

➤ A past participle is derived from the base of the infinitive with a prefix *ge-* and a suffix *-t*.

➤ Some past participles are irregular and add an *-en* suffix instead of a *-t*, with a slight change in pronunciation of the base as well.

Chapter 12

A Table for Ten

> ## In This Chapter
>
> ➤ Preparing for a culinary experience
>
> ➤ Learning about religious laws concerning meat and dairy
>
> ➤ Introducing common words
>
> ➤ How Jews toast each other—and why they use that word

Ever hear this classic line used by Jewish comedians: "When it comes to food, what's the favorite thing Jewish women love to make? Reservations." The truth is, there's nothing wrong with that. It's hard to always prepare meals at home, and restaurants are a welcome break for the difficult labors of daily living. Going out is good not only for the body, but also for the soul. Families and friends have a chance to not only leisurely eat, but to *shmooze* as well. (And just in case you don't know what *shmoozing* means, I can only tell you that *shmoozing* is to conversation what lovemaking is to kissing.)

When Jews go to synagogue, they require a quorum of ten for prayer, called *a minyan*. A service to God without being surrounded by friends is unimaginable. When Jews go out to eat, they'll just as readily feel the need to order a table for ten to turn two hours of dining into a social event. Here, the menu takes the place of a prayer book, the waiter serves his "congregants" instead of the rabbi, and the experience—if it lives up to expectations—inspires everyone to be grateful to God.

Pick a Restaurant

Some years back, a Yiddish song became very popular among Jews. Its title, as well as oft-repeated refrain, was "Vuahin Zol Ikh Geyn?" ("Tell Me Where Shall I Go?") It expressed the dilemma of Jewish history as a people who was forever forced to decide on a land for their next possible haven. Thankfully, today, when that phrase is used, it usually refers to the difficult choice that has to be made between competing eating establishments.

One option, of course, is always the deli. A word created by a sign painter who had difficulty with the longer form, delicatessen, it still maintains its link with the original German via French via Latin, *delicatus*, which means giving pleasure. German, and then Yiddish, added the word *esen* (to eat) to the root of this Latin term, and *voilà*—if you'll forgive a French word in this melange of languages—a *delicatessen*, a place giving pleasure for eating, was born. (What I've always wondered is how a deli could possibly give pleasure if it leaves out the *esen!*)

Because Jews associated meat meals with festive occasions (on the Sabbath and holidays, it is religiously required to eat meat to acknowledge the special joy of the day), delis tended to specialize in meat products—salami, pastrami, corned beef, as well as chicken soup. If they observed the rules of Kashrut, which prevented them from serving dairy foods at the same time, the deli was a strictly *fleishig* (meat) restaurant.

If you're more in the mood for cheese blintzes than chicken soup, you go to a *milkhik*, or *milkhidiker*, restaurant. Here you'll definitely have to give up your diet because most of the dishes, just like the blintzes, require a heavy portion of *smetene* (sour cream). (Even the *borsht*, great with meat, tastes absolutely fantastic when mixed with cream.)

Just as many Jews don't feel themselves bound to follow the laws of dieting, quite a few of them ignore the religious dietary laws as well. That means they eat *treyf*, the Yiddish (and Hebrew) word for non-kosher food.

With a Shmaykhel

It could have happened only in a Jewish deli:

The customer frantically calls the waiter to his table. "Look, look."

"So I'm looking already. Should I be seeing here the Olympics?"

"No, here in my soup. What's that *fly* doing there?"

"To me, I wouldn't swear, but I think it's doing a backstroke."

A Gut Vort

Treyf literally means "torn" and refers to an animal killed not by the painless, ritually required method of slaughtering, but torn apart by another beast in the field. *Treyf* has become a generic word to describe food that is non-kosher for a host of other reasons as well, including its method of preparation and the use of forbidden ingredients.

When Jews want to describe a restaurant that is strictly kosher and that abides by all the rules, it is called *glatt kosher* in Yiddish. If a place is so non-kosher that it serves even ham, the most forbidden of meats, it is referred to *khazer treyf*, pig *treyf*.

Two Sets of Silverware

You can't dine without cutlery. You'll need a *meser* (knife); of course, you can't do without a *gopel* (fork) either. For the soup, you need a *lefel* (spoon). Better yet, if it's a big bowl of soup, make sure you have a *groyser lefel* (a large spoon). For the tea, you'll need a *lefele* (teaspoon). All these will come into use when *der kelner* (the waiter) brings you a *teler* (plate) with the huge servings that betray this order as Jewish food rather than French cuisine.

It often amazes people to discover how strict religious Jews are concerning the law of not mixing meat and milk. Not only are meat and dairy products not eaten together, but even silverware may not be switched off from use for one to the other. Religious Jews are required by tradition to have two sets of silverware as well as dishes, one for meat and one for dairy.

Oy Vey

"Watch out for the pig," say the rabbis. Of all the non-kosher animals, it is the one to be most wary of because of its capacity for deception. To be kosher, an animal needs two signs: It must have split hooves and chew its cud. Almost all non-kosher animals have neither of these signs. The pig *does* have split hooves. It sticks them out as if to say, "Look, I'm kosher." Beware, say the rabbis, of the hypocrite who wants to pass as pious because he can point to one thing that seems to declare him righteous.

To make matters more interesting, religious Jews would usually also have dishes for daily use as well as those for *Shabes*, holidays, and special occasions. That makes four sets right there. Add another two sets for the special requirements of Passover use—when dishes and silverware that came into contact with bread products are off-limits—and you get a grand total of six sets of dishes! Now you understand why Jews so often went into merchandising and became the founders of some of the most famous department stores originally specializing in household supplies.

Want to know how serious this aspect of the dietary law is? Don't make me swear for the truth of this story, but it's a great way to get a lesson in reading a Yiddish tale, while hopefully getting a good laugh at a Yiddish reworking of an American legend.

The Yiddish Pocahontas

Yiddish	English
A mol zaynen geven dray Indians. Di mama, Pocayenta, der tate, Geronowitz, un di tokhter, Minihorowitz. Ein mol, kumtaheym Minihorowitz un zogt, "Mama, ikh vil khasene hobn!"	Once there were seven Indians. The mother, Pocayenta, the father, Geronowitz, and the daughter, Minnie Horowitz. One day, Minnie Horowitz comes home and says, "Mama, I want to marry."
"Khasene hobn! Es iz shoyn tsayt! Du bist itst an alte moyd! Zekhtsen yor alt! Ver iz der bokher?"	"Marry! It's high time! You are now already an old maid! Sixteen years old! Who is the young man?"
"Oy, mama, hob ikh getrofen a bokher! A kresavits."	"Oh, mama, did I find me a boy! Very handsome!"
"Vos iz zayn nomen?"	"What is his name?"
"Siting Bulvon."	"Sitting Bullvon."
"Vos far a yikhus hot er?"	"What kind of a background does he have?"
"Zeyn tate iz Meshugener Ferd, der gantser makher fun di shvartsfus trayb."	"His father is Meshugener Horse, the whole boss of the Blackfoot Tribe."
"Oy, velen mir hoben a khasene! Ale di Shvartsfus, ale di Shomohawks, un di gantse meshpokhe. Oy, oy, oy, mir hoben eyn tsore."	"Oy, will we have a wedding! All the Blackfoots, all the Shmohawks, and the whole family. Oy, oy, oy, we have a problem!"
"Vos iz?"	"What's the matter?"
"Di tipi iz nisht groys genug far ale di gest fun khasene. Geronowits! Geronowits, shtey oyf fun dayn tukhes un gey krig far mir a bufalo!"	"The teepee isn't big enough for all the guests of the wedding! Geronowitz, get off your backside and go bring for me a buffalo."
"Farvos wilstu a bufalo?"	"Why do you want a buffalo?"
"Mitdem fleysh fun bufalo, ken ikh makhen a gut gedempte bufalo tsimis. Un mitdem pelts ken ikh makhen greser di tipi. Un mir velen kenen laden di gantse velt tsuder khasene!"	"With the meat of a buffalo, I can make a good steamed buffalo tsimis and from the fur I can make the teepee bigger, and we will be able to invite the whole world to the wedding!"
Geyt avek Geronowitz. Eyn tog. Tsvey teg. Nisht kayn Geronowitz. A vokh shpeter, kumt aheim Geronowitz, mit gornisht in zayne hent.	Geronowitz goes away. One day. Two days. No Geronowitz. A week later, Geronowitz comes home with nothing in his hands.
"Shlemil! Vu iz mayn bufalo?" fregt Pocayente.	"Schlemiel, where is my buffalo?" asks Pocayenta.
"Du un dayn bufalo tsimis! Ikh hob aykh beide in bod!"	"You and your buffalo tsimis! I have you both in a bath!"
"Vos iz?"	"What's the matter?"

Yiddish	English
"Ershten tog, hob ikh gezen a bufalo. Nit groys genug far a tipi, nit gut genug far tsimis. Tsvayten tog, hob ikh gezen an andere bufalo. Gut genug, groys genug, ober mit aza farfoylten pelts! A miskayt fun a bufalo vos ikh hob keynmol nit gezen! A por teg speyter, hob ikh gezen an andere bufalo. Groys genug, gut genug, a poifect bufalo!"	"First day, I saw a buffalo. Not big enough for a teepee, not good enough for *tsimis*. Second day, I saw another buffalo. Good enough, big enough, but with a spoiled pelt! Such an ugly buffalo have I never seen before! A few more days, I saw another buffalo. Big enough, good enough, a perfect buffalo."
"Nu, vos iz geshen?"	"So, *nu?*"
"Bin ikh gegangen tsu shekhten dem bufalo. Hob ikh gekukt in mayn tash, un Goyishe kop! Ikh hob genumen mit mir dem milkhediken tomahawk!"	"I went to slaughter the buffalo. I looked in my bag and non-Jewish head! I brought with me the dairy tomahawk!"

Words to Remember

Of course, you know the meaning of *tepee* and *tomahawk*. Tell the truth, are you just as clear about the word *tsore* and *tsimis*? I love the story because it has such wonderful words and expressions sprinkled throughout, and I can't resist clarifying them in just a little greater detail:

With a Shmaykhel

The women are sitting around a table discussing their families. Everyone proudly relates the accomplishments of their children until Sadie confesses, "Unfortunately, God did not see fit to bless me with children." "No children? I can't believe it," cries Becky. "What do you do with yourself? How do you cope? Where do you get your *tsores?*"

➤ *Tsimes*, from the old German, *zumessen*, is a stew of fruit and/or vegetables served as a side dish for dessert. That hardly explains its flavor, or gives any clue of its extended meaning. As a culinary dish, it is usually made as sweet as candy and adds the sugary taste to everything else on the plate. Its composition, as a mixture of many items, leads to its usage as a synonym for "a big deal," an overcomplicated, mixed-up situation: "I disagreed with her and she made a whole *tsimes* out of it." "I showed up five minutes late and you should have seen the *tsimes*." "It started out as a small engagement party, but then she rented the *Queen Elizabeth—oy*, did she make a *tsimes!*"

Oy Vey

Be careful when somebody uses the initials TOT: They're telling you to put up or shut up. This is a very strong expression that tells you to lay your cards on the table, to come up with the money, to prove that you really mean what you're saying. The last two initials, OT, stand for *ofn tish*, on the table. The first T—I'm sure you can figure out for yourself.

➤ A *tsore* is the singular of *tsores*, and to tell you the truth, I never knew anyone who had it only in the singular. "*Oy*, is he *oyf tsores*" applies to the man whose business is going bankrupt, as well as to the man who can't explain to his wife where he was last night.

➤ *Tokhes*, I'll admit, had a tough time making it into this book. It's semi-vulgar, yet often used. In some contexts, it's highly insulting. Other times, it's lovingly cooed to a baby. I finally decided that if Pocayenta could tell her husband to get off his *tokhes*, I can include the word for "backside" or "bottom." Granted, *kush mir in tokhes* won't be translated here (although the word *kiss* is in there, it's not an endearing comment), I will tell you that it's pretty legit to pat the baby on his behind and say, "Zayde is allowed to give you a little *patch in tokhes*." However, almost nobody will be upset if you use the euphemism for *tokhes*—*tushy*—unless they are people who are overprotective and pushy.

➤ *Ikh hob dikh in bod* translates literally into "I have you in the bath." That hardly makes any sense at all. What it wants to convey, though, is anger, lack of respect, and perhaps even total contempt. The closest you can come to this expression in English is probably, "Go to hell." How did it come to have this meaning? It's probably related to the phrase, "I took a bath," if someone loses a fortune, or "I got cleaned out in Las Vegas," if someone suffered severe gambling losses. It seems that "taking a bath" is hygienically sound but not economically healthy. Perhaps that's because in a bath we're totally naked and completely vulnerable.

At the Restaurant

We got a little "buffaloed" by Pocayenta and the problem of the dairy tomahawk, but it's time for us to get back to our meal at the restaurant. Here is a list of phrases you'll need to make sure you're comfortable and get good service:

Yiddish	English
Mir hoben gemakht a rezervatsye.	We made a reservation.
Ven vet zayn fray a tish?	When will there be a free table?

Yiddish	English
Vu iz der hoyptkelner?	Where is the head waiter?
Ikh vil a tish in droysen.	I want a table outside.
Ikh vil a tish neben a fenster.	I want a table by the window.
Ikh hob lib tsu zitsen in vinkel.	I like to sit in the corner.
Zayt azoy gut, badint undz gikh.	Please serve us quickly.
Vos iz di spetsialitet fun restoran?	What is the specialty of the house?
Brengt mir dos menyu.	Bring me the menu.
Tsi ken ikh dos oysbayten oyf _____?	May I change this for _____?
Bet dem hoyptkelner tsu kumen aher.	Ask the head waiter to come here.
Dem kheshbon, zayt asoy gut.	The check, please.
Tsi iz dos trinkgelt arayn-gerekhent?	Is the tip included?

I love the story of the stingy old man who was told he had to leave a tip, so on his way out, he told the waiter: "Buy low, sell high." That's not the kind of tip you should leave. Be generous, and you will be *gebentsht* (blessed).

Constructive Criticism

The scene is a Jewish restaurant. The waiter has just completed a marathon back and forth to the kitchen to serve his large table seven courses. Before handing over the check, he asks, "Was anything satisfactory?"

The religious mission of a Jew is to improve the world. That concept is called *tikun olam*. Transferring it to the mundane, Jews believe that complaining is more than a right; it is a religious obligation.

To criticize the food preparation today means that perhaps when the Messiah comes tomorrow, the food will be better and worthy of this royal guest. *Shem dikh nisht* (don't be embarrassed) is the slogan of every Jewish critic. Learn the following comments, and use them to show that you are a member of the tribe, a critic who can't be easily fooled and whose mission is to make every restaurant live up to its potential for excellence:

Khap a Nash

It's a rare Jew who orders meat served rare. Why? Probably because Jews have a religious aversion to blood. To be kosher, meat must be salted to remove as much blood from it as possible. Bloody meat seems too close to forbidden meat. That's why when Jews see meat burned beyond recognition, they say, "Well done."

Khap a Nash

Letters in Hebrew have a numerical value. The letters of the word *khai* add up to 18. That's why 18 is a symbol of life. Every *bobe* will tell you that it is a source of blessing to give money to charity that is a multiple of the number 18—the ideal is 36, twice *khai*, symbolizing a doubling of your life.

A Gut Vort

Simkhe, from the Hebrew root *someakh,* means happiness. It is usually used to describe an occasion with religious significance, such as a wedding. However, it can be extended to any life moment that *is* cause for celebration: "It's our 50th anniversary. Please come join us at our *simkhe*." The possibilities are as extensive as our gratitude to God for our many blessings.

Yiddish	English
Es iz nit genug gekokht.	This is undercooked.
Es iz tsu hart.	This is too tough.
Es iz tsu zees.	This is too sweet.
Es iz tsu zoyer.	This is too sour.
Es iz tsu kalt.	This is too cold.
Es iz tsu heys.	This is too hot.

I hope you see the pattern here. No matter what it is, it's just a little too, too … something. It may, in fact, be bad enough for you to say:

> *Nemt es avek, zayt azoy gut.* (Take it away, please.)

And then, the ultimate criticism, to be used only if the food is actually inedible or if you are really impoverished:

> *Ikh batsol nit far aza esen.* (I'm not paying for such a meal.)

L'Khayim

Better you should order *a glesel vayn* (a glass of wine), have a few drinks, make a *l'khayim*, and enjoy. Every culture has its favorite toast. For Jews, as anyone who has seen *Fiddler on the Roof* surely knows, the prayer "To life, to life, *l'khayim*," is the wish that is most repeated in every social setting.

Life is God's greatest gift. Life offers opportunities for divine service and the accumulation of good deeds that will stand us in good stead as tickets to heaven. The English call for "cheers," the Swedes yell out, *skoal*, Spaniards say *salud*. Yiddish takes the word *khai* (life) and doubles it with the plural Hebrew ending -*im* so that we will be blessed with twice as much as expected.

A *l'khayim* is particularly in place at every *simkhe*. A *simkhe* is a joyous occasion, be it a *bris*, a *bar mitzvah*, or a wedding. To share a *simkhe* is to acknowledge that human beings best serve God when they demonstrate love for fellow human beings. And that truth is so obvious, I'll drink to it!

The Least You Need to Know

➤ Eating out encourages conviviality, conversation, and closeness between people that makes it almost a spiritual experience.

➤ Religious Jews who observe the scriptures of Jewish law make a total separation between meat and dairy, including even different dishes and silverware.

➤ The inadequacies of a meal can be described with pungent Yiddish expressions.

➤ Be sure to share your happy moments of life with others, and never forget to toast them with the traditional *l'khayim*—prayer for life.

Chapter 13

Let Me Entertain You

In This Chapter

➤ Going out on the town speaking Yiddish

➤ All about adjectives

➤ Studying comparisons and superlatives

➤ How to be an expert shopper

➤ Going to a beauty parlor

Judaism is a religion of joy. The founder of the Hassidic movement of the seventeenth century, Rabbi Israel Baal Shem Tov, summarized it simply: "Whoever lives in joy does his Creator's will." That means not only at times when performing religious rituals, but throughout every moment of life. After all, when God created the world, he reviewed his work every day and proclaimed, "Behold, it is good." Who are we, say the rabbis, to dare disagree with the Almighty's verdict?

Asceticism is a sin. To have a good time is to make use of life as God Himself intended. So, *loz undz zikh freyen*—let us be happy. *Es iz gut tsu zingen un tantsen*—it's good to sing and dance. As the Yiddish proverb puts it, *Es iz beser tsu leben in nakhes aider tsu shtarben in tsar*—it's better to live in joy than to die in sorrow. In this spirit,

let's spend a chapter having a ball and really enjoying ourselves. After all, like the girl in the commercial says, "I'm worth it"—and, as we would say it in Yiddish, *Ikh bin es vert.*

How About a Movie?

Es zenen do azoy fil Yiddishe shoyshpiler (there are so many Jewish actors and actresses), *ken zein siz a mitzve tsu geyn tsu di muvis* (it could be it's a religious good deed to go to the movies). Besides, helping Steven Spielberg to make a few more dollars is assisting a fellow Jew financially, and I'm sure he'll give a lot of it to charity as well.

Before you go, it would be wise to check the *tsaytung* (newspaper) to find out if there is a review of the film you want to see. *Vifil shtern hot men dos gegeben?* (How many stars did they give it?) Is it a movie that has you *lakhen* (laughing) or *veynen* (crying)? Perhaps, like an ideal Jewish play, it will make you do both. *Dos iz b'emes gut* (that's really good) *vayl azoy iz dos leben* (because that's the way life is).

Here are some questions you should be prepared to ask when you get to the cinema:

Yiddish	English
Vifil kost dos?	How much is it (does it cost)?
Iz dos biliger far z'keynim?	Is it cheaper for senior citizens?
Ven heybt zikh on der film?	When does the movie start?
Vi lang doyert der film?	How long is the movie?

Once you're in, you'll want to ask the usher:

Yiddish	English
Tsi ken ikh fun do zen?	Can I see from here?
Iz dos nisht tsu noent?	Isn't this too near?
Iz dos nisht tsu vayt?	Isn't this too far?
Vi azoy gayt men tsum balkon?	How does one get to the balcony?
Tsi iz do a hafsoko?	Is there an intermission?
Vos zogen mentshen ven zey kumen aroys?	What do people say when they come out?

Let's Go to the Theater Instead

True, *dos teyater* (theater) *iz asakh tayerer* (is a lot more expensive), *ober es iz vert* (but it's worth it). In the theater, *zenen do lebedike mentshen* (there are living people).

Here are some things you'll need if you're going to treat yourself to the theater, *oder bay nakht* (either at night), *oder far a matiney* (or for a matinee):

Yiddish	English
rezervirter ort	a reserved place (seat)
a program	a program
a binokal	opera glasses
parterplats	orchestra seat

What you're really hoping for in both the theater and the movies is an experience with a wonderful adjective, so that leads us with a perfect segue into the grammatical rules for those descriptive words that tell how we feel about things.

Agreeable Adjectives

Good and bad, big and small, happy and sad—no matter what the adjective is, it must agree with the noun in gender. We've already learned that every noun has a "sexual identity" of its own. It's not something that's obvious or even predictable. It just is, and we have to memorize its gender. Usage will make it a habit, and sometimes even intuition will get it right. We know that masculine nouns are preceded by *der*, as in *der man* (the man). Feminine nouns are preceded by *di*, as in *di meydel* (the girl). Neuter words take *dos*, as in *dos land* (the land). Finally, you remember that every plural uses the definite article *di*, as in *di meydlekh* (the girls).

Now let's move ahead a little and see what happens when we want to add the adjective *gut* to each of these nouns:

➤ **Masculine nouns**—A good man is a *guter man*. The base form of the adjective, *gut*, gets an *-er* ending added whenever the adjective is to describe a masculine noun. For example, the good Jew is *der guter yid*, the good odor is *der guter reyakh*, the good day is *der guter tog*, and the good father is *der guter tate*.

➤ **Feminine nouns**—An adjective before a feminine noun has an *-e* (pronounced "eh") added to the base word as the suffix. For example, the big city is *di groyse shtot*, the long hand is *di lange hant*, and the hard work is *di shvere arbet*.

➤ **Neuter nouns**—Neuter nouns get the same ending as feminine nouns do when preceded by the definite article; for example, the big country translates as *dos groyse land*, the beautiful child is *dos shayne kind*, and the holy book is *dos heylige bukh*.

Khap a Nash

Jews are known as "people of the book." One of the reasons they deserve this description is because they treat books in their tradition as holy objects. Whenever a book is closed, it is customary to kiss it as if temporarily saying goodbye to a lover. When you close the pages of this book, please do it gently—and come back soon because I'll miss you.

Note carefully this strange exception: An adjective that modifies a neuter noun preceded by the *indefinite* article—that is, the word *a* instead of *the*—remains in its base form without any additional letters added. For example, it's a *groys land* (a big country), not a *groyse land*. Likewise, it's a *sheyn kind* (a beautiful child), a *heilig bukh* (a holy book), and a *freylekh lid* (a happy song).

Who Says It's Not Nice to Compare?

Now that you know how to describe nouns with their adjectives, you're ready to make comparisons. After all, something can be large, but there's always something else that's larger—and then there's something that is the largest. Some women are beautiful, but others are even more beautiful—and then, somewhere in the world, there must be the most beautiful woman. (I'm very lucky because she happens to be living with me in my house, and I call her *mayn vayb* [my wife].)

You'll need to know how to turn the base word of an adjective into its comparative form, as in "heavy" to "heavier," and then to get to the superlative, the "heaviest." (In this case, it may seem a little out of place to use the word *superlative* for "heaviest," especially if it refers to a person).

Comparative adjectives take the ending *-er*. For example, *shver* (heavy) becomes *shverer* (heavier); *reyn* (clean) becomes *reyner*; *varm* (warm) becomes *varmer*. The superlative adds the ending *–est*. To illustrate, note the following:

Positive	Comparative	Superlative
shver (heavy)	*shverer* (heavier)	*shverest* (heaviest)
reyn (clean)	*reyner* (cleaner)	*reynest* (cleanest)
orm (poor)	*ormer* (poorer)	*ormest* (poorest)
raykh (rich)	*raykher* (richer)	*raykhest* (richest)

Some popular adjectives also go through a small vowel change in their comparative and superlative forms. Remember these because they are very common:

Positive	Comparative	Superlative
alt (old)	*elter* (older)	*elster* (oldest)
gezunt (healthy)	*gezinter* (healthier)	*gezintster* (healthiest)
groys (large)	*greser* (larger)	*grester* (largest)
hoykh (tall)	*hekher* (taller)	*hekhster* (tallest)
yoong (young)	*yinger* (younger)	*yingster* (youngest)
lang (long)	*lenger* (longer)	*lengster* (longest)
noent (near)	*nenter* (nearer)	*nenster* (nearest)
frum (religious)	*frimer* (more religious)	*frimster* (most religious)
kalt (cold)	*kelter* (colder)	*keltster* (coldest)
kurts (short)	*kirtser* (shorter)	*kirtster* (shortest)
klug (smart)	*kliger* (smarter)	*kligster* (smartest)
kleyn (small)	*kleiner* (smaller)	*klenster* (smallest)
sheyn (beautiful)	*shener* (more beautiful)	*shenster* (most beautiful)
shmol (small)	*shmeler* (smaller)	*shmelster* (smallest)

There are just a few—very few, I promise—irregular comparatives and superlatives in both Yiddish and English. The adjective itself, for some reason, changes from its base form to another word. For example, you don't say good, goodier, and goodest, but you switch from good to better and best. Likewise, in Yiddish, you say *gut, beser,* and *bester.* The same thing, interestingly enough, happens to the antonym of *good* in English as well as in Yiddish. In English, events take turns from bad to worse and then to the worst. In Yiddish, they go from *shlekht* to *erger* to *ergster.*

Now that you learned all this, you can finally say, *Ikh bin der grester khokhem*—I am the greatest wise person. Saying it, though, will clearly mark you as a *kleyner onov,* a small humble person.

Where Else Can We Go?

It's up to you now to decide *vos iz gut, vos iz beser, un vos iz der bester.* As we say in English, different

With a Shmaykhel

Rather than using superlatives, Jews very often prefer to make comparisons. Richest became **raykh vi** Rothschild. The poor Hebrew school teacher, though, claimed that if he had Rothschild's money, he would be even richer than this paradigm of wealth because, "I would still give some lessons on the side to make a few more rubles."

strokes for different folks—or, as we say in Yiddish, *nisht yeder eyner est mit di zelbe tseyner* (not everyone eats with the same teeth, meaning people have different tastes). If you want other diversions than the movies or the theater, you should explore the following options.

Let's Have a Ball

Do you like sports? Are you sure you're Jewish? Actually, Jews love all kinds of sports. They could sit and watch them for hours. It's only physically doing things that seems so off-putting. Interestingly, baseball, football, golf, and tennis remain in Yiddish *beyzbol, fusbal, golf,* and *teniz.* Guess it didn't pay to make up new words for activities that aren't primarily Jewish sports.

There is a Yiddish word, though, for skating—*glitshen*—although it means not only skating but also skidding or slipping, which may be a wry comment on Jewish skill with this sport. Strangely enough, skiing does have a Yiddish word, *nartlen.* Who knows? Maybe Jews living in the frigid climes of Russia had to learn to ski to get out of town in a hurry at times of *pogroms* and persecutions.

Life's a Gamble

Jews like to gamble, probably because the precariousness of their existence made life an ongoing constant gamble. Also, it reflected the cultural need of those struggling to make a living to find a way to make "one big easy killing." *Shpilen di ferdlekh* (playing the horses) is a challenge too good to be missed. *Ver vet gevinen* (Who is going to win)? is a question whose correct resolution offers the reward of a *sakh gelt* (a lot of money).

With a Shmaykhel

Little Jacob came home excitedly and told his grandpa the good news. "The Yankees won, the Yankees won." "Tell me," asked the **zayde,** "now that the Yankees won—*dos iz gut far di yiden* (this is good for the Jews)?"

Wise Sayings

"**Gelt** and guilt are the two most popular Jewish pastimes."

—Anonymous

Other Diversions

Let's not forget cultural activities. There are always *muzayem* (museums). You want to go see *moleray* (paintings), or perhaps some *skulptur* (sculpture). You probably should buy *a firer-bikhl* (a guide book). Make sure to ask before you take photographs: *Tsi meg ikh fotografiren* (May I take pictures)?

Hooray, It's on Sale

Of all the things to do, shopping is surely one of the most enjoyable. You not only have a good time, but you come home with something. Shopping is a religious experience. After all, God created the world, and it's our obligation to own and appreciate more of it. The Yiddish word you will want to know that is sexier than sexy is *oysfarkoyf*. That means sale! The proper response to *oysfarkoyf* is *Ikh vil koyfen* (I want to buy).

Here are some key words you'll need in your negotiations:

biliger (cheaper)	*fayner* (finer)	*greber* (thicker)
enger (tighter)	*shtarker* (stronger)	*laykhter* (lighter)
loyzer (looser)	*enlikh* (similar)	*andersh* (different)
a por (a pair)	*a tuts* (a dozen)	*a halber tuts* (half dozen)

You may also find the following phrases quite useful on your shopping spree:

Yiddish	English
Mir gefelt dos nit.	I don't like that.
Vayzt mir andere.	Show me some others.
Tsi ken ikh dos onmesten?	Can I try this on?
Tsi ken ikh es bashtelen?	Can I order one?
Ven zol ikh es opnemen?	When can I call for it?
Vi lang vet es gedoyeren?	How long will it take?
Tsi kent ir es hoben greyt oyf heynt in ovent?	Can you have it ready this evening?
Es past mir.	It looks good on me.
Pakt es ayn, zayt azoy gut.	Wrap this up, please.
Ikh vil es mitnemen mit zikh.	I'll take it with me.
Tsi kent ir mir dos shiken?	Can you send it to me?
Vemen zol ikh batsolen?	Whom do I pay?
Shikt mir a kheshbon.	Bill me.
Git mir a farkoyf-tsetel.	Let me have a sales slip.
Pakt dos forzikhtik.	Pack this carefully.
Zayt azoy gut, nemt fun mir a mos.	Please take my measurements.
Es past mir nit.	It doesn't fit me.

Where Did You Buy It?

So where do you go to buy all the beautiful things you own? Rule number one, if you're Jewish, is that you have to buy everything wholesale. If that's not available, you look for the four-letter word that means "it's permissible to make an exception and purchase here even though it's retail." In both English and Yiddish, that word, of course, is *sale. Vi kumt es az du host gekoyft in* Bloomingdale's? (How come you bought in Bloomingdale's?) *Vayl es iz geven oyf a sale!* (Because it was on sale!)

Before you can shop in Yiddish, though, you first need to know the generic names of the different stores you'll be going to. So study this list carefully:

Yiddish	English
der universalkrom	the department store
der kleyderkrom	the clothing store
di shnayderay	the tailor shop
di shnayderke	the dressmaker
der shukhkrom	the shoe store
der shuster	the shoemaker
di hutkrom	the hat shop
di tsirungkrom	the jewelry store
der zeygermakher	the watchmaker
der shpilkrom	the toy shop
di opteyk	the drugstore
der ayzenvargkrom	the hardware store
der bikherkrom	the bookshop
dos antikengesheft	the antique shop
di tsukernye	the candy store
di bekeray	the bakery
der fleyshmark	the meat market
di shpayzkrom	the grocery
der kosherer katsev	the kosher butcher

With a Shmaykhel

Cohen goes to Rabinowitz, the tailor. He describes the kind of suit he wants and asks how much it is. "Ten thousand dollars," replies Rabinowitz.

"Are you crazy? Ten thousand dollars for a suit?"

"You don't understand what kind of a suit I have in mind for you. First, I order the finest silk from Kyoto, and then I have it dyed in India. From Australian shepherds I choose a young sheep with the finest wool, which I send to be woven in Scotland. I myself fly to the deepest part of the Mariana Trench to find the most lustrous oysters for buttons. You will have a suit the likes of which no one has ever seen."

Cohen is convinced, but he has one problem. "Too bad, I would take it, but I need it for a *bar mitzvah* this coming *Shabes*."

Without missing a beat, Rabinowitz replies, "You'll have it, you'll have it."

Look for a *Metsiye*

One final note: Whatever you buy, make sure you get a *metsiye*—a find, a bargain, a really great buy! *Goyim* (that's non-Jews, if you still don't know) wait for Godot. Jews wait for a *metsiye*. That's the ultimate thrill. It isn't even so much that you're buying something at a good price. Finding a *metsiye* means that you're beating the system, that you managed to outwit someone else, that you found something that's a real conversation piece because you can use it as a great story at hundreds of Hadassah meetings.

Some years ago, an enterprising man decided to open a Japanese restaurant on Long Island. He thought long and hard about an appropriate name with an oriental flavor. He finally decided on *Take a Metsiye*. His *bobe*, who suggested it to him, knew that it was really Yiddish for "What a Bargain." Almost everyone else thought it was an exotic Japanese phrase connoting luxury and good dining. But to find a dual purpose name like that, now that's a *metsiye*!

With a Shmaykhel

Chaim walks by a store with a large clock in the window. He goes in and asks if the owner can fix his watch.

"What do I know about fixing watches? I'm not a watchmaker. I'm a *mohel*—I perform circumcisions."

"So why, in your window, did you put a clock?"

"So what else do you suggest I should put outside in the window?"

It's Time for a Makeover

Still not happy? Shows and shopping didn't do it for you? Maybe you need to spend some more time on yourself. Fran Lebowitz, the biting satirist of our day, claims, "All God's children are not beautiful. Most of God's children are, in fact, barely presentable." But that's not really so, or it certainly doesn't have to be. Almost anyone today can become *sheyn* or, at the very least, *shener*. "Ugliness," the Yiddish giant Isaac Peretz said, "is the greatest of all sins." So why not take time out for a little makeover—because it's a *mitzve*.

Wise Sayings

"Each conception of beauty is a glimpse of God."

—Moses Mendelssohn, eighteenth-century philosopher and Bible scholar

With a Shmaykhel

How can you tell which Jews are afraid of surgery? They have long noses!

See which of the following phrases you'll want to use soon:

Yiddish	English
Tsi ken ikh makhen a bashtelung?	Can I make an appointment?
Ikh vil a naye frizur.	I want a new hairstyle.
Ikh vil opfarben mayne hor.	I want to dye my hair.
Tsi ken ikh zen di koleer-musteren?	Can I see the color samples?
Ikh vil a permanente ondulirung.	I want a permanent wave.
Ikh vil a shampu.	I want a shampoo.
Ikh vil a bahandlung oyfn ponim.	I want a facial.
Ikh vil a manikir.	I want a manicure.
Ikh vil a masadzh.	I want a massage.
Ikh vil a naye noz.	I want a new nose.

Having said all that, though, King Solomon—known by the Jews as the wisest of all men—probably put it best when he wrote in his Book of Proverbs, "Grace is deceitful, beauty is vain, but a woman that feareth the Lord she shall be praised." True beauty emanates from an inner glow of contentment, of kindness, and of being at peace with oneself and with God.

A Sheyner Yid

The classic Yiddish story says it beautifully:

Yiddish	English
A Yid kumt fun Minsk tsu Pinsk.	A Jew comes from Minsk to Pinsk.
A Pinsker fregt im, "Du kumst fun Minsk? Efsher kenst du mayn khaver Chayim?"	A man from Pinsk asks him, "You come from Minsk? Perhaps you know my friend, Chaim?"
"Chayim ... Chayim, es klingt mir epes in kop az ikh ken em. Dermont mir vi er zet oys."	"Chaim ... Chaim, it rings a bell in my head that I know him. Remind me what he looks like."
"Er iz a gor shmoler un darer Yid."	"He is a very small and skinny Jew."
"Vos nokh kent ir mir zogen als simen?" zogt der Minsker.	"What else can you tell me as a sign?" says the man from Minsk.

Yiddish	English
"Er hot pristshiklekh oyf zayn ponim," *zogt der Pinsker.*	"He has pimples on his face," says the man from Pinsk.
"Ikh bin als nokh nish zikher zogt mir *nokh epes," zogt der Minsker.*	"I'm still not sure, tell me something else," says the man from Minsk.
"Er hot oykh a parakh un a hoyker."	"Yes, he also has no hair and a hunch back."
"Ah, yo, yo," shrayt der Minsker, "der *Chayim. Zikher ken ikh em.* *A sheyner Yid!"*	"Ah, yes, yes," yells the man from Minsk, "that Chaim. Sure I know him. A beautiful Jew!"

The Least You Need to Know

➤ Adjectives agree with the nouns they modify according to gender.

➤ Masculine nouns have adjectives that end in *-er*.

➤ Feminine nouns have adjectives that end in *-e*.

➤ If neuter nouns are preceded by the indefinite article (a), their adjectives remain in their base form.

➤ If neuter nouns are preceded by the definite article (the), their adjectives have an -e ending.

➤ Comparative and superlative adjectives end in *-er* and *-est* respectively.

➤ Assure yourself that beauty is only skin deep and that you're judged by far more than your external appearance.

Chapter 14

Let's Go on Vacation

In This Chapter

➤ Learning about the four corners of the earth

➤ Preparing for a trip by plane, boat, or train

➤ More about the past tense

➤ Yiddish and the Israel connection

➤ Getting comfortable in a hotel

All work and no play doesn't only make Jack a dull person—according to Judaism, it is also strictly forbidden. Jews gave the world the concept of Sabbath, a day of rest. Jews still commemorate Passover as the festival of freedom that brought their slavery in Egypt to an end. Life is meant for more than physical exertion. Every week, the Bible teaches us, "six days shall you labor and do all your work, and the seventh day is a Sabbath to the Lord your God, you shall do no manner of work." The weekday work days allow us to make a living. The day of rest allows us to find a life.

Yet, even the weekly cycle somehow doesn't suffice. Sometimes we just need to get away, to have a change from our regular routine, to clear our heads and *tsu geyn of a vakatsye* (to go on a vacation). Vacations are meant for recreation. The word *recreation* is really re-creation, the opportunity to re-create oneself anew. If God is the original Creator, what could be a holier and more important task than to imitate Him by re-creating ourselves?

Tell Me, Where Shall I Go?

Choices, choices, choices. Before you travel, you have to decide where you want to go. (And, no, it's not true that all Jews have a homing instinct that automatically takes them to Miami Beach!) We might as well start by considering which direction

Khap a Nash

Every synagogue had a special reserved section for the most prominent people of the congregation. To this day, if you are a VIJ (a very important Jew), you may be asked to sit by *der mizrakh vant* (the eastern wall). To sit among the notables in this exclusive area is to reach the heights of social status. Believe me, a seat *bayn mizrakh vant* is worth more than a World Series ticket behind home plate at Yankee Stadium!

A Gut Vort

A *mizrakh,* literally "east," is the name of the "reminder" cloth placed on an eastern wall in Jewish homes to indicate the proper direction for prayer.

we want to go and learning the words for the four points of the compass. Interestingly enough, although most Yiddish words come from old German, Yiddish chose to remain true to biblical Hebrew for directions. Maybe that's the language's way of reminding us that when it comes to knowing where we're going, it's only the words of God that can serve as our ultimate guide.

Mizrakh is east. For Jews, this direction has a very special meaning. Tradition demands that wherever Jews may be, they must face in the direction of Jerusalem and the holy temple whenever they stand in prayer. As Jews were expelled from Israel and scattered throughout the world, they found themselves most often west of the Holy Land. That meant they had to always remember to face *mizrakh*, to the east. Because Jews build their synagogues with an ark in the front containing the Torah, the five books of Moses, synagogue architecture always demanded that houses of worship be built in such a way that the worshippers facing the ark looked to the east.

Throughout the ages, religious Jews would have a special embroidered cloth in their homes called a *mizrakh*, with the word *mizrakh* prominently displayed on it in different styles of calligraphy. Placed on an eastern wall in Jewish homes, this cloth, also known as the "reminder" cloth, served to identify the direction to which people should pray when they worshipped at home. The first Jewish posters weren't pictures of pop stars, but had a religious purpose!

Mayrev is west. Yes, in countries to the east of Israel, Jews pray to *mayrev*. It's only because historically Jews have far more often found themselves west of the Holy Land and therefore have been forced to face east that *mizrakh* has assumed such a holy connotation. For Jews who are east of Israel, the advice to "go west, young man" still applies.

Dorem is south. Another name for it in Hebrew is *negev*. That is probably more well-known because of its association with the southern portion of Israel, most commonly referred to as the Negev. Contrary to what some people believe, *negev* doesn't mean barren or desert land. It just so happens that the Negev is—at least for now—undeveloped and desert-like. The word *negev* itself simply means *south*.

Tsofen is north. The Hebrew word also means "hidden." North was the hidden, elusive area, the place the ancient Jews didn't know too much about.

Jews may decide to travel in any direction—*mizrakh, mayrev, dorem, tsofen*. Yet, if they go to Israel and visit the site where the holy temple once stood, there is one spot in particular to which they will always be drawn. It's the *koysel marovi* (the western wall).

This wall is the last remaining wall of the original four walls surrounding the ancient house of God. Tradition has it that every other part of the temple was built from the contributions of the rich. The poor pleaded for the right to contribute something from their meager funds to beautify the temple. Their hard-earned monies went for the construction of the western wall, the wall on the *mayrev* side. God then promised that *that* wall built with the greatest demonstration of sacrificial giving would never be destroyed. And so it was!

With a Shmaykhel

Cohen went to his travel agent and asked him to recommend a nice country to visit on vacation. Pointing to a globe on his desk, the agent recommended a trip to beautiful Spain.

"Spain? The country of the inquisition that expelled our people in 1492? Are you crazy?"

"Alright, then, how about France?

"France? You want I should remember the crusades? The killings and the cruelty?

So it went from country to country. Whatever the agent recommended, Cohen refused because of its antisemitic associations. In desperation, he finally says to Cohen, "*Nu*, so maybe you have a better idea?"

To which Cohen replies, "So maybe, *efsher*, you have another globe?"

Getting There Is Half the Fun

Everybody knows the real reason why you need a vacation: It's to recuperate from the trip you have to take to get there. Whether you are traveling by car, by train, by boat, or by plane, you need tickets, luggage, lots of patience, and even more money. Here are some important words and expressions you'll need for your travels:

Yiddish	English
Vu ken ikh koyfen a guten tshemedan?	Where can I buy a good suitcase?
Tsi kent ir mir zogen vu es gefint zikh a rayze-bero?	Can you tell me where to find a travel agency?
Ikh vil tsukumen tsum flee-plats.	I want to get to the airport.
Tsi iz der wagzal nont?	Is the railroad station nearby?
Vifil iz dos forgelt?	How much is the fare?
Ven velen mir onkumen?	When are we going to arrive?
Ikh darf a treger.	I need a porter.
Tsi iz der ort farnumen?	Is this seat taken?
Tsi darf ikh zikh iberzetsen?	Do I have to change?
Zayt azoy gut, zogt mir vu aroptsugeyn.	Please be good enough to tell me where to get off.
Vifil kost a bilet in ayn rikhtung?	How much is a one-way ticket?
Vifil kost hin un tsurik?	How much is it there and back? (a round trip)
Ikh vil forn ershte klas.	I want to travel first class.
Fun velkher toyer for ikh op?	From which gate do I leave?
Vifil bagazh meg ikh mitnemen?	How much baggage am I permitted to take?
Ot iz mayn pas.	Here is my passport.
Ikh bin a turist oyf vakatsye.	I'm a tourist on vacation.
Ikh hob nit vos tsu deklariren.	I have nothing to declare.
Dos alts iz far mayn eygenem banuts.	All this is for my personal use.
Dos zaynen matones far di kinder.	These are gifts for the children.
Tsi muz ikh alts efenen?	Must I open everything?
Dos ken ikh nit efenen.	I can't open that.
Ikh vil iberlozen di tshemedanes oyf a vayl.	I want to leave these bags for a while.
Yener iz mayner dorten.	That's mine over there.
Ikh vil foren bay shif.	I want to travel by boat.
Ven muz ikh aroyf oyf der shif?	When do I have to board?
Vu zitst der kapitan?	Where does the captain sit?
Ikh vil an aybertshte dek.	I want an upper-deck seat.
Ikh hob an untershte dek.	I have a lower-deck seat.
Ikh vil dingen a dekshtul.	I want to rent a deck chair.
Ikh bin yamkrank.	I am seasick.
Vu gefint zikh a rate-shifel?	Where is a lifeboat?
Ikh darf a ratering.	I need a life preserver.

Thank God, It's Past Tense

Now that you've made the trip, you can honestly say, *Ikh bin gegangen* (I went). Notice anything unusual about the way I phrased that past tense? It's time to teach you another very important grammatical rule.

In Chapter 11, "How Should We Go?" you learned that to form a past tense, you use an auxiliary verb, the Yiddish *hoben* for "to have," and add it to the past participle of the root of the infinitive. For example, the root of the infinitive of *lakhen* (to laugh) is *lakh*; the past participle (formed by adding the prefix *ge-* and the suffix *-t*) is *gelakht*. The various conjugated forms are *Ikh hob gelakht* (I laughed); *du host gelakht* (you laughed); *er hot gelakht* (he laughed); *zi hot gelakht* (she laughed), and so on.

Wise Sayings

"Fame is not to the wise, nor favour / To the men of skill / Save only to them that have skill / To swim."

—Judah Halevi, *Selected Poems* (Spanish poet, philosopher 1085–1140)

Now here's the new rule you have to learn for some irregular verbs: Some past tenses are conjugated not with the auxiliary verb *hoben* (to have), but with the auxiliary verb *zayn* (to be).

Verbs that use *zayn* as the helping verb in the past tense are generally identified by the following three characteristics:

1. Verbs of motion or being
2. Verbs that are almost always intransitive
3. Verbs that involve the whole body

An example is the verb *geyen* (to go). The past participle is *gegangen*. Here's how you would express the various forms of the past tense, using conjugated forms of the auxiliary verb *zaynen* (to be):

Yiddish	English
Ikh bin gegangen	I went
du bist gegangen	you went
ir zayt gegangen	you (formal) went
er iz gegangen	he went
zi iz gegangen	she went
mir zaynen gegangen	we went
ir zayt gegangen	you (plural) went
zey zaynen gegangen	they went

151

Going All the Way

There aren't that many verbs that use conjugated forms of the verb *zaynen* instead of *hoben* to create the past tense. As I've said, the common denominator for this irregular category of "to be" words is that they involve motion, are intransitive, and include the entire body. Any verb that is conjugated with *zaynen* also has its opposite conjugated the same way. For example, because *geyen* (to go) is in this group, so too is *zitsen* (to sit).

If you have trouble figuring out whether the past participle of a verb is conjugated with *zaynen* or *hoben*, consult the following table that lists those verbs that are conjugated with *zaynen*. It's almost all-inclusive and, as you can see, contains some very common words used in everyday conversations:

English	Yiddish (Infinitive)	Yiddish (Past Participle)
to stay, to remain	*blayben*	*gebliben*
to go, to walk	*geyen*	*gegangen*
to like, to appeal	*gefelen*	*gefelen*
to happen	*geshen*	*geshen*
to hang	*hengen*	*gehongen*
to grow	*vaksen*	*gevaksen*
to become	*veren*	*gevoren*
to ride (an animal)	*rayten*	*geriten*
to swim	*shvimen*	*geshvumen*
to die	*shtarben*	*geshtorben*
to be	*zayn*	*gewen*
to sit	*zitsen*	*gezesen*
to run	*loyfen*	*gelofen*
to lie (opposite of to stand)	*ligen*	*gelegen*
to travel	*foren*	*geforen*
to fly	*flien*	*gefloygen*
to come	*kumen*	*gekumen*
to stand	*shteyn*	*geshtanen*
to sleep	*shlofen*	*geshlofen*
to jump	*shpringen*	*geshproongen*

To make it all stick, use each of these verbs and construct simple sentences using the past participle and conjugated forms of the auxiliary verb *zaynen*.

Now tell me, *vu bist du geforen letsten zumer* (to where did you travel last summer)?

How far did he swim?

Where did they go to take a walk?

What was the fastest time that you ran?

How long did they lie in bed?

What airline did you all fly?

When did they go to sleep?

Would you kindly be good enough and *enfer mir oyf Yiddish*—answer me in Yiddish only!

Milk and Honey

If you're going to travel far, why not make it a vacation to the Holy Land? Yiddish has many words for this religious experience.

To identify Israel properly in both Yiddish and Hebrew, call it *Erets Yisroel*. *Yisroel* (Israel) is the name of the third patriarch of the Jewish people, also known as Jacob. It was his children, all 12 of them, who are the ancestors of the Children of Israel. *Erets* (source of the German word *Erde* and later the English *earth*) means land. As we say in Yiddish: *Yeder Yid vil foren khotsh eyn mol in leben kaynrets Yisroel* (Every Jew wants at least once in his or her lifetime to go to the Land of Israel).

Israel is described in the bible as flowing with "milk and honey." In Yiddish, that's *milkh un honig. Milkh iz gut far kinder* (milk is good for children). Both words, milk and honey, symbolize important blessings for the land. It is their original source of nourishment and the bearer of life. *Honig iz zees*, honey is sweet, delicious and enjoyable. Can you think of two better things to which to compare the Promised Land?

Jews—and even non-Jews—who visit Israel should spend some time going to see the *kvorim*, the graves of great and holy people buried throughout the land. One of the holiest sites, revered by people of many faiths is the *moras hamakhpelah*

A Gut Vort

The name **Israel** literally means "fighter for God." It was added to Jacob's name when he finally recognized that passivity was not always the best option, and he was willing to wrestle with the angel who came to attack him.

Oy Vey

Don't confuse the word *Jews* with the Children of Israel or Israelites. Israelites describes all twelve children of Jacob. When ten of the tribes were lost through dispersion and exile, almost all the ones remaining were descended from Judah. That's why they're called Jews. All Jews are Israelites, but if you're really careful about using words properly, all Israelites aren't Jews.

in Hebron, the Cave of the Couples in which are buried Adam and Eve, Abraham and Sarah, Isaac and Rebeccah, and Jacob and Leah.

Khap a Nash

During the course of its history, Israel has had many names. Before the Israelites came to it, it was known as Canaan. For many centuries, it was Palestine, land of the Philistines. When the Jewish people returned in 1948 and founded the state, they called it Israel to affirm their link with the land going back to Jacob/Israel of old.

Khap a Nash

Leah was much grieved during her lifetime that her sister Rachel, also married to Jacob, was more beloved by him. God pays special heed to the prayers of the oppressed and the down-trodden, so according to tradition He rewarded Leah by granting her the right to be buried side-by-side with her husband in place of Rachel.

Jerusalem is *ir hakoydesh* (the holy city), for it is the city of *tsadikim* (saintly people). Jerusalem was the city in which *Shlomo hamelekh* (King Solomon) built *der heyliger beys hamikdosh* (the holy Temple).

Going to Israel isn't just a trip, it's an *aliyah* (an ascent). Even if you're not on a mountain top but in a valley, you've still gone up, if not physically, then at least spiritually.

Room and Board

No matter where you go, you still have to deal with the petty details of lodging. You don't want to be told, "There's no room in the inn" and that you have to sleep in the street or a stable.

Instead, you'll want to *machen a rezervatsye in a hotel vos iz nit zu tayer* (make a reservation in a hotel that's not too expensive). Perhaps you'll want to be *in tsenter shtot* (in the center of town). Make sure though that it's a place that isn't too *tumeldik* (noisy). Specify whether you want a room with *moltsayten* (meals) or *on moltsayten* (without meals). Indicate whether you'll require a *topelbet* (a double bed) or *an eyntsike bet* (a single bed). Make clear if you want *a vane* (a bath) as well as *a shprits* (a shower). Ask *oyf vifelten gorn* (on what floor) and whether you have to take the *trep* (the stairs) or if there is *a lift* (an elevator).

Hopefully you can take for granted that there is *heis un kalt vaser* (hot and cold water). Nevertheless, be firm in your demand that *Ikh vil zen dem tsimer eyder ikh bin maskim* (I want to see the room before I agree).

If you don't like the room (and even if you do but you'd like to get an upgrade) say *der tsimer gefelt mir nit* (I don't like this room). Ask for a room *mit mer likht* (with more light) or *mit mer luft* (with more air). You're not being a *tsorelayt* (a real pain in the you-know-what) if you ask for these essentials: *bod-hantekher* (bath towels), *vashtikhlekh* (washcloths), hantekher tsum ponim (face towels), *ayz* (ice), and *ayz-vaser* (ice water), as well as where to find a *shikyingel* (a messenger), in case you need some special service.

Whatever you do, don't forget that if the service was good, you've got to leave *trink-gelt*, the Yiddish word for tip that literally means "money for a drink." Please be nice and don't make that just enough for a Coke, but preferably a bottle of single malt scotch—or better.

The Air Raid Siren

Almost every vacation has its horror story. Sometimes it's just a snafu with the schedule. Other times it can be something dangerous and even death-defying. Let's close this chapter with a story about an incident that could have happened in a hotel in Israel:

A Gut Vort

Aliyah, literally "going up," is used both for going to Israel as well as for being called up for the honor of reciting blessings upon the Torah in the syna-gogue. The land and the Bible represent the two spiritual mountains that every Jew is meant to scale.

Yiddish	English
Sam un Seydy zenen geven in zeyr tsimmer in hotel in Erets Yisroel.	Sam and Sady were in their room in a hotel in Israel.
Plutsling hoben zey gehert fun droysen a geshray un di sirene vos bavornt an onfli.	Suddenly they heard from the outside a scream and a siren that warns of an oncoming air raid.
Gelofen zenen zey bald beyde zikh tsu rateven in keyler, er in zayne pidzhames, zi in ir nakhthemd.	They both ran immediately to save themselves in the cellar, he in his pajamas, she in her nightshirt.
Loyfentig, shtelt zikh inmiten op Seydy un zogt zi ken nish geyn vayter. Zi muz zikh tsurik umkeren tsum shloftsimer.	Running, Sady stops in the middle and says she can't go any farther. She must return to the bed-room.
"Vos bis du meshugge," shrayt Sam. "Es iz a sekone. Es iz an onfli. Vos iz azoy vikhtig?"	"What, are you crazy?" screams Sam. "It's dan-gerous. It's an air raid. What is so important?"
"Du farshteyst nisht, Sam. Ikh hob nish kayn breyre. Ikh hob fargessen mayne tseyner."	"You don't understand, Sam. I have no choice. I forgot my teeth."
"Dayne tseyner," shrayt Sam. "Far vos darfs du di tseyner? Vos meynst du, as di Araber geyen varfen sandvitsches?"	"Your teeth," screams Sam. "Why do you need your teeth? What do you think, the Arabs are going to throw sandwiches?"

The Least You Need to Know

➤ Each one of the four directions has special significance for Jews.

➤ Some irregular verbs use conjugated forms of the verb *zaynen* to construct the past tense.

➤ Israel, as the Promised Land, is known by many different descriptives.

Part 5

That's Life

The word life, it has been pointed out, has the shorter word if right at its center. That's because life is filled with so many imponderables. To be human is to recognize the "ifs" of existence.

Language has the obligation to deal with all of life's contingencies. We pray for good health, but, unfortunately, sometimes we get sick. Part 5 teaches you how to identify what ails you, how to talk to the doctor, and how to deal with your pain. You'll hopefully be able to get back to work, so this section will also teach you all about the different ways to find employment, the various jobs and professions, and the beautiful insights of Yiddish about the value of human labor and creativity.

Life is a challenge, but it is also a gift. Jews spend a great deal of time praying for health and for years, and "God talk" is an essential component of Yiddish. Part 5 will also help you become familiar with the many different ways of talking to the Almighty, just as Tevye did in the unforgettable Broadway smash hit, Fiddler on the Roof.

All the while, as you move on to learning new words and expressions, you'll be introduced to important rules of grammar you'll need to speak clear and comprehensible sentences.

Don't Get Sick!

Gezunt iz beser fun gelt (health is better than wealth). Who can argue the wisdom of this Jewish proverb? Small wonder that for thousands of years, the dream of every Jewish mother has been that her child grow up to be either a doctor or a rabbi. And if she was really blessed by God, then she might even be as fortunate as the mother of Moses Maimonides, whom Jews consider next to Moses of the Bible in importance. This twelfth-century giant actually achieved greatness as both a rabbinic scholar as well as a medical master. In his master work *The Guide for the Perplexed*, he wrote: "The well-being of the soul can only be obtained after that of the body has been secured." To be holy, one has to first be healthy.

That explains the Jewish obsession with healing. That explains the Jewish mother's overprotectiveness. That explains the Yiddish emphasis on words, expressions, idioms, and proverbs that all center around the theme *zay gezunt* (be well).

Discussing Body Parts

Every day when a pious Jew rises from bed, blessings are recited for the use of every part of the body. Just thinking about how everything functions so perfectly makes us realize that we don't have to look for miracles: We ourselves are a miracle. As we say in Yiddish, *a mentsh iz a nes.*

Let's get to know the various parts of the body so that we can tell the doctor what hurts when we have a problem—and so that we can thank God for their proper functioning when we are well:

Yiddish	English	Yiddish	English
dos knekhel	the ankle	*di blinde kishke*	the appendix
der orem	the arm	*di pleytse*	the back
dos blut	the blood	*der beyn*	the bone
di brust	the breast	*di bak*	the cheek
di brust	the chest	*dos kin*	the chin
der kolnerbeyn	the collar bone	*dos oyer*	the ear
der elnboygen	the elbow	*dos oyg*	the eye
di bremen	the eyebrows	*di ve'es*	the eyelashes
dos oygenledel	the eyelid	*dos ponim*	the face
der finger	the finger	*der fus*	the foot
der shtern	the forehead	*di hor*	the hair
di hant	the hand	*der kop*	the head
dos harts	the heart	*di pyate*	the heel
di lend	the hip	*dos eyngeveyd*	the intestines
der kinbeyn	the jaw	*dos gelenk*	the joint
di nir	the kidney	*dos kni*	the knee
der fus	the leg	*di lip*	the lip
di leber	the liver	*di lung*	the lung
dos moyl	the mouth	*di muskel*	the muscle
der nogel	the nail	*der naken*	the neck

Yiddish	English	Yiddish	English
der nerv	the nerve	*di noz*	the nose
di rip	the rib	*der aksel*	the shoulder
di hoyt	the skin	*der sharben*	the skull
der rukenbeyn	the spine	*der mogen*	the stomach
di dikh	the thigh	*der haldz*	the throat
der grober finger	the thumb	*der finger fun fus*	the toe
di tsung	the tongue	*di mandlen*	the tonsils
dos hantgelenk	the wrist	*der boykh*	the belly

Now practice this section by using your *moyl*. Say the words aloud, and you'll soon know them in your *kop*.

S'tut Vey—It Hurts

Sometimes a diagnosis isn't really that difficult. It may literally be pointing a finger at you with the correct answer. Read this story in Yiddish, and you'll not only get a good review of some important words but also, hopefully, a chuckle:

Yiddish	English
A yid kumt tsum doktor un baklogt zikh. "Ikh hob groyse tsores," zogt er.	A Jew comes to a doctor and complains. "I have big problems," he says.
"Vos tut aykh vey?" fregt der doktor. "Zogt mir genoy vel ikh aykh kenen helfen."	"What hurts you?" asks the doctor. "Tell me exactly and I'll be able to help you."
"Avade un avade. Ikh vel aykh zogen vos tvrt mirve. Ober ikh muz aykh zogen foroys az es is zeyer modne."	"Surely and surely. I will tell you what bothers me. But I must tell you beforehand that it is very strange."
"Vos iz azoy modne?" fregt der doktor.	"What is so strange?" asks the doctor.
"Vayl ikh hob a min krankhayt vos iz aponim iber mayn gants kerper. Ven ikh gib a druk oyf mayn kop, tut vey. Ven ikh gib a druk oyf mayn halz, tut vey. Oyf mayn boykh, tut vey. Oyf mayn harts, tut vey. Oyf mayn fus, tut vey. Ikh hob shtark moyre, doktor, vos iz mit mir?"	"Because I have a kind of sickness that is apparently over my whole body. When I give a push on my head, it hurts. When I give a push on my throat, it hurts; on my belly, it hurts; on my heart, it hurts; on my foot, it hurts. I am very afraid, doctor, what is with me?"
"Siz poshut," enfert der doktor. "Es tut aykh vey vu ir tapt vayl ayer grober finger is tsebrokhen."	"It's simple," answers the doctor. "It hurts you wherever you touch because your thumb is broken."

And be sure to remember these words:

baklogt (complains)

genoy (exactly)

avade (surely)

vos hart mir (what bothers me)

modne (strange)

krankhayt (sickness)

tsubrokhen (broken)

siz poshut (it's simple)

Wise Sayings

"Oh God, You have formed the body of man with infinite goodness. You have united in him innumerable forces incessantly at work like so many instruments, so as to preserve in its entirety this beautiful house containing his immortal soul, and these forces act with all the order, concord and harmony imaginable. If weakness or violent passion disturb this harmony, these forces act against one another. Send Your messengers, the diseases which announce the approach of danger and bid man prepare to overcome them."

—Physician's prayer of Moses Maimonides

And That's the Truth

Now that you know the words for so many body parts, you'll be able to understand the wisdom of Yiddish proverbs that include them. Here's a small sampling, together with a few observations about doctors, health, and healing:

➤ The tongue:

A beheyme hot a langen tsung un ken nisht reden; der mentsh hot a kurtse tsung un tor nisht reden.

(Animals have long tongues but can't speak; men have short tongues and shouldn't speak.)

Di tsung iz di feder fun harts.

(The tongue is the pen of the heart.)

➤ The heart:

A biter harts ret a sakh.

(A bitter heart talks a lot.)

➤ Teeth:

A hunt on tseyn iz oys hunt.

(A dog without teeth is no longer a dog.)

Az men ken nit baysen, zol men nit vayzen di tseyn.

(Those who can't bite shouldn't show their teeth.)

➤ The mouth:

A kleyne vaybele ken oykh hoben a groys moyl.

(A small woman can also have a big mouth.)

➤ Hands:

A kind vert geboyren mit kulyaken un a man shtarbt mit ofene hent.

(A baby is born with clenched fists, and a man dies with his hands open.)

This proverb is based on a famous passage in the *Talmud*. The rabbis of old saw a profound message implicit in the form of our hands at birth and at death. When we come into the world, we clench our fists as if to indicate that we plan to conquer it all. Our clenched fists declare, "It will be mine." As we leave this earth, our hands open up as if to declare that now we understand, "You can't take it with you." All our strivings for material possessions were in vain. What we can hold in our hands is meaningless. Only what we have acquired spiritually remains as the legacy of the soul.

➤ The fingers:

Ale finger tuen glaykh vey.

(All fingers hurt alike.)

The saying was used with reference to children. All children are equally dear to parents. Favoring one child over another is not only bad parenting, but it's also a sin.

➤ The head:

Az es kumt tsonveytik, fargest men kopveytik.

(When a toothache comes, you forget your headache.)

In the face of a greater pain, smaller difficulties become almost negligible. This proverb, you can readily realize, served as an almost constant refrain for a people whose problems seemed only to intensify with the passage of time. Its corollary became at least equally famous: *Es ken shtendig zayn erger*—It could always be worse. Realizing that, even tragedy becomes bearable as a grim reality that usually has even worse possibilities.

A Gut Vort

The ***Talmud,*** literally "teaching," is a collection of rabbinic teachings comprising Jewish law and lore as discussed by sages in academies of Israel and Babylonia, from the first through the end of the sixth century of the Common Era.

Oy Vey

Why did the brothers in the biblical story of Joseph hate him so? Because his father Jacob loved him more than the other children and gave him a coat of many colors as a sign of his special status. Because of this improper show of favoritism, the rabbis declared that the Jewish people were forced to endure their slavery in Egypt. Let that be a lesson!

➤ The eye:

Vos dos oyg zet nit, dos harts filt nit.

(What the eye doesn't see, the heart doesn't feel.)

With a Shmaykhel

The prominent Park Avenue physician completed his hour-long examination. Presented with the bill, Cohen explains that he doesn't have a penny and can't possibly pay anything.

"If you have no funds, why in the world did you come to one of the most expensive doctors in the city?"

"To tell you the truth, doctor," Cohen explains, "when it comes to my health, money is no object."

Gloyb eyn oyg mer vi tsvey oyren.

(Believe one eye more than two ears.)

Oygen zenen greser vi der boykh.

(The eyes are bigger than the stomach.)

➤ Doctors:

A doktor un a kvoresman zaynen shutfim.

(Doctors and gravediggers are partners.)

Di tsayt iz der bester doktor.

(Time is the best physician.)

Ven hungert an oysher? Ven der doktor heyst im!

(When does a wealthy man go hungry? When the doctor orders him!)

➤ Health:

Gezunt kumt far parnose.

(Health comes before making a living.)

Abi gezunt—dos leben ken men sikh aleyn nemen.

(Be sure to stay healthy—you can kill yourself later.)

➤ Sickness:

A make bay yenem iz nit shver tsu trogen.

(Another man's disease isn't hard to endure.)

A foylen iz gut tsu skhiken nokh dem malekhhamoves.

(It's a good idea to send a lazy man for the angel of death.)

I'm Not a Hypochondriac

Alright, maybe Jews overreact a little. We're an emotional people. But with a *krankheit* (a sickness), who says you should take a chance? Remember, in Yiddish you *never* say *Ikh vil zen a doktor.* The correct phrase is

Ikh vil zen a spetzyalist. Above all, memorize the warning of Jackie Mason, the famous Jewish comic: If a doctor has time to see you right away, he's no doctor!

To help the doctor determine what's wrong, here's a list of possible problems:

Yiddish	English	Yiddish	English
a kopveytik	a headache	*a virus*	a virus
an alergye	an allergy	*apenditsit*	appendicitis
galkrankayt	gall bladder	*a bis*	a bite
a penkher	a blister	*a bluter*	a boil
a breh	a burn	*tsiteren*	chills
a farkilung	a cold	*farshtopung*	constipation
a hust	a cough	*a kramf*	a cramp
shilshul	diarrhea	*disenterye*	dysentery
an oyerveytik	an earache	*hits*	a fever
heyzerkayt	hoarseness	*boykhveytik*	indigestion
nitgutkayt	nausea	*lungen-entsindung*	pneumonia
haltsveytik	a sore throat	*an oyslinkung*	a sprain
zunshlok	sunstroke	*flektifus*	typhoid
oysbrekhen	vomit		

(If you want to, you can add more than your own symptoms just to see if he's really a good doctor and knows if you're faking.)

Now just because you read about these ailments, don't *red zikh ayn a krenk* (talk yourself into sickness).

If You Don't Know, Ask

Nor a nar halt zikh aleyn far a doktor (only a fool considers himself a doctor). You may know what hurts you, but have the good sense to ask how to treat it. Be sure to ask your doctor to answer these questions:

Yiddish	English
Vos iz mayn krankhayt?	What is my sickness?
Vos muz ikh ton?	What am I supposed to do?
Tsi muz ikh ligen in bet?	Do I have to stay in bed?
Tsi darf ikh geyn in a shpitol?	Do I have to go to a hospital?
Tsi meg ikh oyfshteyn?	May I get up?
Ven rekhent ir vet mir veren besser?	When do you think I'll be better?

continues

continued

Yiddish	English
Ven vet ir vider kumen?	When will you come again?
Vos iz mayn retsept?	What is my prescription?
Zol ikh dos nemen far oder nokh dem esen?	Should I take this before or after meals?
Vifil lefel zol ikh nemen?	How many teaspoons full should I take?
Muz ikh hoben rentgenshtralen?	Do I have to have x-rays?
Kent ir varten a bisel eyder ikh batsol aych?	Can you wait a little before I pay you?

Gevalt!

The word *gevalt* can probably be written only with an explanation mark alongside of it. It's a scream, a cry, a protest. It's an all-purpose word for shock, astonishment, amazement, upset, and fear. It's also a desperate cry for help. How can one word do all that? It's just one of those wonders of Yiddish. If it didn't exist, we'd have to scream *gevalt!*

With a Shmaykhel

The Goldbergs made a fortune and wanted to begin to mingle with high society. The first thing they did was to change their name to Grant. Elocution lessons and surgery to correct their Jewish features soon followed. At last they were invited to the social ball of the country club season.

Without warning, a waiter spilled a bowl of soup on the newly assimilated couple. "*Gevalt!*" the former Goldberg screamed, to which he immediately added, "Whatever that means."

Gevalt is what you scream out when you see an *umglik* (an accident). But you'd better not stop at that. That would make you a *shlemiel* (an ineffectual nerd) and a *nebbish*. (You want a definition of a *nebbish*? He's the person in a group you always forget to introduce.)

If you want to be a real *mentsh*, you make sure to do the following:

Yiddish	English
ruf a doktor	call for a doctor
shik nokh an ambulans	send for an ambulance
gefin a koldre	find a blanket
gib dem farvundeten vaser	give the injured person water
helf oyb es geyt blut	help if there's bleeding
ze oyb du kenst gefinen mit vos tsu farbandazhiren	see if you can find something to make a bandage
helf trogen dem farvundeten oyf a trogbetel	help carry the wounded on a stretcher
un tsum sof telefonir dem man oder der froy fun farvundeten	and, last of all, telephone the husband or wife of the wounded

Remember, not doing the right thing is as bad as doing the wrong thing. A *mentsh helft andere* (a *mentsh* helps others).

Don't Make Me Younger

Sometimes it seems like we expect our doctors to perform miracles. The following anecdote makes clear what we really hope for:

Yiddish	English
Seydi Cohen bet dem doktor er zol ir helfen.	Sadie Cohen begs the doctor to help her.
"Vos vilt ir fun mir?" zogt der doktor. "Ir zend shoyn zibetsig yor alt. Ale eyvorim zenen shoyn alt. Ir meynt az ikh ken makhen nisim un makhen aykh yinger?"	"What do you want of me?" asks the doctor. "You are already seventy years old. All the parts of your body are old. You think that I can make miracles and make you younger?"
"Neyn, does meyn ikh nisht un dos vil ikh gor nisht. Tut mir a toyve, makht mir nisht yinger. Ir vil nor kenen veren elter!"	"No, that's not what I mean and not what I want. Do me a favor, don't make me younger; I only want to be able to get older!"

The Expensive Funeral

No matter what you do, *men ken nish obkoyfen dem malokh hamoves* (you can't buy off the angel of death). Death is inevitable. Judaism helps to ease the pain of the mourners with rituals. There is comfort in the procedures of the *levay* (the funeral). To die with dignity and to be accorded a proper Jewish burial are the universal prayers.

Pity the poor Jew in our concluding story:

Yiddish	English
Moyshe ligt in bet un er veys er geyt bald shtarben.	Moses is lying in bed and knows he will soon die.
Di kinder shteyen neben zayn bet un veynen. Zey veysen az der tate lost zey bald iber.	The children stand near his bed and cry. They know that their father will soon be leaving them.
Fort, darf men trakhten fun der levaye. Tzu fil gelt is nisht do un sayvisay di kinder zenen gor karg.	Nevertheless, they have to think about the funeral. They don't have much money, and the children are extremely miserly.
Heyben zey on tsu shmusen. "Vifel ken dos kosten?" fregt eyner. Entfert an andarer, "Efshar hundert dolar."	They begin to discuss: "How much can it cost?" asks one. Answers another, "Maybe a hundred dollars."

continues

167

continued

Yiddish	English
"Vey es mir, azoy feel. Efshar krigt men a biligerer levaye. Lomir zen oyb siz meglikh tsu gefinen a beser preys," tanet nokh a kind.	"Woe is me, so much. Maybe we can get a cheaper funeral. Let's see if it's possible to find a better price," argues another child.
"Ir veyst vos," zogt der tate mit zayn letzer koyakh, "Siz nish azoy vayt tsum beys hakvores. Efshar is besser ikh gey aleyn vet ir kenen shporen di por dolar."	"You know what," says the father with his last bit of strength. "It's not so far to the cemetery. Perhaps it's better that I go by myself so that you'll be able to save the few dollars."

The Least You Need to Know

➤ The words for many body parts are almost identical in Yiddish and English.

➤ Yiddish has many profound and beautiful proverbs about doctors, health, and healing.

➤ Aches, pains, and illnesses can be described just as easily in Yiddish as in English.

➤ *Gevalt* is an all-purpose word and a cry for help that deserves an exclamation mark after it.

Chapter 16

Get a Good Job

In This Chapter

➤ Identify the most common occupations

➤ Find out what Jews think about work and different career choices

➤ Discover why *gelt* is both good and bad

➤ Discover plural nouns and rules

Jews didn't only teach the world the sanctity of rest and the Sabbath. They also emphasized the importance of work and the sacred responsibility to add something of one's own efforts to improving the world. The very same biblical verse that commands, "You shall do no manner of work on the Sabbath," prefaces that statement with, "Six days shall you labor." Even in the Garden of Eden, the divinely created Paradise, Adam and Eve were given a job, "to tend it and to guard it." Without a task to perform, human beings lose their humanity. Without a purpose in life, life becomes meaningless. As the Yiddish proverb so beautifully puts it: *Di shverste arbet iz arumgeyn leydik* (The hardest work is to walk around idle).

Ben Gurion, the first Prime Minister of Israel, summed up Judaism's views on labor in these meaningful words: "We don't consider manual work as a curse, or a bitter necessity, not even as a means of making a living. We consider it as a high human function, as the basis of human life, the most dignified thing in the life of the human being, and which ought to be free, creative. Men ought to be proud of it." That's why a *leydikgeyer*—a person with no trade, profession, or means of support—is contemptible. *A yid muz davenen tsu Got un dernokh geyn tsu der arbet* (A Jew must pray to God and then go to work).

Doctor, Lawyer, Indian Chief?

Nu, so what do you want to be when you grow up? *Vos vilst du zayn?* Maybe you'll be a doctor. *Oy, halevay!* An *advokat* (a lawyer) is also not a bad *fakh* (vocation). An Indian Chief? *Fe!* That's about as bad as being a bartender. *Es past nisht.* It's just not appropriate for a nice Jewish boy.

What Should I Become?

It's not easy to decide what one's lifetime occupation should be. You've got to take into account your personal preferences, your abilities, as well as your opportunities for making a living. The following famous Yiddish song nicely illustrates the problem:

Yiddish	English
Vos Zol Ikh Zayn	*What Shall I Become*
1.	
Zol ikh zayn a rov,	Should I be a rabbi,
Ken ikh nit keyn Toyre.	I don't know any Torah
Zol ikh zayn a soykher,	Should I be a merchant,
Hob ikh nit kayn skhoyre.	I don't have any wares.
Der Refren	*The Refrain*
Un kayn hey hob ikh nit,	And I have no hay
Un kayn hober hob ikh nit,	And I have no oats
Un di vayb shilt zikh,	And the wife curses
A trunk bronfn vilt zikh,	A drink of whisky I'd love
Ze ikh mir a shteyn,	I see a stone,
Zets ikh mir un veyn.	I sit myself down and cry.

Yiddish	English
2.	
Zol ikh zayn a shoykhet,	Should I become a *shoykhet* (ritual slaughterer),
Halt ikh nit kayn khalef,	I don't hold a knife.
Zol ikh zayn a melamed,	Should I become a *melamed* (Hebrew teacher),
Ken ikh nit kayn alef.	I don't know an *aleph* (the first letter of the Hebrew alphabet).
(Der Refren)	*(The Refrain)*
3.	
Zol ikh zayn a shuster	Should I become a shoemaker
Hob ikh nit kayn kopete,	I don't have a hoof.
Zol ikh zayn a beker,	Should I become a baker,
Hob ikh nit kayn lopete.	I don't have a paddle.
(Der Refren)	*(The Refrain)*

A Gut Vort

A ***melamed*** is a teacher, usually of elementary Hebrew. As a corollary to George Bernard Shaw's famous quip, "Those who can, do; those who can't, teach," the Yiddish version would be: "Those who can, *a rabbi*; those who can't, *a melamed*."

So Many Choices

Of course, if you don't prepare yourself, you won't be able to find *arbet* (work). That's why school is so important. Make sure you finish *mitelshul* (high school). If you're so inclined, register in a *fakhshool* (trade school). Don't miss out on *kaledzh un der universitet* (college and university). Here are some of the subjects you might want to specialize in:

Yiddish	English	Yiddish	English
aritmetik	arithmetic	*kunst*	art
khemye	chemistry	*ekonomik*	economics
shprakhen	languages	*geshikhte*	history
matematik	mathematics	*muzik*	music
filosofye	philosophy	*fizik*	physics
leynen	reading	*sotsyale limudim*	social studies
zhurnalism	journalism	*gezets*	law
meditsin	medicine	*visenshaft*	science
elektronik	electronics	*limudey koydesh*	religious subjects

Call Me ...

After you've studied, you can become a professor or a practitioner, an expert in a particular field, and a person with a title. Depending on your major or field of study, here are your options:

Yiddish	English	Yiddish	English
der doktor	the doctor	*der tsondoktor*	the dentist
der advokat	the lawyer	*der khezhben-firer*	the accountant
der zhurnalist	the journalist	*der muziker*	the musician
der oygen-doktor	the oculist	*der optiker*	the optometrist
der apteker	the pharmacist	*der druker*	the printer
der visen-shaftler	the scientist	*der khirurg*	the surgeon
der kinstler	the artist	*der mekler*	the broker
der bankir	the banker	*der khemiker*	the chemist
der tentser	the dancer	*der aktyor*	the actor
di aktrise	the actress	*der beker*	the baker
der stolyer	the carpenter	*der tsivil-dinster*	the civil servant
der modelen-tsaykhener	the designer	*der katsev*	the butcher
der oyfzeher	the foreman	*der mekhaniker*	the mechanic
der rehren-shloser	the plumber	*der shnayder*	the tailor
der tekhniker	the technician	*der makhshirim-makher*	the toolmaker
der kremer	the storekeeper	*der farkoyfer*	the salesman
der lerer	the teacher	*der rov*	the rabbi
der arbeter	the worker		

With a Shmaykhel

What did the first Jewish astronaut say to his wife when she asked him where he was going? "*Ikh gey orbiten,*" of course.

Happiness Is ...

For some people, happiness may be a warm puppy. For others, for many years it was simply being able to make a *parnosse* (living) in a dignified and not too difficult manner. To have a *shtele* (job), to get decent *loyn* (wages), to be able to provide for one's family—what more could one ask for? Just listen to the wisdom of these simple folk sayings:

Yiddish	English
Der vos hot lib zayn arbet iz gebentsht.	He who loves his work is blessed.
A melokhe iz a melukhe.	To have a trade is to own a kingdom.
Es iz gornisht shver, az me ken.	Nothing is hard, if you have the know-how.
Az men iz a mayster, iz ful der tayster.	If you are a craftsman, your wallet is full.
Az s'iz in droysn a blote, freyen zikh di shusters.	When the streets are muddy, the cobblers rejoice.

Wise Sayings

"It's remarkable that Hebrew has but one word, **avodah,** for both work and worship."

—Hugo Bergman, twentieth-century Israeli philosopher

Show Me the Money

No matter how much you enjoy your work, you still want to get paid. When George S. Kaufman explained why he loved to write together with Moss Hart, he said, "It's because I love *gelt* by association." *Gelt, shekels, mezumem*—call it by whatever name you want, it's still the universal language. As Sholom Aleichem put it, "Like an elevator shoe, it makes small people appear taller than others."

Wise Sayings

"Money legitimates a bastard in the eyes of people."

—Babylonian Talmud

Yiddish proverbs are filled with keen insights about *gelt* and its power:

Yiddish	English
Far gelt bakumt men alts, nor keyn seykhel nit.	Money buys everything except brains.
Gelt firt di gantse velt!	Money rules the whole world!
Gelt geyt tsu gelt.	Money goes to money.
Gelt iz di beste zeyf vos nemt aroys dem gresten flek.	Money is the best soap, it removes the biggest stain.
Gelt tsu fardinen iz gringer vi tsu halten.	It's easier to earn money than to keep it.
Gelt balaykht vi zun mayn velt.	Money lights up my world like the sun.
Gelt iz kaylekhdik—amol iz es do, amol iz es dort.	Money is round—sometimes it's here, sometimes it's there.
Gold probirt men mit fayer; a froy mit gold.	Gold is tested with fire; a woman—with gold.

continues

continued

Yiddish	English
Gold shaynt fun blote.	Gold glitters even in the mud.
Kinder un gelt iz a sheyne velt.	Children and money make a nice world.
Oyf dray zakhn shteyt di velt; oyf gelt, oyf gelt un oyf gelt.	The world stands on three things; money, money, and money.

Oy Vey

Want to make sure you don't lose your money? Then give some of it away to **tsedakah** (charity). The Bible promises that those who give will receive; those who keep only for themselves will lose what they have.

Get the idea that *gelt* is nothing to feel guilty about? After all, money, says Jewish tradition, isn't only the root of all evil; it can just as well be the basis of great blessing. That's why coins have two sides. There are always two sides to whether having lots of money is a curse or a gift from God.

Lots and Lots

What better place to study some grammar about plurals than when we're talking about money. We haven't said a word about it until now, and you must have noticed from the many Yiddish quotes that there are a number of ways to express a plural form in Yiddish.

Because Yiddish stems from so many different languages, it has absorbed different plural endings. For example, English words that were assimilated into Yiddish maintain their plural *-s* ending. *Radiyo* becomes *radiyos*. Yiddish pronunciation, however, gives the *-s* ending a slightly different sound, somewhere between an "s" and a "z." Transliteration will usually stick with the "s," but if you can, give it a bit more of a "z" flavor than a harsh "s" sound, and you'll come across as a more fluent speaker.

The same *-s* plural ending is also used for family names. So, for example:

Mister Goldberg	Mr. Goldberg	*di Goldbergs*	the Goldbergs
Mises Rabinovits	Mrs. Rabinowitz	*di Rabinovitses*	the Rabinowitzes
Sam Rapoport	Sam Rappaport	*di Rapoports*	the Rappaports

The -en Ending

The most common ending for Yiddish words to make them plural (used for almost all nouns ending in a consonant or a stressed vowel) is adding the suffix *-en*. Here are some examples:

Singular	Plural
armey (army)	*armeyen* (armies)
ban (train)	*banen* (trains)
bet (bed)	*beten* (beds)
gas (street)	*gasen* (streets)
mentsh (person, good human being)	*mentshen* (persons)
shul (synagogue)	*shulen* (synagogues)

Now, change all these singulars to plurals on your own:

di tir (door)	*di teeren*
der tish (table)	*di* _____
dos yor (year)	*di* _____
der lomp (lamp)	*di* _____
di fabrik (factory)	*di* _____
di froy (wife)	*di* _____
di tsaytung (newspaper)	*di* _____
dos tsimer (room)	*di* _____
dos shif (ship)	*di* _____
di shprakh (language)	*di* _____
der dolar (dollar)	*di* _____

Ten Dollars, Lots of Dollars

Remarkably enough—and I know no logical reason for this—the Yiddish word for *dollar* stays in the singular when it is modified by a number. For example, in Yiddish we say *tsen dolar, hundert dolar,* or *milyon dolar.* No matter how high you're going to go, the Yiddish word for dollar keeps it singular. Say you have a couple of dollars, and the rule still holds: *Ikh hob a por dolar.* Only when the plural is unmodified or modified by something other than a precise number, the plural form, *dolaren,* is used:

American dollars is *amerikaner dolaren.*

A lot of money is *a sakh dolaren.*

Old dollar bills are *alte dolaren.*

New dollar bills are *naye dolaren.*

What makes this rule more important is that it's applied equally to time. Guess it's the Yiddish way of teaching us that time is money! So if you're going to be ready in five minutes, say *Vart finf minut*. If it's two hours, say *Tsvey sho*. If you don't know how long, but you're certain it will be many minutes or hours, say *A sakh minuten* or *A sakh shoen*.

Move Your -s

While the *-en* ending is extremely common in Yiddish, the *-s* suffix of English is also used for many words aside from the ones we've already mentioned. If the Yiddish word already ends with the *-en* in the singular, as in *volken* (cloud), you simply add an *-s* to get *volkens*. The same goes for *kishen* (pillow), which becomes *kishens*.

Here's a list of other words that, for various reasons, receive an *-s* ending in the plural. Don't worry about rules; just say them aloud. You'll get a feel for them and other words like them.

English	Yiddish singular	Yiddish plural
worker	*arbeter*	*arbeters*
grandmother	*bobe*	*bobes*
watch (noun)	*zeyger*	*zeygers*
grandfather	*zeyde*	*zeydes*
father	*tate*	*tates*
life	*leben*	*lebens*
teacher	*lerer*	*lerers*
mother	*mame*	*mames*
peddler	*pedler*	*pedlers*
pen	*feder*	*feders*
storekeeper	*kremer*	*kremers*
rain	*regen*	*regens*
writer	*shrayber*	*shraybers*
summer	*zumer*	*zumers*
church	*kloyster*	*kloysters*

Some plural nouns, mostly of Slavonic origin, require not just the *-s* ending, but a lengthier *-es* ending. For example, the plural of *khuligan*, which became the English hooligan, is *khuliganes*. A *nudnik* (someone who is only outdone as a bore by a *phudnik*, a *nudnik* with a Ph.D.), if allowed to multiply, becomes a group of *nudnikes*.

To -er *Is Human*

Okay, okay, I know it's a lot for one chapter. But what can I do, there are lots and lots of ways to say lots and lots in Yiddish. Let's just do one more for now, and then we'll let you rest and review. The suffix *-er* is also quite common and very often causes a vowel change for the singular word as well. The following list shows nouns that add the *-er* ending for the plural:

With a Shmaykhel

Sam goes to see a psychiatrist. "What's your complaint?" the doctor asks. "Oy, doctor, I can't stand it any more. All day, all night I talk to myself." Reassuringly, the doctor tells him, "Not such a problem. Don't be so upset. A lot of people talk to themselves." "Yes," answers Sam, "but you don't know what a *nudnik* I am!"

English	Yiddish Singular	Yiddish Plural
picture	*bild*	*bilder*
hundred	*hundert*	*hunderter*
wife	*vayb*	*vayber*
song	*lid*	*lider*
child	*kind*	*kinder*
stone	*shteyn*	*shteyner*

The following list shows nouns that change vowels when forming the plural with the *-er* ending:

English	Yiddish Singular	Yiddish Plural
land	*land*	*lender*
man, husband	*man*	*mener*
plane	*plan*	*plener*
place	*plats*	*pletser*
bottle	*flash*	*flesher*
garden	*gorten*	*gertener*
hole	*lokh*	*lekher*
wheel	*rod*	*reder*

continues

continued

English	Yiddish Singular	Yiddish Plural
book	*bookh*	*bikher*
hen, chicken	*hun*	*hiner*
tongue	*tsung*	*tsinger*
stomach	*boykh*	*baykher*
house	*hoyz*	*hayzer*
mouth	*moyl*	*mayler*
tree	*boym*	*beymer*
tooth	*tson*	*tseyner*

Leave Me Alone

The good news is that there are some words that don't require anything to form the plural. They are identical whether the word is used for one or for many. You can just leave them as they are. As a general rule, words describing human beings that already end in *-er* do not have a separate plural form. For example, *amerikaner* is both *American* and *Americans*. *Worker* and *workers* are both *arbeter*. *Vegetarier* (vegetarian), *tenser* (dancer), *shvester* (sister), and *shrayber* (writer) can all refer to one or to many.

Interestingly enough, there are a very few words that don't end in *-er*—and yet, for some inexplicable reason, have no plural form. The most used of these is the word *fraynd* (friend). It doesn't distinguish between singular and plural. Maybe Yiddish in its own way is using this to make a profound observation: When it comes to friends, one good one is as precious as hundreds. Or, maybe it's even more profound than that. Perhaps it's grammatically expressing the same thing the Hebrew poet Joseph Zabara wrote in the thirteenth century: "True friendship is but one heart in many bodies."

The Least You Need to Know

➤ Work is not a curse but a blessing affording human beings many options for self-fulfillment.

➤ Money isn't the root of all evil but the subject of a good many proverbs, some of which you surely can remember.

➤ To turn a singular word into a plural Yiddish, use the *-en*, *-s*, and *-es* or *-er* suffix.

➤ Some words in Yiddish, such as those ending in *-er* that describe people, are the same for both singular and plural.

Chapter 17

God Bless You

In This Chapter

➤ Learn what to call God—as well as what *not* to call him

➤ Study the wise sayings that summarize Jewish beliefs about God

➤ Learn the words that are based on religious beliefs or superstitions

---

For almost a thousand years, Yiddish has been spoken by a God-intoxicated people. Yiddish was created by those who believed deeply in a personal God. It developed and was refined in a culture that treasured the Bible above all books and revered God above all possessions. Yiddish came not only from the lips, but also from the hearts of the pious, the saintly, the trusting, and the believing. Small wonder that God, His law, His values, His will, and the nature of His relationship to man play such an important role in Yiddish words, phrases, and expressions.

Yiddish speakers didn't simply believe in monotheism—that there is one God and no other. Central to Jewish thought is the acceptance of a God with a number of all important attributes. God is the Creator of the entire universe. He is the King who judges the whole world—not only Jews, but gentiles as well. He is omnipotent, able to do whatever He pleases and to perform miracles of His choosing. He is omniscient, aware of our innermost thoughts and desires. He is just, merciful, and benevolent. He is our ultimate Provider, in whose hands rests the decision whether we are to be wealthy or poor, sated or hungry. He is the true healer who determines whether medical ministrations will be successful. He is Protector, Redeemer, and Father in whom we can place our trust. Most remarkable of all, He is omnipresent.

As King David put it in his Book of Psalms, "Whither shall I go from Thy spirit, or flee from Thy presence?" (Psalm 139:7). God is with us every moment of every day. How can the language of the Jewish people not mirror this closeness, this personal link, this remarkable relationship between the all-powerful Creator of the universe and His humble subjects?

Wise Sayings

"Human lips are now forbidden to utter His name, for being the only God He needs no name."

—Isaac Peretz, nineteenth-century Polish-Yiddish novelist

Khap a Nash

According to Jewish legend, the seventeenth-century Rabbi Judah Low of Prague turned a mound of clay into a **golem,** a living robot who followed his master's every command and took revenge on oppressors of the Jews as the time. The secret of the *golem*'s creation was the rabbi's mystical use of the name of God. Mary Shelley used this tale as the basis for the famous Frankenstein story.

What Should We Call You, God?

In English, the name God is a contraction of the word *good*. Of all the attributes of the Almighty, we define Him most succinctly by His goodness, kindness, mercy, and compassion. These are the things we most highly value. That's why whenever we take leave of a friend we say "goodbye," yet another contraction for the phrase, "God be with ye."

An alternative name found in English is Lord. While used for human beings as well—for example, lord of the manor or, in England, the House of Lords—with reference to God it suggests the supreme owner. The Lord is the ultimate Ruler of the world. Calling Him Lord affirms our acceptance of the Almighty as Creator, Master, and King.

The Bible, written in Hebrew, also has two different names for God. One of them, just like in English, is meant to stress His goodness and mercy. The other similarly emphasizes His strength and His power. Yet, strangely enough, although these names are liberally sprinkled throughout the entire Bible, Jews have for centuries abided by a strict rule that forbids their recitation.

Thou Shalt Not Take My Name in Vain

Only as part of a religious service may God's names as they appear in the Bible be spoken. Otherwise, they are simply too holy for everyday use. Mystics offer numerous possible explanations. Some even believe that using God's name indiscriminately invokes spiritual powers so strong they may be misused by laymen.

What do you do then if you want to talk to God throughout the day or talk about Him to family and friends? Pretty difficult to have one of the most important topics of conversation so severely limited. As the song says, "Hello, I love you … won't you tell me your name?" We love you, dear God; now what should we call You?

"Kosher" Nicknames

Of course, Jews found not one, but many acceptable ways to avoid using God's "real" name in vain. Here are the most popular alternatives:

➤ *Hashem*, **literally "the name"**—It's *the* name, the one you realize I can't say. *Hashem vet helfen* (God will help). *Hashem in himel* (God in heaven). Even when speaking directly to Him, this roundabout reference is common: *Hashem, hob rakhmonus* (God, have mercy).

➤ *Adoshem*—Using *Adoshem* is a little more daring. The first three letters, *ado*, are actually part of God's real name as it appears in the Bible. It's as if we are about to say it all, and then we complete it with the word *shem* (name). *Adoshem* is a little clearer in its intent and backs off at the last minute, as if to say now that you know who I'm talking about, so finish it in your own mind with "the name" of the Holy One. *Adoshem* is used in any phrase where *Hashem* is appropriate, and they are, for all intents, interchangeable.

➤ *Elokim*—This alternative uses another little trick to avoid being guilty of using God's name—changing a letter. The biblical version is spelled with an "h" instead of the "k." One little sound different and now it's kosher! Because *Elokim* is the biblical name for God in His attribute of strict justice, it's not the one usually chosen in Yiddish to beseech God for blessings. Instead, one is more likely to use *Elokim* in a phrase like, *Elokim, farvos host Du mir ibergelost?* (God, why did You forsake me?)

➤ *Ribonoy Shel Oylam*, **literally "Master of the World"**—This is the most usual form of address when speaking to God personally. It expresses the required humility of a servant to master while acknowledging the power of the one being spoken to, to fulfil even the most difficult request: *Ribonoy Shel Oylam meyn kind iz zeyer krank, shik im a refua shleyme* (Master of the World, my child is very sick, please grant him a complete recovery).

Wise Sayings

"The center and soul of all religion, the belief in a personal God, is the pillar of the religion of Israel. And it fathomed this truth with incomparable and triumphant energy, and expressed it with incomparable poetic power."

—Carl Cornill, twentieth-century German theologian

Khap a Nash

Among the other names of God, there's one comprised of 72 letters that *is* so holy that it was pronounced in the Temple only once a year by the High Priest on Yom Kippur, the Day of Atonement, in the Holy of Holies, the chamber where the ark and the commandments were kept. Does anyone still know that name with which, it is said, miracles can be performed? No one will say!

A Gut Vort

A **shadkhen** is a professional matchmaker who arranges "appropriate" marriages for a fee. Not to worry, though, that he'll make a mistake in judgement. Jewish tradition has it that the ultimate matchmaker is none other than God, who decrees 40 days before the birth of every child whom that person will marry!

➤ *Tate*—*Tate, Tate in himmel* (Father, Father in heaven). Look, it's not like we're strangers. You told me that we are your children and that You are our Father. Would a father allow this to happen to us? Would a father not hear our cries? So what if we sinned and rebelled against you? Remember when the Jews told Jeremiah, the prophet, that they didn't dare approach the Almighty because they had sinned so grievously. God responded, "Tell them, when you come to me, do you not come to your Father in heaven?" *Tate* is presumptuous yet prophetically permissible. *Tate* is intimate and is used for the most personal requests and confessions. "I know God will provide for us. After all, He is our *Tate*. A father *must* take care of His children. I only wish He would provide *until* He provides."

➤ *Hakodesh Baruch Hu*, **Hebrew for "The Holy One Blessed Be He"**—This alternative is a little more formal, a little more respectful, a little more synagogue- and prayer-oriented, and maybe even a little more complimentary to get on His good side. Using this descriptive marks you, the speaker, as just a bit more pious. This is usually not used in direct conversation with God, but more often in philosophic observations *about* Him.

➤ *Borey Oylom*, **The Creator of the World**—So what if all the nations of the world gang up on Israel? So what if the Jews comprise less than a quarter of 1 percent of the world's population? *Der Borey Oylom vet helfen* (The Creator of the World will help us). He is a universal God, not just a Jewish one. We'll talk about God by this name when the issues are complex and we need to remind ourselves of the Almighty's power.

➤ *Got*—This is the all-purpose word, straight from the German, but with oh, so much more meaning! *Got* is not a concept. *Got* is not a philosophic entity. *Got iz mayn pastekh* (The Lord is my shepherd), as the twenty-third psalm assures me.

Therefore, *ikh vel keyn mol nit darfen* (I will never want). *Got* is there for me always in good times and must be thanked—*Got tsu danken* (thank God). *Got* will see to it that evil will be averted, so I pray to Him, *Got zol ophiten* (God forbid). *Got veyst* (God knows everything). *Got*, You are so dear to me that I don't hesitate to call you *Gotenyu* (with the suffix *-enyu* emphasizing special affection). And one last thing, *Gotenyu*—if you don't mind my asking. If You really love us so much, how come we've been suffering for so long?

The Respectful Son-in-Law

Let's try reading a story in Yiddish that makes a humorous point about God and our identification with him. For some of you, it might even evoke memories of a personal experience, God forbid.

Yiddish	English
Der shadkhen hot forgeshtelt dem yungen man als a pasendik shidekh far Mister Goldberg's tokhter.	The professional matchmaker (*shadkhen*) introduced the young man as a suitable mate for Mr. Goldberg's daughter.
"Zog mir," fregt Mister Goldberg tsum tsukunftigen eydem, "fun vos makhst du parnose? Vi azoy vest du oyshalten mayn tokhter als froy?"	"Tell me," says Mr. Goldberg to his prospective son-in-law, "from what do you earn a livelihood? How do you hope to support my daughter as a wife?"
"Tsu zogen dem gantsen emes," entfert der yunger man, "kayn fakh hob ikh nit un funvanet makhen a leben veys ikh nit. Ober zorgt aykh nit. Ikh bin zikher Got vet helfen."	"To tell you the whole truth," answers the young man, "I have no trade and I don't know how to make a living. But don't worry—I'm sure God will help."
"Un mit vos," fregt Goldberg vayter, "meynst du tsu koyfen a dira tsu voynen?"	"And with what," asks Goldberg further, "do you intend to buy a dwelling in order to live?"
"Oykh nit tsu zorgen. Zikher Got vet helfen."	"Also not to worry. Surely God will help."
"Un tsu helfen mit gelt ke shtelen a khupa, iz epes do fun dayne elteren?" iz nokhamol a kashe fun shver. "Neyn, dos iz oykh nit meglikh. Ober ikh hob bitokhon in Riboyno Shel Oylom. Got vet helfen."	"And to help with money in order to put up a *khupa* (bridal canopy), is there anything possible from your parents?" is again a question from the father-in-law. "No, that is also not possible. But I have confidence in the Master of the World. God will help."
Der bokhur lost iber di shtub un Goldberg trakht zikh iber als vos men hot geret. Kumt arayn zayn vayb un fregt, "Nu, vi hot dir gefelen der yunger man?"	The young man leaves the room, and Goldberg thinks over everything that had been spoken. His wife comes in and asks, "*Nu*, how do you like the young man?"

continues

183

continued

Yiddish	English
Entfert Goldberg: "Tsu feel veys ikh nokh nit vegen em. Ober eyn zakh ken ikh dir shoyn zogen hundert protsent: Koved hot er far mir in an umgloyblikhen oyfen. Fun zayn reden iz klor as er halt mir far Got!"	Answers Goldberg: "Too much I don't know about him. But one thing I can already tell one hundred percent: Respect he has for me in an unbelievable manner. From his speech it's clear that he already considers me God."

God Talk

We love Him, we fear Him. We need Him. We pray to Him. God is the focus of so much of our lives that Yiddish has an almost endless array of *shprikhverter* (folk sayings) revolving around the Almighty. Some are profound theology. Others are daring in their lightheartedness and even border on the sacrilegious. To read them is to be stirred by the prominence Yiddish speakers give to their relationship with God:

A Gut Vort

A **khupa,** the bridal canopy, is usually made of white silk or satin and is held above the bride and groom as they perform the marriage ritual. It symbolizes the presence of God above their heads as they commit themselves to their lifelong partnership. It also symbolizes a royal canopy because the bride and groom on their wedding day are considered as king and queen.

Yiddish	English
Ven es zol helfn Got betn, volt men shoyn tsugedungen mentshn.	If it would help to pray to God, then people would be hiring others to pray to Him.
Ven freyt zikh Got? Az an oreman gefint a metsie, un git es op.	When does God rejoice? When a poor man finds a treasure and returns it.
Vos Got tut bashern, ken kayn mentsh nit farvern.	What God decrees, man can not prevent.
Der mentsh fort un Got halt di leytses.	Man rides, but God holds the reins.
Emes iz nor bay Got, un bay mir a bisl.	Truth is found only with God, and with me a little.
Er gleybt nit in Got, nor bet Zayn genod.	He doesn't believe in God, but he asks for His mercy.
Far Got hot men moyre, nor far mentshn muz men zikh hitn.	Fear God, but be wary of men.
Oyf Got tor men kayn kashes nit fregn.	On God, one isn't permitted to ask any questions.
A mentsh trakht un Got lakht.	A man thinks and God laughs (meaning man proposes and God disposes).

184

Yiddish	English
Az Got vil, shist a bezem.	If God wills it, even a broom can shoot.
Oyb Got volt geven oyf der erd, volt men Im ale fenster oysgeshlogn.	If God lived on earth, all His windows would be broken.
Az s'iz a regnboygn, vayst Got dem simen, az Er iz undz moykhl.	If there is a rainbow, it's a sign that God has forgiven our sins.
As es shneyt, meynt es as Got flikt di kishens, un lozt aroys di federn.	When it's snowing, it means that God is letting the feathers out of the pillows.
Far der velt muz men yoytse zayn mer vi far Got.	It's more important to please people than to please God.
Far morgn, vet Got zorgn.	Let God worry about tomorrow.
Fun dayn moyl in Gots oyern.	From your mouth to God's ears.
Got hot bashafn a velt mit kleyne veltelekh.	God created a world with many little worlds.
Got nemt tzu mit eyn hant, un git mit der anderer.	God takes away with one hand and gives with the other.
Got shikt di kelt nokh di kleyder.	God sends the cold in accordance with the clothes (meaning God sends the weather according to your needs).
Got zitst oybn, un port untn.	God sits on high and makes matches below.
Far Got veynt men, far mentshn lakht men.	Before God one cries, before people one laughs.
Bay Got tor men kayn kashe nit fregn, vayl Er vet zogn, az du vilst an entfer, "Kum aroyf tsu Mir."	You mustn't ask questions of God, for if you want an answer, He might say, "Come up to Me."
Got, shrek, nor nit shtrof.	Lord, frighten but don't punish.
Vemen Got vil shtrofn, nemt Er bay im tsu dem seykhl.	Whom God wants to punish, from him He takes His reason.
On Got's viln rirt zikh afile a flig nit oyf der vant.	Without God's will, even a fly on the wall does not move.
Got zol helfn, keyn mol nit erger; beser hot kayn shir nit.	God should help, never worse; there's no end for better.
Vos tsu Got iz tsu Got, vos tsu layt iz tsu layt.	What pertains to God is to God what to man is to man.
Er iz tsu Got un tsu layt.	He is to God and to people.
Er meynt az er hot Got bay di fis.	He thinks he has God by His feet.
Az s'iz a groyse hits, zogt men az Got raybt oys dem putershisl.	When it is extremely hot, it is said that God rubs out the butter dish.

According to the Bible, the rainbow first made its appearance as a sign to Noah from God after the flood almost destroyed the entire world. God promised Noah He would never again repeat a similar punishment. The rainbow, with its many colors, peacefully coexisting alongside each other, is a symbol of a time in the future when hopefully human beings will learn this lesson of peaceful coexistence between all peoples, no matter their color, race, or creed.

Spiritual Words

Even the most everyday, secular conversation in Yiddish couldn't help but be filled with words of spiritual content. A *vos makhst du* (how are you)? is most often answered with a *Borukh Hashem* (blessed be God), even if the respondent is a non-believer. (Someone answered me once mixing Yiddish and English *Borukh Hashem* lousy—proving that a Jew thanks God for everything, both the good and the bad.)

If Jews agree to meet the following day, they'll invariably propose it with *imyirtse* (God willing). *Imyirtse* is a great sentence opener or closer: *Imyirtse,* you'll find a good job. *Imyirtse,* you'll meet a nice boy/girl. *Imyirtse,* you'll finish this book and you'll speak Yiddish like someone who "just got off the boat."

You can also add *imyirtse* to the end of the sentence, simply delaying the punch line. I'm telling you it's going to happen, and just to make sure I'm adding a little bit of Godspeak.

Interesting—and to be expected—is that Yiddish uses Hebrew rather than German or any of its other source languages to express ideas relating to God, Jewish law, or spiritual matters. Here is a list of some of the most important words you ought to know:

➤ *Olov hasholem,* literally "on him peace"—The phrase is added automatically when talking about someone who is dead. It is the equivalent of the English "of blessed memory" but used far more frequently. The phrase is rooted in the religious belief that people are judged after death and that their souls go through a period of spiritual purging and cleansing. The hope is to find peace from this process and achieve the rest of the righteous seated in the presence of God. So ingrained in common speech is this prayer for the departed that it is used even when you'd least expect it: "Sam was a miserable no-goodnik, a thief and a liar, *olov hasholem."* So who says the wicked don't deserve a kind word after they're gone?

➤ *Omeyn* **(amen)**—The English word *amen* comes from the Hebrew "to believe." *Amen* is an affirmation of what was just said, and therefore the proper response to any and every blessing. Used outside the synagogue and independent of liturgy, it's a way of forcefully expressing agreement. To the statement "He should live and be well," you certainly should immediately respond with *Omeyn.* If the conversation is about an enemy and someone happens to express the hope that "All his teeth should fall out except for one so that he can have a toothache," an *Omeyn* on your part is optional.

➤ *Amorets,* **an ignoramus, an uneducated person**—*Amorets* is a Yiddish condensed version of the Hebrew *am ho'orets,* "people of the soil." According to the Biblical version, Adam was created by God as a combination of soil and spirit, dust of the earth and breath of the Almighty. An *amorets* is concerned only with his "earthly" origin and ignores the image of God in which he was created. The word has a particularly negative connotation because it refers not so much to someone who is uneducated as to someone who simply doesn't care and refuses to become more knowledgeable.

Khap a Nash

The Ten Commandments were given on two tablets because the first five deal with obligations of man to God, and the second five concern human responsibilities of people to others. To be religious, in Jewish thought, is to be responsive to both categories.

Khap a Nash

The Babylonian Talmud forbids an **amorets** to eat meat. What right, it declares, does someone who is no better than an animal have to kill an animal for food in order to sustain himself?

➤ *Apikores* **(heretic)**—Here's a word with a long history, from Ancient Greek to Aramaic to Hebrew to Yiddish. *Apikores,* in slightly altered form, is the Greek philosopher Epicurus, who gave the world his version of the ideal life as "Eat, drink, and be merry, for tomorrow you may die." Judaism turned the statement on its head by declaring that, "Tomorrow you *will* die, so make your eating and drinking and merriment secondary to your spiritual growth." Epicurus denied life after death and a final accounting to God. That made his views the ultimate heresy. Today the word *apikores* is used loosely (in all certainty, *too* loosely) to describe anyone whose religious practices are somewhat more lenient than yours.

With a Shmaykhel

The non-believer told the rabbi there was no point in discussing religion because he was an **apikores.** The rabbi asked him, "Tell me, have you completed studying the entire Talmud? Did you go through the works of Maimonides? Have you thoroughly digested the Bible and its commentaries?" When the answer to all these was a firm no, the Rabbi firmly declared, "No, you definitely are not an *apikores.* You are only an *amorets.*"

Wise Sayings

"If time is money, then everybody lives beyond his means."

—Ludwig Fulda, twentieth-century German dramatist

➤ *Aveyre* (sin)—An *aveyre* doesn't have to be as severe as desecrating the *Shabes* or eating on *Yom Kippur*, the Day of Atonement. My childhood was filled with motherly admonitions to finish what was on the plate in front of me because *es iz an aveyre dos aroys tsu varfen* (it's a sin to throw it out). If I didn't listen to her, then she concluded that *es iz an aveyre tsu reden mit dir* (it's a sin to talk to you, meaning it's useless, a waste of time, and therefore an *aveyre*). Because the most precious commodity of all and the one thing that's truly irreplaceable is time, you'll frequently hear the phrase, *an aveyre di tsayt*—"it's a sin the time," meaning that it's a sin to waste the time involved in what we're talking about or what we're doing because it will certainly come to nothing.

➤ *Bentsh* (bless)—Jewish life is filled with moments in which we are called upon to *bentsh*. On Friday nights, we *bentsh likht*, we bless the candles lit before the Sabbath to symbolize its light and its warmth. After every meal, we *bentsh*, we bless God for the food granted bountifully to us. When spared from catastrophe, sickness, car accident, or the like, we *bentsh goymel*, a blessing of thanks for divine intervention. Whenever anyone does us a kindness, we say *zol dir Got bentshen* (may God bless you). Whoever gets a blessing like that is truly a *gebentshter!*

➤ *Beys din*, literally "house of judgement," a court—If we can't agree on how to resolve our dispute, we'll have to go to *beys din*. Three rabbis comprise a Jewish court, and their decisions are based on talmudic and biblical law. *Ikh nem dikh tsu beys din* is usually more of a threat than a fact, almost like a mother warning her child that if he doesn't behave, she's going to go call a policeman.

➤ *Beys medresh*, literally "house of study"—The *beys medresh* and the *shul* (synagogue) used to be one and the same. In it were holy books too expensive to be owned individually. The *shul* served as an open library to which everyone could come and fulfill the religious obligation of study. When a Jew says *Ikh gey tsum beys medresh*, he usually means he's going to synagogue for prayers; but he'll probably grab a little bit of study time as well.

➤ *Bris* (circumcision)—A *bris* goes back to Abraham, the first Jew, who was commanded to circumcise himself as a physical sign of his covenant with God. Thankfully, his descendants didn't have to perform this procedure upon themselves when they were advanced in years. It is now performed on an infant who is eight days old. (Amazingly enough, that's the exact day, scientists have discovered, that vitamin K, the blood-clotting agent, is present in greatest quantity during our lifetime.)

➤ *Khale* (braided bread)—A *khale* can't be described, it can only be tasted. It's the bread for the *Shabes* meal that turns eating into a spiritual service. Because American Jews very often can't pronounce the "kh" sound, they end up calling this wondrous bread "holly," as if it had kinship with the gentile custom of celebrating Christmas. What a *mishmash*—an incredibly confused mixture. A *khale* is a *khale*, glazed with egg white, soft, delicate, seeded with poppy, sometimes with raisins, and always, always (at least if homemade) filled with the love of the person who made it.

➤ *Khilul Hashem*, literally "profaning God's name"—A *khilul Hashem* is worse than any individual sin. It's to act in such a way that your misdeed reflects discredit not only upon yourself, but upon God and the Jewish people. A Jew is publicly exposed as a pornographer? That's a *khilul Hashem*. A rabbi is caught committing an immoral act? That, too, is a *real khilul Hashem*. In fact, the Talmud teaches, the greater the person, the more possibility for *khilul Hashem*. In the Bible, Moses was punished very severely for a seemingly small infraction. Why? Because for Moses to hit the rock instead of speaking to it as God had commanded, the smallest of sins is a grave one. As a public figure, it's also a *khilul Hashem*.

➤ *Kidush Hashem*, literally "sanctification of God's name"—A *kidush Hashem* is the exact opposite of a *khilul Hashem*. It can be something as major as martyrdom or as minor as helping a blind man to cross the street when other people can clearly see that you're Jewish.

➤ *Daven* (to pray)—A word whose origin is lost to us, *daven* is something every pious Jew does three times a day. In the European *shtetel*, shopkeepers would often put up a sign with the first four letters of the Hebrew alphabet—*alef, beyz, gimel, daled*. Everyone who saw the sign knew immediately that it was an acronym. Instead of saying "out to lunch," it stood for the words *"Ikh bin gegangen davenen"* (I went to pray). That, after all, was the ABCs of Jewish life.

➤ *Gan Eden* (**Garden of Eden**)—Granted, Adam and Eve were kicked out of the original Garden of Eden, but that doesn't mean we can't find at least some of its pleasures in our own daily lives. The cakes my wife bakes—*oy, tam gan eden* (oh, it's the taste of paradise). Go to a *shvits* (a steam bath), *tam gan eden!* Want to give your hostess the ultimate compliment? Tell her *es iz geven gan eden.*

➤ *Get* (**divorce**)—Strange that in English "to get" means to receive and in Yiddish *tsu get* means to get rid of, to divorce. One of the greatest geniuses of Jewish history, the eighteenth-century Rabbi Elijah, the *Gaon* (genius) of Vilna, made the amazing observation that the two Hebrew letters which form the word *get*—the *gimel* and the *tes*—are the only letters that never appear side by side in the entire Bible. Because they can't be together, they're the perfect letters to stand for divorce.

➤ *Gilgul* (**reincarnation, a reincarnated soul**)—Some Jews believe in reincarnation; others don't. Judaism, as a religion of life, doesn't take a clear stand. Yet there were many Jews, who, well before Shirley MacLaine popularized the idea, accepted the belief that people can come back again after death, in human form, or sometimes as an animal, to atone for past misdeeds. Just in case they're right, be very kind to your dog. He may be a repentant sinner who has seen better times and deserves a little compassion.

➤ *Kadish* (**the prayer for the dead**)—*Kadish* is a mourner's prayer that, amazingly enough, doesn't mention death at all! It reaffirms belief in God, in the presence of death. It expresses faith at a time when people might most waver. In Jewish tradition, the recitation of *kadish* by a child achieves a great measure of blessing for the soul of a departed parent. Jews consider this prayer so important that parents would often refer to a child affectionately as my *kadishl*—the one I'm counting on to say *kadish* for me eventually and bring me into heaven.

➤ *Keyn ayn hore/kinehora,* **literally "with no evil eye"**—Yes, it's probably superstitious, but *kinehora,* whenever I've said it, no harm befell me. Do I believe in the evil eye? What's the difference? If it's true, I've used the magic formula to ward off evil spirits. If it's not true, it doesn't matter, and who is the worse for it? So if you ask me whether I think your child looks well, of course, I'll tell you *kinehora zi iz a sheynkayt* (without an evil eye, she is a real beauty).

➤ *Shehekheyonu,* **literally "that He allowed us to live"**—*Shehekheyonu* is the key word in the blessing recited for anything performed for the first time that gives us great joy. When moving into a new home, putting on a new suit, or eating the first cherry in spring, thanks are given to God "who has kept us alive to this time." Every first demands a *shehekheyonu.* Yiddish allows us to borrow the word from its liturgical frame of reference and apply it to everyday experiences. He finally paid me back what he owes me, *ikh darf makhen a shehekheyonu* (I have to make a *shehekheyonu*). What does she look like? She's absolutely gorgeous, she's worthy of my making a *shehekheyonu.*

Oy Vey

Be careful. Don't give anyone a canary. What's the origin of this strange expression? In all probability, it's a variant of **kinehora.** Then again, some people think the whole idea of an evil eye is for the birds!

Is this really the last entry in this long chapter? *Borukh Hashem,* I think we both should make a *shehekheyonu.*

The Least You Need to Know

➤ God's name is too holy to be spoken in its pure, original form, so we have to use alternatives.

➤ The different names for God reflect various different aspects of His attributes and the nature of His relationship with human beings.

➤ Yiddish folk sayings highlight Jewish attitudes to God and His role as Ruler of the universe.

➤ Many Hebrew words have become part of conversational Yiddish, carrying with them religious beliefs as well as superstitions.

You Gotta Follow the Rules

There's an old fable about an owl and a centipede. The owl watches the centipede walk and can't contain his amazement. He asks the hundred-legged creature, "How do you possibly do it? So many legs, so many choices. How do you decide which to move first? Do you go in regular sequence, do you do your left ones first and then the ones on the right? Do you do consecutive rows? I think it's absolutely brilliant how you manage to do it so flawlessly. What's your secret?" The story has it that from that day forward, the centipede never walked again.

The moral is particularly relevant to the way in which we use language. How do we know which grammatical rule to apply? How do we make sentences so quickly when we're presented with dozens of different possibilities? How do we keep track of irregular verbs, adjectives, and prepositions? How do we recall exactly which ending it is that makes the plural of a word we're about to use? If we really had to stop and think about every one of these questions, I don't know whether we'd ever be able to utter a word again! That's why it's so important to learn a language the way small children do it. We certainly don't stuff the head of a 2-year-old with rules of grammar. We just let the child speak, mistakes and all. When we hear an error, we laugh and think it's cute.

Before long, in some mysterious way that proves our innate linguistic ability, children end up speaking correctly and obeying grammatical rules they hardly even know exist.

That's why I've spent far more time actually having you get the flavor of Yiddish sentences and speech than burdening you with memorizing countless rules to be applied for different situations. Rules are, of course, helpful, but oft times they are too confining. So you'll make a mistake. Go ahead. Fall down once in a while. That's the only way you'll learn how to walk. Talk a little. And if you don't know your nominative from your genitive, your dative from your accusative, who's going to accuse you of a capital crime? Having said all that, however, we can't escape a little dose of grammar we need to understand the usage of some all-important words. If you had learned Yiddish as a child, you'd just naturally understand these things. Because you're an adult, I'll have to explain them to you in adult language.

Let's Be Definite

In Chapter 5, "The Basic Words," you learned about the definite article. That's the word *the*, without which you'd hardly be able to talk about anything. With the exception of some *oyfgeblozene shoytim*—some overblown, self-inflated fools whose favorite word is *I*—I'm sure for everyone else the word *the* is probably the single most frequently used word.

Wise Sayings

"The great principle of Judaism is nothing but the belief in revelation and acceptance of the burden of the *mitsves*, the commandments."

—Samuel David Luzzatto, nineteenth-century Italian Hebrew scholar

You've seen that the definite article in Yiddish comes in three flavors. It has to agree with its noun in gender (sex somehow always seems to find a place everywhere), so you have the words *der, di,* and *dos* for masculine, feminine, and neuter nouns respectively.

You may have already figured out from some of the Yiddish sentences quoted that the definite articles *der, di,* and *dos* can also serve double duty as demonstrative pronouns. For example, if you say *der man* and emphasize the first word, you mean not just the man, but *this* man. If you say *di latke* and stress the *di* part, you won't be satisfied with any other *latke* except the one you are pointing at. *Dos pekel* can be just the package, but if it's addressed to you, you obviously mean *this* one. Remember that the definite article for all plurals—masculine, feminine, or neuter—is *di*. When *der yid* changes to *di yiden* for many, it can also mean "the Jews" or "these Jews," depending on inflection.

All these examples have one thing in common: They are in the *nominative* case. That's the grammatical term linguists use when the noun is the subject of the verb in its sentence. In the sentence "The man put on his shoe" the *man* is the doer, and both the noun *man* and the descriptive *the* are in the nominative case. The soldier takes his gun; the artist chooses his paints; the sculptor chisels his stone. *Soldier, artist, sculptor* are all the movers and shakers, the actors and doers of their respective activities. They are the subjects of their sentences, and it is their definite articles that we have been discussing until now. Let's see what happens to the gun, the paint, and the stone when they are the *objects* of someone's activity.

Being Accusative

Just remember being accusative isn't the same as being argumentative. Accusative is just the word grammarians use to indicate the case where a noun and its definite article directly receive the action expressed in the verb. For example, "I see the boy." You would expect that to be, *Ikh ze der bokher.* Sorry. That's wrong. As a direct object—and, therefore, in the accusative case—the nominative *der* (the) is replaced by a new word—*dem,* pronounced just the way Brooklyn Dodger fans years ago used to speak about "dem Bums."

Note that the accusative case changes the masculine singular word only for *the.* It's just the *der* that becomes *dem.* The feminine *di,* the neuter *dos,* and the plural *di* all remain the same whether they are in the nominative or the accusative, whether the word *the* refers to the one doing the action or the thing acted upon.

Make yourself a mental image of a man, have something happen to him (if you're angry at your husband or boyfriend right now, the sky's the limit), and say to yourself, "*Dem* it, he deserves it." That's your memory aid for restricting the accusative change of *dem* to the masculine singular.

It's time to move on and make a date with the dative.

Making a Dative

A date , and a dative aren't the same at all. A date usually comes with a proposition; a dative has to follow a preposition. When a noun and its definite article receive the action indirectly, following a preposition, they are spoken of as being in the dative case. The book is on the table. I like sugar with the tea. Please walk me to the store. Note that in all these examples, the nouns *table, tea,* and *store* are the indirect objects following the prepositions *on, with,* and *to.*

Now here's the rule for the dative: Masculine singular *der* words again become *dem* (just as in the accusative). Neuter *dos* words in the singular now join the masculine words and get the *dem* as well. Feminine singular *di* words in the dative, strangely enough, turn to *der.* Again, all the definite articles in the singular change for the dative case. *Der* and *dos* become *dem,* and *di* becomes *der.* No matter what you do, though, don't touch the plurals! They all remain *di.*

The following exercise helps you practice using the accusative and dative in Yiddish. If you have eight correct answers out of ten, feel free to proceed with this chapter. If you're still having trouble, go over it one more time and make sure that you understand everything. Here's a list of words you should know for this exercise:

Yiddish	English	Yiddish	English
dos kleyd	the dress	*der kholem*	the dream
di shleykes	the suspenders	*der veg*	the road
der sendvitsh	the sandwich	*di sardinke*	the sardine
di televisye	the television	*der shnaps*	the whisky
dos vayb	the wife	*dos shaytel*	the wig

Khap a Nash

Among orthodox Jews, it is the custom for many married women to wear a *shaytel* (wig). That's not because they're going bald, but because they consider natural hair to be too erotic to be seen by anyone other than their own husband.

With a Shmaykhel

"Why is it, Chaim," asked Yankel, "that the Yiddish word for television is feminine?" "Simple," Yankel replied. "That's because it keeps on talking and talking even when nobody there is listening."

1. *Zi trogt _____.*
   (She wears the dress.)

2. *Er hot lib _____ vos du host gekoyft.*
   (He likes the suspenders you bought him.)

3. *Er tut on a hut oyf _____.*
   (He puts a hat on the wig.)

4. *Er trinkt _____.*
   (He drinks the whiskey.)

5. *Er hot gezen sayn gelibte in _____.*
   (He saw his beloved in the dream.)

6. *Er iz gegangen oyf _____.*
   (He walked on the road.)

7. *Er hot tsugegeben salts tsu _____.*
   (He added salt to the sandwich.)

8. *Vos kenst du zen oyf _____?*
   (What can you see on the television?)

9. *Vu iz _____ fun hoyz?*
   (Where is the wife of the house?)

10. *Ikh hob gegessen _____.*
    (I ate the sardine.)

Please Cut It Short

Now that we know all about *dem* words, let me share with you one of their very interesting characteristics: *dem* words simply love to be merged with prepositions. (Maybe they really do confuse preposition with proposition!) In English, we tend to contract frequently used words for the sake of convenience—*isn't* that so? Of course, you could always stick with the more formal—is that not so?—but hardly anyone does that—isn't that true? Similarly, Yiddish conversation will almost always choose the easier option of contraction. That's why the list of contractions in the following table is absolutely essential for you:

With a Shmaykhel

What's the definition of a pessimist? Someone who wears *shleykes and a gartel*—suspenders and a belt.

English Words	Yiddish Words	Yiddish Contraction
until + the	*biz + dem*	*biz'n*
by way of/through + the	*durkh + dem*	*durkh'n*
after + the	*nokh + dem*	*nokh'n*
before + the	*far + dem*	*far'n*
in + the	*in + dem*	*in'm*
to + the	*tsu + dem*	*tsum*
with + the	*mit + dem*	*mit'n*
on + the	*oyf + dem*	*oyf'n*
from + the	*fun + dem*	*fun'm*

The Ingenious Genitive

Okay, I promise this is the last case. Probably because you have to be a genius to understand them all, linguists call it the genitive case. (Why is it that grammarians always try to complicate things by choosing descriptives that only serve to confuse you?) Simply put, the genitive case is when a noun and its definite article show possession: the man's beard, the woman's hair, the child's toy. The correct way to express these relations in Yiddish is: *dem manz bord, der froyz hor, dem kindz shpilkhel.*

With a Shmaykhel

The rabbi tells the *mohel* (the man who performs circumcisions), "I envy you." "Why is that?" asks the *mohel*. "Because," says the rabbi, "every time I get up to give a sermon, people tell me to cut it short. Bet they never say that to you!"

Note what happened here. The *der* word *man* changed to *dem* because the case is genitive, showing possession. The *di* word *froy* changed to *der*, and the *dos* word *kind* became *dem*. Confused? Don't be. Look at the following table for a handy quick reference and summary of what you need to know:

Case	*Der* words (masculine) Singular	Plural	*Di* words (feminine) Singular	Plural	*Dos* words (neuter) Singular	Plural
Nominative	*der*	*di*	*di*	*di*	*dos*	*di*
Genitive	*dem*	*di*	*der*	*di*	*dem*	*di*
Dative	*dem*	*di*	*der*	*di*	*dem*	*di*
Accusative	*dem*	*di*	*di*	*di*	*dos*	*di*

An important reminder: Remember what I said at the beginning of this chapter. If you're going to try to be a perfectionist and get hung up on always doing the definite articles correctly, you will never again speak a word of Yiddish. Don't be too hard on yourself. Allow for mistakes. The truth is, even people who speak Yiddish fluently often don't pass the scrutiny of strict grammarians. The way you'll get most of them right is by practicing reading and speaking. Just like a baby who learns how to talk, it'll come naturally to you and you will get a feel for the right word in every situation.

Learn to Be More Possessive

You've just learned the genitive case and know a little bit about possessives, so let's broaden our sights a little bit and fill in some information about possessive adjectives. After all, you can't have a conversation without making clear that what's mine is mine and what's yours is yours.

Let's start first with the possessive adjectives in their base forms. Those are the "real" words without anything added to them to agree with any words that follow:

Yiddish	English
mayn	my
dayn	your (singular)
zayn	his
ir	her
zayn	its
undzer	our
ayer	your (plural)
zeyer	their

These base forms are all used when they precede a noun in the singular: my mother, your house, his car, our friend, their book. With plural nouns, however, you have to add an *-e* ending—more like an "eh" sound—to the base of the possessive adjectives. For example:

mayn khaver
(my friend)

mayne khaverim
(my friends)

dayn zakh
(your thing)

dayne zakhen
(your things)

zayn kind
(his child)

zayne kinder
(his children)

> **Khap a Nash**
>
> An important synagogue prayer asking for God's help in redeeming the oppressed and speedily bringing about the Messianic Age closes with these words: *khaverim kol Yisrael* (all Jews are friends). Sages debate whether that's the precondition for bringing the Messiah or a description of what will at long last happen once he arrives.

When Yiddish Is Hebrew

In one of the examples we just gave, you may have noticed that the word for friend, *khaver*, became *khaverim* in the plural. That must have surprised you. After all, the *-im* ending wasn't one of the plural suffixes you've learned before (and God knows we saw that Yiddish already has quite a number of endings to express plurality). Well, this time there's a very good reason to account for the suffix I haven't taught you yet.

In Chapter 17, "God Bless You," I revealed that many words in Yiddish are taken over almost exactly from the Hebrew. These words always maintain the plural endings of their original language: *-im* for masculine words and *-os* (slightly altered in pronunciation to "es") for feminine words. The following two tables provide examples of masculine and feminine words, respectively:

Singular English	Yiddish	Plural English	Yiddish
boy	*bokher*	boys	*bokherim*
friend	*khaver*	friends	*khaverim*
body	*guf*	bodies	*gufim*
room/schoolroom	*kheder*	rooms	*khedorim*
groom	*khosen*	grooms	*khasanim*
holiday	*yontev*	holidays	*yontoyvim*
king	*melekh*	kings	*melokhim*
prophet	*novi*	prophets	*nevim*
miracle	*nes*	miracles	*nisim*

Note that in many of these examples, there is also a slight vowel change in the word itself when it becomes plural, caused by the addition of an extra syllable.

Singular English	Yiddish	Plural English	Yiddish
generation	*dor*	generations	*doyres*
dwelling	*dire*	dwellings	*dires*
wild beast	*khaye*	wild beasts	*kheyes*
dream	*kholem*	dreams	*khaloymes*
strength	*koyekh*	strengths	*koykhes*
bride	*kale*	brides	*kales*
good deed/ commandment	*mitsve*	good deeds/ commandments	*mitsves*
work	*melokhe*	works	*melokhes*
war	*milkhome*	wars	*milkhomes*
family	*mishpokhe*	families	*mishpokhes*
gift	*matone*	gifts	*matones*
prayer	*t'file*	prayers	*t'files*

A Gut Vort

Kapores, literally "atonement" in Hebrew, is the name of a ceremony practiced by some on the day before *Yom Kippur*, the Day of Atonement. A chicken is symbolically slaughtered in place of a person and then given as a gift to the poor so that the merit of this act might help the doer be worthy of life and blessing for the coming year. Others consider this superstition and claim that it helps *oyf kapores*, that it is good for nothing.

As an interesting aside, a word such as *koyekh* (strength)—which in Yiddish is masculine, *der koyekh*—retains its feminine plural because that's what it has in its original Hebrew form.

As Long as You're Well

We've had so much about genitive cases and possessives in this chapter that I'm afraid you might think that owning things is all that really matters. So let's bring this section to a close with a song made famous by the great Yiddish actress and comedienne, Molly Picon:

Yiddish	English
Abi Gezunt	As Long as You Have Your Health
A bisel zun, a bisel regen	A little sun, a little rain
A ruyik ort dem kop tsu legen	A quiet spot the head to lay
Abi gezunt	As long as you have your health
Ken men gliklikh zayn.	One can be really happy.

Yiddish	English
A shukh, a zok	A shoe, a sock
A kleyd on lates	A dress without patches
In keshene, a drey, fir zlotes	In the pocket, three-four *zlotes* (dollars)
Abi gezunt	As long as you have your health
Ken men gliklikh zayn.	One can be really happy.
Di luft is fray	The air is free
Far yeden glaykh	For everyone the same
Di zun zi shaynt far yeden eynem	The sun shines for everybody
Orem oder raykh	Poor or rich
Raykh, raykh, raykh.	Rich, rich, rich.
A bisel freyd, a bisel lakhen	A little joy, a little laughter
A mol mit fraynt a shnapsel makhen	Sometimes with friends to share a whisky
Abi gezunt	As long as you have your health
Ken men gliklikh zayn	One can be really happy.
Eyner zukht ashires	Someone seeks riches
Eyner zukht g'vires,	Someone seeks wealth
Aynemen di gantse velt	To capture the entire world
Eyner meynt dos gantse glik	Someone thinks that all of happiness
Hengt nor op in gelt.	Depends only on money.
Zolen ale zukhen	Let everyone search
Zolen ale krikhen	Let everyone crawl
Nor ikh trakht bay mir	Only I think to myself
Ikh darf es oyf kapores	I need it for nothing
Vayl dos glik shteyt bay mayn tir.	Because happiness awaits by my door.
A bisel zun, a bisel regen	A little sun, a little rain
A ruyik ort dem kop tsu legen	A quiet spot the head to lay
Abi gezunt	As long as you have your health
Ken men gliklikh zayn.	One can be really happy.

The Least You Need to Know

➤ The best way to learn a language is to learn from your mistakes.

➤ The definite article in Yiddish (*der, di, dos*) means not only *the* but also *this* and *these*.

➤ In the accusative case, a noun and its definite article directly receive the action expressed in the verb.

➤ In the dative case, the noun and its definite article receive the action of the verb indirectly, following a preposition.

➤ In the genitive case, a noun and its definite article show possession.

➤ Plurals of words with Hebrew origin maintain their Hebrew plural endings.

Part 6

The Popular, the Powerful, and the Profound

Language best conveys the culture of a people in its pungent words, its pithy expressions, and its profound proverbs. Part 6 is a gold mine of these all-important "Yiddish-isms." You'll learn perfect put-downs and curses, as well as beautiful blessings and good wishes. You'll delight in everyday similes and metaphors that can make you sound like a philosopher, a comedian, or a biblical scholar. You'll chuckle at the fine shadings of meaning Yiddish possesses as it describes the morons and misfits, the shlemiels *and the* shlemazels, *as well as the heroes and heroines—the true* mentshen *of life.*

Most important of all, you'll treasure the magnificent proverbs that have been transmitted from generation to generation. They powerfully illuminate the brilliance of a people who view the world with humor, with love, with faith, with optimism, and with a zest for living.

Comparisons, Curses, and Blessings

Picture a people who for centuries lacked any real power. Constantly victims, they were persecuted and oppressed by those far more numerous and mighty. They sought refuge in the only weapon available to them: not by way of the sword, but by the strength of the word. The Bible had already made clear to them, "How forcible are right words." (Job 6:25) Words could hurt, and words could heal. Words could comfort and console. And so, Yiddish, the language of a people beset by many enemies and inured to suffering, perfected the usage of words as the most precious of skills and the most prized of talents.

King Solomon, considered by Jews to be wisest of all men, wrote in his Book of Proverbs, "A word fitly spoken is like apples of gold in settings of silver." (Proverbs 25:11). For those who lacked real gold and silver, words were considered almost their equals. That's why Yiddish is filled with colorful expressions, magnificent metaphors, brilliant word plays, and incredible insights. In it, you'll find the loftiest ideas as well as the most imaginative curses. Superlative praises are matched by powerful putdowns. Pungent aphorisms are as popular as morbid meditations. In short, Yiddish expressions are the very soul of a people. They identify its past, in no small measure have created its cultural present, and, for all we know, may presage its future. Let's devote this next chapter to familiarizing ourselves with some of the most popular examples.

Biblical Similes

Similes compare everyday events, people, or objects to well-known equivalents. Of course, Yiddish speakers will never liken anything to "a pig in a poke." They will, however, turn to allusions easily recognizable to anyone familiar with Jewish culture.

Khap a Nash

When two women argued over a baby, each one claiming it was hers, Solomon ruled, "Let the child be cut in half to satisfy both claimants." When one of the women screamed out, "Spare the child, I renounce my claim," Solomon wisely decided that she was the real mother.

Some of the following expressions are obvious and simple to understand. Others require a little knowledge of the Bible or Jewish history to grasp the point they're making. All of them are commonly used today. Show your expertise by inserting them into your conversation at the appropriate time.

➤ *Er iz klug vi Shlomo hamelekh.* (He is as wise as King Solomon.)

King Solomon, son of King David, is responsible for building the first Temple, writing the biblical Book of Proverbs, and—most important of all—bringing about a lengthy period of peace for the Land of Israel during his reign. By coincidence (or was it really Divine providence?), his name *Shlomo*, like the Hebrew *shalom*, means peace. Isn't someone who can achieve all that the smartest of human beings?

➤ *Er iz raykh vee Korakh.* (He is wealthy as Korakh.)

In the Bible (Numbers 16), a rebellion against the leadership of Moses was led by an extremely rich but immoral Jew named Korah. The fact that his punishment was to be swallowed up by the earth is probably a good reason why the simile chooses him as illustration. Wealth can mislead people to seek undeserved power, and when all is said and done, "you can't take it with you."

➤ *Shikor vi Lot* (Drunk as Lot)

To get some idea of how much getting drunk can degrade you, just think of the story in Chapter 19 of Genesis. In his drunken stupor, Lot had incestuous relations with his own two daughters! What could serve as a more powerful warning than that?

➤ *Shlekht vi Yerovem ben Nvot* (Evil as Jereboam, the son of Nevot)

Jereboam's story of rebellion against God, in the book of Kings I (11:26), makes clear why he deserves this "honor." What a punishment, though, to have your crimes commemorated to this very day, by serving as the epitome of evil!

➤ *Groys vi Oyg melekh haboshen* (Tall as Og, King of Bashan)

No, Dorothy, it's not the Wizard of Oz, but of Og. He was a *real* giant, so every Jew over six feet is linked with this biblical oddity (see Deuteronomy 3:11).

➤ *Gezunt vi Shimshon hagibor* (Healthy as Samson the mighty)

It didn't happen often in Jewish history, but at least once Jews had a real macho hero, an unlikely Yiddish Superman named Samson. To show you how undependable physical strength is, the man who tore apart lions and—with the jawbone of an ass—slew a thousand Philistines, was overcome by Delilah, a member of what the world laughingly calls "the weaker sex." Just goes to show that between brawn and brains, brains will win every time!

➤ *Ikh hob Eeyov's tsores.* (I have the problems of Job.)

Wise Sayings

"Woe to them that rise early in the morning to follow strong drink, that tarry late in the night until wine inflame them!"

—Isaiah 5:11

Oy Vey

Be very careful of the sins you commit. According to Jewish tradition, they'll define your punishment. Samson couldn't control his passion and followed his eyes to lust after Philistine women. The result? He was blinded by his enemies.

Tsores are one thing, but the *tsores* of Job (Eeyov in Yiddish)—they are in a league by themselves! What makes the comparison more palatable is the fact that the travails placed on Job turned out not to be caused by any wrongdoing. They were merely a test meant to prove to Satan, the accuser, the unwavering piety of this saintly believer. I hope my problems, like Job's, are merely a test of my sincerity and are only temporary.

➤ *A gantse megile* (A big deal, a lengthy story)

The *megile* is the Book of Esther, which recounts the story of an attempt, in approximately the fifth century before the Common Era, to destroy the Jewish people by Haman, the wicked adviser to the Persian king, Ahasuerus. The entire

Megile literally means "scroll." The Book of Esther is publicly read from a parchment scroll handwritten by a scribe as a reminder of the original form in which it was written.

lengthy tale, from beginning to end, is read twice on the holiday of Purim. On this festive holiday, when Jews are commanded to eat and drink in celebration of their victory, they have to take time out, not only to listen to the reading of the entire story twice in the synagogue, but to hear the *gantse megile*. That's why when we want someone to cut a story short, or to get to the point, we say, please, *nisht di gantse megile*.

Descriptive Expressions

For the expressions that follow, you don't need any special knowledge. Just a sense of humor and a quirky way of looking at things will do. Here goes:

➤ *Shenere leygt men in drerd.* (They bury better-looking ones.)

The people you're talking about have to be pretty ugly to deserve this.

➤ *Sheyn vi ziben velten* (Beautiful as the seven worlds)

Mystical tradition has it that there are seven worlds. The number may be off, but there's almost total agreement that our earthly existence isn't the only one. The movie *Star Wars* isn't as far-fetched as you might think.

➤ *Me vert tsugevoynt tsu di tsores.* (We grow accustomed to our troubles.)

We had better. If we didn't, with our history we'd never survive.

➤ *Me makht a gants yontev derfun.* (They are making a big deal out of this.)

What could be a bigger deal than a *yontev* (a holiday)? But a holiday is decreed by God and deserves to get all its attention. It's criminal to confuse petty problems or stories with really holy moments.

➤ *Meh ken leben nor men lost nit.* (You could live, but they don't let you.)

Life, as God created it, could be so beautiful. It's not His fault that people mess up the world.

➤ *Di goldene medine* (The golden country)

Used only with reference to America, the expression emphasizes the very special love Jews came to have for the one country in the world that offered them a haven, freedom, and the opportunity to make a better life for themselves.

➤ *Vos gikher, alts beser* (The faster, the better)

Every wasted moment is a wasted opportunity to perform good deeds, and it can never be recaptured.

➤ *Es past zikh vi a patsh tsu gut shabes.* (It's as appropriate as a slap in response to a greeting of "good Shabes.")

If someone is kind enough to greet you and wish you well, it's really ludicrous to respond with a slap in the face.

➤ *Es vet nit shaten tsum shidekh.* (It won't hurt in arranging a marriage.)

Children have to get married, or else there'll be no continuity for the Jewish people. A *shidekh* (an arranged marriage) is the most important agreement of all. Anything that can destroy this arrangement is a catastrophe. If you want to describe a minor imperfection in a person, a deal, or even a product, you can reassuringly say, *Es vet nit shaten tsum shidekh.*

➤ *Es past vi a khazer.* (It's as appropriate as a pig.)

How can anything be more unsuitable for a Jew than a *khazer*? A miniskirt for the *rebbetzin*, the rabbi's wife? *Es past vi a khazer.* A Jew in the Mafia? *Es past vi a khazer.*

➤ *Dos heyst gelebt.* (That's what I call living.)

See someone driving a nicer car than yours? *Dos heyst gelebt.* Hear that your neighbors are going on a cruise while you're stuck at home in the snow? *Dos heyst gelebt.* There's a tinge of envy in the statement unless you use it to describe your own good fortune.

➤ *Ale montik un donershtik* (Every Monday and Thursday)

Monday and Thursday are special in Jewish life. On those days, the Torah is publicly read in the synagogue in addition to the Shabes. That's such a regular, repeated event that it's a paradigm for anything that can be expected to recur all the time.

With a Shmaykhel

Sam Cohen is at the cemetery visiting his father's grave. As he leaves, he sees a magnificent tombstone nearby carved out of the most expensive marble. Alongside are beautiful flowers and manicured bushes. With a sigh, Sam enviously exclaims, "*Oy, dos heyst gelebt.*"

Khap a Nash

Jews feel they can't live without the Torah, just as people die without water. The longest time people can go without drinking is three days. So, too, the longest period without a public reading of the Law is three days, from Monday to Thursday.

➤ *A lek un a shmek* (A lick and a smell)

If the hostess served almost nothing, she gave you a *lek un a shmek*. If the show for which you paid a hefty fee to see was far too short, they only gave you a *lek un a shmek* for your money. True, it's not nothing, but it may be even worse than that because it teased you with the merest taste and then left you unfulfilled.

Khap a Nash

The most famous *kashes* (questions) are the four reserved for the youngest child at the Passover Seder. *Kashes* are encouraged as the ideal way to transmit information from generation to generation. Questions are even more important than answers because they stimulate us to think and to probe.

➤ *Bilig vi borsht* (Cheap as borsht)

In a society where almost everything was scarce, at least beets were fairly plentiful. That made borsht the perfect example of something that's cheap, *bilig*, especially because of its alliteration.

➤ *Es iz nit geshtoygen un nit gefloygen.* (It never rose and it never flew—that is, it just doesn't make sense.)

Wouldn't it be remarkable if this expression had its birth in attempts by some early precursors of the Wright brothers to build a flying machine? For want of a better explanation, I offer it as a possibility. I'm sure, though, that many readers will scoff and say that my idea *iz nit geshtoygen un nit gefloygen.*

➤ *For gezunterheyt.* (Travel in good health.)

Journeys were always fraught with danger. Arriving safely at one's destination required a blessing of thanksgiving to God. Starting out warranted the good wishes of friends.

Rewarding the Philanthropist

The custom of wishing people a safe journey as they embark on a trip is at the heart of this delightful anecdote. Read it carefully to improve your knowledge of Yiddish in complete sentences.

Yiddish	English
A gor rayker yid fun Amerika is gekumen kein Erets Yisroel oyf Bazukh.	A very rich Jew from America came to Israel on a visit.
Ze'endik dos land, iz er geven zeyer iberasht. Hot er bashlosen tsu geben der medina a groyse sume gelt als matone.	Seeing the land, he became very impressed. He decided to give the country a large sum of money as a gift.

Yiddish	English
Demols iz geven Golda Meir der praym-minister. Hot er ir geshriben a brif un gezogt er iz berayt tsu shrayben a "tshek" far fir milyon dolar. Dos iz demols geven an umgloyblikhe sume.	Then Golda Meir was prime minister. He wrote her a letter and said he was ready to write a check for four million dollars. That was, at that time, an unbelievable sum.
Golda Meir hot shtark gevolt krigen dos gelt. Ober es iz geven nit laykht.	Golda Meir very much wanted to receive this money. But it turned out not to be such an easy matter.
Der Amerikaner hot gegebin tsu zayn matone eyn tnay. Er vil, tsulib der dem geldkrigen a shtele in Kabinet fun der medina. Un nokh epes. Es zol khotsh zayn a bkovedike shtele, fir milyon dolar is fort a hipshe nedova.	The American added to his gift a condition. Because of his donation, he wants to get a position in the cabinet of the State of Israel. And one more thing: It must at the least be an honorable position. Four million dollars is still a considerable donation.
Vos tut men, hot zikh Golda Meir shtark farvundert. Trots dem vos der yid hot a sakh gelt, iz er a groyser shoyte. Vi ken men im araynloyzen in kabinet?	What does one do? Golda Meir strongly wondered. In spite of the fact that the Jew had a lot of money, he was a great fool. How can he possibly be allowed into the cabinet?
Plutsing iz ir ayngefalen an eytse. Zi hot gerufen dem yid un gezogt as zi is maskim tsu zayn tnai. Di nekste vokh, git zi ir vort, vet zayn a groyse tsere-monye un men vet instaliren dem yid tsu zayn groysen un bkovedikem posten.	Suddenly an idea fell into her mind. She called the Jew and said that she agreed to his condition. The next week, she gave her word, there will be a large ceremony and he will be installed to his great and honor-able position.
Mit gor groys freyd hot der yid kom gevart di por teg. Gekumen, endlikh, iz der moment fun dem kovedgeben.	With great joy, the Jew was just, just able to wait out the few days. There came, at long last, the moment of his honor.
"Un vos," fregt der Amerikaner, "iz mayn vikhtiger posten? Tsu bin ikh der balabos fun der politsay, der armey oder etvos enlekh?"	"And what," asked the American, "is my important position? Am I in charge of the police, the army, or something similar?"
"Neyn, nish genoy dos," entfert Golda Meir. "Far aykh hoben mir a shtele vos iz efshar mer vikhtig far di gantse medina. Ir vet zayn der minister fun gezunt un fun religiyon."	"No, not exactly," answered Golda Meir. "For you we have a position that is per-haps more important than these for the entire country. You will be the Minister of Health and of Religion."
"Take, azoy hoykh un azoy groys a shtele? Zogt mir, vos genoy iz mayn tafkid? Vos muz ikh ton als minister fun gezunt un religiyon?"	"Really, so high and so great a position? Tell me, what exactly is my responsibility? What do I have to do as Minister of Health and Religion?"

continues

continued

Yiddish	English
"Yeden tog," entfert Golda, *"foren shiffen fun Erets Yisroel ariber der gantser veld. Ir, als minister fun gezunt un religiyon, darft shteyn baym breg yam, un shrayen azoy loyt vi meglekh, 'Mit Got's hilf, fort gezunterheyt!'"*	"Every day," answered the prime minister, "ships embark from Israel round the entire world. You, as Minister of Health and Religion, have to stand by the seashore and scream as loud as possible, 'With God's help, travel in good health!'"

It's Imperative

Notice how the last story ended with the words, *fort gezunterheyt.* Giving a command, a directive, or an instruction is the imperative form in grammar. Let's take this opportunity to learn a simple rule about how to form this tense.

The singular imperative is always the same as the base of the verb. To travel is *foren,* and the base is *for.* To tell someone to travel, you say *for.* To insist that he sing, you tell him *zing,* from the infinitive *zingen. Esen* is eating, and every Jewish mother for centuries has been telling every one of her children, *es* so that it takes years of adult dieting to undo the damage of youth.

A Gut Vort

The word **kheyrim** means excommunication. It was a severe form of punishment meted out by the Jewish courts and resulted in the excommunicant being in total isolation. It is almost never used in modern times.

When the imperative is used in the plural, you simply add a "t" to the base. Tell the choir to sing, and it's *zingt.* Insist that all your children eat, and it's *est.* If the base word already ends in a "t," as in the word *arbet* (work), then you don't have to change it at all when speaking to a group. *Arbet* is the imperative for both singular and plural.

Just so that it will not be too easy, there are two very common irregular verbs that you must remember: the singular *hob* (have) becomes *hot* in the plural, and the singular *gib* (give) becomes *git* in the plural. Now that you know the plural, don't you feel good being able to order everyone around?

Put-Downs and Perfect Squelches

So, I don't like you, I can't stand what you're telling me, and I don't have time to make long speeches. Just a few little words will have to capture my meaning. Yiddish is great at doing that. Use these when the going gets rough, and then, if the person you're talking to is bigger than you, get going!

Yiddish	English
Drey nit keyn spodik.	Don't confuse me (literally, don't turn the cap around).
Es geyt mir in pupik arayn.	It doesn't hurt me at all (literally, it goes into my belly-button).
Er iz im shuldik di lokh fun beygl.	He owes him nothing (literally, he owes him the hole in the bagel).
Es hart aykh?	Does it disturb you?
Es iz nito mit vemen tsu redn.	You just don't understand (literally, there's no one with whom to talk).
Fardrey zikh dayn kop.	Drive yourself crazy (literally, twist your head around).
Freg mir bekheyrim.	No matter what, I can't answer (literally, ask me even under the threat of excommunication).
Gey strashe di gens.	Go threaten the geese (because you're not threatening me).
Gib mir nit keyn eyn hore.	Don't give me the evil eye.
Hak mir nit in kop.	Don't talk so much (literally, don't bang me on my head).
Hak nit keyn tshaynik.	Don't be long-winded and boring (literally, don't bang on the tea kettle).
Ikh darf es vi a lokh in kop.	I need it like a hole in the head.
Ikh vel dir gebn kadokhes.	I'll give you nothing (literally, I'll give you a malarial fever).
Ikh zol azoy lang lebn.	I should live so long.
Freg mir nit keyn kashes.	Don't ask me any questions.
Ikh zol azoy visn fun tsores.	I have no idea (literally, I should know as little about trouble).
Me krikht oyf di glaykhe vent.	You're asking the impossible (literally, you're climbing on the straight wall).
Red mir nit arayn keyn krenk.	Don't talk me into illness (literally, don't talk a disease into me).
Shem zikh in dayn vaytn haldz.	You should be ashamed of yourself (literally, you should be ashamed to the bottom of your throat).
Shlog mikh nit, un lek mikh nit.	Do me no good and do me no evil (literally, don't hit me and don't lick me).
Shlog zikh kop in vant.	Go bang your head against the wall (and don't bother me).

continues

213

continued

Yiddish	English
Vet moshiakh geboyrn vern mit a tog shpeter.	Don't be in a hurry (literally, so the Messiah will be born a day later).
Vu krikhst du mit dayn krume fis?	Since you're not capable, what are you trying to accomplish? (Literally, where are you climbing with your crooked feet?)

Curses for All Seasons

Judaism never preached the Christian ideal of "turn the other cheek." In fact, the Talmud makes clear that if you passively accept a slap to your face, you yourself are responsible for the ones that follow. Yet Jews found it difficult to fight back. They were always better with words than with weapons. So Yiddish developed some of the most magnificent curses as a way of getting back at enemies. Psychologists call it compensatory verbalized hostility. I call it the intelligent man's response to attack, a way of saying you may be stronger, but I'm still much smarter.

A Gut Vort

Moshiakh, literally "the anointed one," is the Hebrew and Yiddish way to refer to the Messiah. One of the most fundamental beliefs of Judaism, it maintains the hope of the prophets that the world will someday be blessed with peace and the universal recognition of God.

Collections of these maledictions have been compiled, but I wouldn't dare make too many available to you. Trust me, though, when I tell you that they are highly imaginative. Can you beat, "You deserve the sweetest death—to be run over, softly, by a truckload of sugar." Or, "Like a beet you should grow—with your head in the ground." Or, "May you always hear music—as your insides churn like a music box."

Very often, Yiddish curses gave away the innate goodness of the one casting the curse as a contradictory softening of the curse was added. "May both eyes drop out of your head, God forbid." "Boils, *khas veshalom* (God forbid), should form on your carbuncles." "Every bone in your body should, *kholile* (God forbid), break." Now that's what I call mixed emotions.

I beg you to please not go overboard with these, but to make you a well-rounded Yiddish speaker, I'll give you a dirty dozen:

Yiddish	English
A brokh tsu dir!	A curse on you!
A kholyere oyf dir!	The cholera on you!
A mise meshune oyf dir!	May a strange death befall you!
A rikh in dayn tatens taten arayn!	A devil should be in your father's father!
Di beyner zolen im oysrinen!	May his bones be drained of marrow!
Er zol vaksn vi a tsibele mit dem kop in drerd!	He should grow like an onion with its head in the ground!
Gey in drerd arayn!	Go into the earth (and die)!
Klap kop in vant un shray gevald!	Go bang your head against the wall and yell for help!
Ver dershtikt!	You should be choked!
Zol er tsebrekhn a linke hant un a rekhtenfus!	He should break a left hand and a right foot!
Zolst farlirn ale tseyner akhuts eynem, un der zol dir vey ton!	You should lose all your teeth except one, and that one should ache!
Zol im klapn in kop vi es hakt mir in oyer!	I hope his head aches as much as my ear does!

Blessings and Good Wishes

Let's end this chapter on a far more cheerful note. Mouths that knew how to curse also were expert at blessing. "To life, to life," *lekhayim* was one way to say it. *Mazel tov* was another. These expressions were constants in Jewish life, without a doubt even more frequently used than any maledictions.

Here are some other nice thoughts you may use as toasts, cheerful greetings, or good wishes:

Khap a Nash

During the Middle Ages, Europe was decimated by a plague of cholera. Because many Jews weren't affected—probably because of their religious hygienic practices—they were accused of being the cause of this outbreak. Cholera remained as an example of the most horrible death.

Wise Sayings

"Strange, when you come to think of it, that of all the countless folk who have lived on this planet, not one is known in history or in legend as having died of laughter."

—Max Beerbohm, twentieth-century English author

Oy Vey

Be careful. Don't wish anyone more than 120 years of life. That's as long as Moses lived, and it would be disrespectful for anyone after him to expect more years than the greatest Jew who ever lived.

Yiddish	English
A gezunt oyf dayn kop!	Be with good health! (Literally, good health on your head!)
A gezunt dir in pupik!	Thanks for your favor! (Literally, good health to your belly-button!)
A lebn oyf dayn kop!	A long life upon your head!
Biz hundert un tsvontsik yor!	For a hundred and twenty years!
Fun dayn moyl in Got's oyern.	From your mouth into God's ears.
Lomir lebn un lakhn.	May we live and laugh.
Men zol nit darfn onkumen tsu kinder!	Pray that you may not be a burden to your children!
Men zol zikh bagegenen oyf simkhes.	May we meet on happy occasions.
Nit far dir gedakht!	May it never happen to you!
Oyf undz ale gezogt gevorn.	It should only happen to all of us (literally, let it be said about us).
Zol dos zayn dayn ergste dayge.	That should be your worst worry.
Zolst nit visen fun keyn shlekhts.	You shouldn't know from bad.

Promise me that you'll use the blessings far more than the curses. As a reward, I pray, *zolst keynmol nit visen fun keyn tsores* (may you never know of any troubles).

The Least You Need to Know

➤ Some Yiddish expressions use similes requiring familiarity with the Bible, such as *raykh vi Korakh* (wealthy as Korah).

➤ Yiddish is rich in descriptive expressions with unforgettable metaphors and allusions.

➤ The imperative in Yiddish is the base word in the singular; add a *-t* in the plural.

➤ Yiddish uses words as weapons in many powerful put-downs and curses.

➤ Everyday blessings such as *mazel tov* and *lekhayim* remain as some of the most frequently used expressions together with others conveying best wishes for long life and good health.

Chapter 20

Morons and Misfits

> ➤ Introducing the fools and the villains of Jewish life

> ➤ Meeting the *nudniks* and the numbskulls

"Mourn for the dead seven days," says the book of Ben Sira in the Apocrypha, "but for a fool all his life." As the People of the Book, Jews not only revere wisdom, but they are also repulsed by stupidity. It's not just that they can't suffer fools gladly; as Ben Sira puts it, "Sand and salt and a weight of iron are easier to bear than a senseless man."

That probably explains why Yiddish has so many different words for morons and misfits, for idiots and incompetents, for the "mentally challenged" and the mindless ignoramuses. The fine shadings of difference between degrees of abnormality, as well as exceptions to the approved norms of a ritualistically oriented culture, provided a need for countless words to do justice to the multitude of character traits, quirks, and personalities. As a matter of fact, illustrations of powerful, one-word descriptions practically run the gamut from A to Z.

Remember that none of these words are used indiscriminately. You must develop a certain feeling for their appropriateness. Just as you've already seen that a *shlemiel* isn't the same as a *shlemazel*, every one of these descriptives has its own degree of animosity, disgust, and disfavor—with some of them even implying a wink of the eye and a kind of envious acceptance. I'll try my best to do justice to not just the translation, but also to the spirit of these capsule summaries.

A Is For ...

➤ *Azas-ponim*—An impudent, disrespectful, brazen person

An *azas-ponim* will not hesitate to walk over to a rabbi after his sermon and tell him, "Rabbi, you don't know what you're talking about." Woe to parents who have *azas-ponim* for children. They'll think nothing of looking you straight in the eye and saying, "Who says I have to listen to you?"

➤ *Alter noyef*—A dirty old man

The word *alter* (old) ordinarily commands respect. When joined to an inappropriate form of behavior, it makes the action all the more repulsive. A sexually promiscuous young person can at times be forgiven for his indiscretions. An *alter noyef* is to be judged so much more severely because he's just not acting his age—and that makes him not just a sinner, but stupid.

➤ *Arumloyfer*—A runaround, a gadabout, an unstable personality

Arumloyfers just don't want to accept responsibility. They very often are one and the same as the *alter bokher*, literally "old young man," or bachelor. The only thing an *arumloyfer* is serious about is having fun.

With a Shmaykhel

How do women get rid of roaches in their New York City apartments? The same way they get rid of unwanted boyfriends, says Jackie Mason, the Jewish comic: They ask them to make a commitment.

B Is For ...

➤ *Bal gayve*—A conceited person

Heard about the *bal gayve* who was involved in a sexual threesome? He and his girlfriend were in love with him!

➤ *Beyze khaye*—Wild animal

Khaye by itself can be used as an insult, but if you add the adjective *beyze* before it, you're really talking about a vicious person. A *beyze khaye* has no self-control and acts out aggression. It's permissible to warn someone who is visibly angry not to become a *beyze khaye*.

➤ *Beheyme—An animal*

The difference between a *khaye* and a *beheyme* is that the former is an undomesticated beast and the latter a domesticated animal. Using *khaye* stresses wildness; calling someone a *beheyme* stresses nonhuman intelligence, that the person has the brains of a cow.

➤ *Balagole—A wagon driver, a coachman, a coarse person*

Balagole as an insult is probably politically incorrect today. It puts down a person by way of his menial profession. It's as if someone would call Eric Hoffer, the brilliant contemporary American philosopher, a *balagole* just because he chose to be a longshoreman. Strangely enough, the word is still used even though I pray for its hasty departure.

➤ *Barabantshik—Drummer in a band, a noisy person*

What a wonderful word for a drummer! Can't you just hear the rhythm and the beat in *barabantshik?* I wouldn't be surprised at all if the English *baraboom,* used to suggest loud and unexpected noise, has its source in the Yiddish.

➤ *Batlen—A nonproductive person, a lazy person*

Notice the negative and positive feelings surrounding this word? Guess it all depends on where you're coming from when you see an unproductive, nonworking person who nevertheless tells you his mind is occupied with more important things.

➤ *Bomer/Bomerke—A bum (masculine and feminine)*

I couldn't resist this American Yiddishism. Somehow the English word *bum* has such a unique flavor that we had to change it just a little and add it to our lexicon.

➤ *Boytshik—Little boy*

This is yet another Americanism with a truly split personality. As a negative, it's like the way the blacks in the South were called "boy" no matter how old they were by their white masters. "He's a *boytshik*" used about a business competitor of your own age is a way of showing lack of respect and indicating your belief that he's a "babe in the woods." The same word, when literally true because you're talking about your infant son, is a diminutive that's endearing: "Look at my *boytshik*—isn't he something special?"

Khap a Nash

The Talmud says that a large town "is one that has 10 *batlonim,* men of leisure who attend synagogue." Even the unemployed have a purpose to serve as the necessary quorum for services in the synagogue.

Wise Sayings

"A mighty man is not delivered by great strength."

—Bible (Psalms 33:16)

➤ *Bulvan*—A man built like an ox; a boorish, coarse, rude person

You'd think that someone blessed with strength would be more appreciated! Just because someone is Superman doesn't mean he can't be as mild-mannered as Clark Kent. Yet, Yiddish almost doesn't forgive the man of strength his blessing. If he's a *bulvan*, he probably always gets his way by being boorish. Ever since Samson's downfall, Jews haven't trusted muscles to make a *mentsh*.

C Is For ...

Note: The following words are all pronounced with the gutteral "kh," not the "ch" as in "church."

➤ *Chazer* (or *Khazer*)—A pig; a piggish person

A pig is filthy and wallows in dirt. A pig is not kosher, off-limits by law. A pig is ranked as the worst of animals forbidden for food, as it has only one of the two signs required for an animal to be acceptable: It has split hoofs, but it does not chew its cud. Pigs have a habit of flinging out their hoofs, which the rabbis saw as a way of trying to ingratiate themselves by saying, "Look at me, I'm kosher." That makes them deceivers and symbols of those who try to be considered pious by virtue of one positive trait, while concealing their inner impurity. A *chazer* (or *khazer*) is someone who may be said to resemble a pig for any of these reasons: He's dirty, religiously lax, or hypocritical.

➤ *Chutspenik* (or *Khutspenik*)—A person with *chutspe* (or *khutspe*)

Okay, so I didn't explain *khutspe*, but that's because I don't think there's any English word that's able to express its full meaning. English itself has given up and adopted the word. Is it impudence? Oh no, it's much, much more than that. The best illustration of *khutspe* is still the classic one of the man who kills his mother and father and then asks the court for leniency on the grounds that he is an orphan. Now that's *khutspe*!

D Is For ...

➤ *Dreykop*—Literally, "turn-head"; someone who confuses, connives, twists, and ignores the simplest logic very often because he doesn't even realize what he is doing himself

A *dreykop* will convince you without a shadow of a doubt that you have to turn left at the crossroad and then assure you, after you have followed his directions and gotten lost, that he really meant right. *Dreykops* can not only turn your head around, but they also can give you a headache like you wouldn't believe!

A Gut Vort

A ***shofar*** is a ram's horn blown on Rosh Hashana, the Jewish New Year, and at the close of *Yom Kippur*, the Day of Atonement. It recalls the biblical story of the near-sacrifice of Isaac, halted when God told Abraham to offer a ram instead of his son.

➤ *Dumkopf*—Literally dumb-head, dumb-bell, dunce

Anyone who has ever seen a German movie will remember this word. It's the expletive used in response to any act of stupidity. It usually is more of a reaction to a specific incident than to the total person. *Dumkopf,* how could you have done this?

➤ *Dybuk*—An evil spirit; in mystic belief, the soul of a dead person or a demon who takes possession of someone and renders him irrational, vicious, and crazy

The idea of a *dybuk* goes back thousands of years. One of the classics of Yiddish theatre, written by S. Ansky, called *The Dybuk*, has been performed around the world in many languages and popularized this idea of Jewish folklore. A *dybuk* has to be exorcised, and there is a powerful ritual including the use of a *shofar*, which is traditionally used to remove the unwanted demon. Calling someone a *dybuk* is pretty strong stuff. It suggests an irrationality so outrageous that it could be brought about only by superhuman forces.

E Is For ...

➤ *Eyzel*—A donkey, an ass

Funny how ass is a dirty word unless you're talking about an animal. If you've ever heard an ass bray, you'll never forget it. So much noise, so little content. That's what I call an *eyzel*.

➤ *Eyngeshparter*—A stubborn person

There's really no point in trying to convince an *eyngeshparter*. Logic just doesn't work. He's right because he thinks so, and how could you possibly know more than he does?

➤ *Ekeldikerparshoyn*—A disgusting person

To be a *parshoyn* is already not such a big compliment. To have the *ekeldiker* added really makes the designated person too disgusting for human contact.

223

If someone eats like a pig, he's a *khazer*. If someone cannibalistically consumes human flesh, that's *ekeldik*.

F Is For ...

➤ *Farbisener*—An embittered, envious, and unhappy person

A *farbisener* never smiles except when he hears of your misfortune. A *farbisener*'s least favorite commandment is "Thou shalt not covet." A *farbisener* doesn't *fargin*—a great Yiddish word for which I know no English equivalent. To *fargin* is to be happy for someone else, to rejoice in another's good fortune. I *fargin* him his Jaguar. I *fargin* him that he won the lottery. *Fargin* is a word you'll never hear from the words of a *farbisener*.

➤ *Farblondzheter*—A lost, bewildered, confused person

A *farblondzheter* doesn't just have to be lost while driving. He can have lost his way spiritually, rationally, career-wise, or on any path of life that he has taken. A *farblonzheter* just doesn't get it. Even signposts won't help. He's off-track and doesn't seem to want to find his bearings.

➤ *Fardreyt*—Crazy

Fardreyt is really turned topsy-turvy. It's mixed-up-crazy. It's the perfect word for the expression *fardrey zikh dayn kop* (drive yourself crazy). Don't hassle me and get me *fardreyt*.

➤ *Farshtopterkop*—Stopped-up head; dense person

A *farshtopterkop* is capable only of holding just so much information and no more. Like the computer whose memory is full and can't absorb another byte, the *farshtopterkop* can't absorb another bit of information.

➤ *Farshtunkener*—Smelly, stinky, malodorous person

Sometimes even *shtunk* will do to make the point. A *shtunk* is a stinker, and he can smell not just because of body odor, but because of repulsive behavior.

➤ *Fartshadeter*—A bewildered, befuddled person

This is a word appropriate even for someone to say about oneself. Highly unexpected events can *fartshader* you. "I'm all *fartshadet* because my daughter told me she's pregnant." "So what's to be *fartshadet*?" "You don't understand—she's still single."

➤ *Feygele*—Literally, a little bird; a disparaging term for a homosexual

Could the word *fag* be related to *feygele*? Both share a profoundly objectionable attitude and join the list of contemporary "incorrect" words.

➤ *Freser*—A huge eater

Normal people eat; *fresers* devour and gorge themselves. When the owner of the kosher deli who had put up the sign, "All you can eat for $10" saw a *freser* approaching, he immediately closed up for the day before he went bankrupt.

➤ *Fonferer*—A double-talker

A *fonferer* is someone who speaks through the nose and is intentionally unclear. In English, you'd say he's full of baloney. In Yiddish, the baloney he's full of is probably not kosher.

Wise Sayings

"Is homosexuality a morally neutral choice for people free to choose? The Jewish answer would surely be no. My gut tells me that the answer is no. But it is not so easy to explain why that is so for committed homosexual partners leading constructive lives and even engaging in rich Jewish observance."

—Harold Shanks, contemporary U.S. publisher of *Moment* magazine

G Is For ...

➤ *Gazlen*—A criminal, a racketeer, a robber

A *ganef* is a dictionary-approved word for a thief. It doesn't have any of the harsh condemnation implicit in *gazlen*. A grandparent can say with a sly grin, *"Oy meyn eynikel iz a ganef."* It's a thief's cleverness without his criminal intent. But a *gazlen* is evil. He's a mugger who accosts you and physically beats you if you don't hand over the money. Unlike a thief, he doesn't use his brains to get into your home when you're not around. That's why, in the words of Rodney Dangerfield, he deserves no respect.

➤ *Geleymter*—Literally, a lame person; a *klots*

A *geleymter* is someone who drops whatever he touches. The note in the crystal shop read, "To *geleymters*—you can touch and pay for it when you leave."

➤ *Geshtrofter*—A punished, cursed person

A *geshtrofter* seems to have far more than his share of misfortunes. The only way you can explain his ill luck is that it must be by way of curse or punishment.

➤ *Goyisher-kop*—Literally, gentile head; a disparaging, chauvinistic way of implying inferior intellect by comparing it to that of a non-Jew

With a Shmaykhel

Abie can no longer take the blows he receives daily because he's a Jew, and so he decides to convert to Christianity. The next day his friends see him going to synagogue to attend services. "What in the world are you doing here?" they ask him. "You're no longer Jewish!" "*Oy,*" Abie bangs his head in acknowledgement of his stupidity. "What are you going to do? I have a *goyisher-kop.*"

Khap a Nash

If you make fun of stutterers, you're also mocking Moses, the greatest Jew who ever lived. Moses had this very same speech defect! Why didn't God cure him of it? So that no one should ever say that Moses convinced the people by way of his eloquence rather than because of the truth of his message.

Okay, before you get too upset with this one, let's give you some background. The word *goy*, used for a gentile, is in itself not a pejorative. In Hebrew, it simply means "nation." Jews in the Bible are called *goy kodosh* (a holy nation). What distinguishes Jew from gentile is not the noun but the presence of the adjective. In time, however, *goy* used alone to describe gentiles came to have very negative associations. That's certainly understandable when Jews were slaughtered, persecuted, and abused on a regular basis by *goyim* (plural of *goy*). For many centuries, Jews lived alongside neighbors who in the main were illiterate, while every Jewish child for religious reasons was taught to read and write by the age of five or six. You can hardly blame victims of barbaric anti-Semitism for their verbal disparagement of their oppressors. For a Jewish child not to want to make study his most treasured pursuit was to make him worthy of being called a *goyisher-kop*.

H *Is For ...*

➤ *Hikevater*—A stammerer, a stutterer

Say the word *hikevater* slowly to yourself and see how appropriate it is to describe a stammerer. Because it's a physical rather than a mental failing, it should never be laughed at. According to the Talmud, to mock a person with a deformity or an ailment beyond his control is the equivalent of making fun of God Himself who created this person.

➤ *Hitsiger*—A hothead

The Talmud teaches that loss of temper leads straight to Hell. That's why a *hitsiger* is in such danger of the *hits*, the heat that awaits him.

I *Is For ...*

➤ *Idiot*—Idiot

Idleness, says the Talmud, leads to idiocy. You're not born an idiot, you only choose to become one. That's why an idiot is condemned. Idiocy is a remediable illness. All you have to do is read the *Complete Idiot's Guide* series and be cured.

➤ *Ipisher*—Someone with a bad odor

Just take away the first letter, see what's left of the word, and understand why you can't stand being near this person!

Wise Sayings

"Anger begins with madness and ends with regret."

—Abraham Hasdai, thirteenth-century Barcelonian Hebrew scholar

K *Is For ...*

➤ *Kalike*—A cripple, a misfit, a terrible craftsman

You gave it to *him* to fix? He's a *kalike*. From one pair of pants he'll make two shorts—neither one of which will fit. A *kalike* has three hands, all of them left ones. A *kalike* has found the secret of alchemists, only in reverse: They tried to turn dross into gold; he knows the secret of turning gold into dross.

➤ *Karger*—A miser, a tightwad

When the Rabbi made an appeal and pleaded that the congregants give "until it hurts," the *karger* said that the thought alone made him sick. A *karger* isn't someone who *won't* give; it's someone who *can't* give—just like the man in this poem by Judah Ben Zeb, the great eighteenth-century Hebrew grammarian:

"A miser once dreamed he had given away
Some bread to a beggar he'd met in the day:
He woke with a start and solemnly swore
That as long as he lived he would slumber no more."

➤ *Khoserdeya*—Lacking brains, feeble-minded

A *khoserdeya* is someone more to be pitied than punished. The descriptive makes clear that the person has no brains, but absolves him somewhat for this deficiency because he can't be blamed for a defect from birth.

➤ *Kibitser*—An intrusive, meddlesome spectator

Kibitsers are self-appointed advisers who think themselves superior. *Kibitser* is such a great word that when it became the title of a play by Jo Swerling in 1929, it made both the title and its star, Edward G. Robinson, famous overnight. When a *kibitser* "stir puts his two cents in," it usually isn't worth even that, especially in today's inflationary times.

➤ *Knaker*—A bigshot, a show-off, a wise guy

Beware particularly of a *groyser knaker*—he's a *knaker* first-class. To the man who tells you how you should have done it when you put up the cash and he sat on his hands, you can say, *groyser knaker*.

➤ *Kokhlefel*—Literally, a cooking ladle; a busybody

A *kokhlefel* is worse than a *kibitser*. A *kibitser* only butts in verbally; a *kokhlefel* does something to "stir things up" a little. What he usually accomplishes is to get you deeper into hot soup.

➤ *Krekhtser*—A moaner, a sigher, a complainer

He's the one in the story who, while travelling on a train, drives everyone crazy by repeating over and over, "*Oy* do I have a thirst, *oy* do I have a thirst." When finally someone gets up, goes to the dining room car and brings him back a glass of water, the *krekhtser* continues his lament, "*Oy* did I have a thirst, *oy* did I have a thirst."

➤ *Kvetsh*—A whiner, a complainer

A *kvetsh* is first cousin to a *krekhtser*. A *kvetsh* doesn't just moan, though. A *kvetsh* is in a constant state of dissatisfaction. A *kvetsh* will be given six choices of main dishes at a fancy wedding reception and complain afterward that they didn't have anything that he liked.

Wise Sayings

"The truth is heavy, therefore its bearers are few."

—Samuel Uceda, sixteenth-century Palestinian preacher

L Is For ...

➤ *Lemishke*—A bungler, a Caspar Milquetoast

A *lemishke* doesn't even know how to take yes for an answer. He's meek, ineffectual, and incompetent. What's worse, it's hard to get mad at him because he is so docile.

➤ *Ligner*—A liar

From telling untruths, the Bible teaches, keep yourself far. Truth is the seal of God. A liar is worse than a blasphemer in Jewish tradition. Even *a halber emes iz a gantser ligen* (a half-truth is a whole lie), according to a famous Yiddish proverb.

➤ *Luftmentsh*—Literally, airman; someone who manages to survive by improbable schemes

A *luftmentsh* is a person with no visible means of support, surviving by improbable schemes and jumping from one wild project to another. A *luftmentsh* is an expert in 50 professions, who is capable of making a living from none of them. Israel Zangwill authored a famous story, *The Luftmentsh*, about a man whose business card read, "Dentist and Restaurateur."

Oy Vey

Be very careful not to be misled by superstition. Jewish law rules that the only people who could be appointed to serve on the *Sanhedrin*, the Jewish supreme court, were those who had a knowledge of the tricks of sorcery, so as not to be misled in their deliberations.

M Is For ...

➤ *Mamzer*—Literally, bastard; an untrustworthy person

Mamzer hovers just on the border of vulgar, taboo words. What saves it is the Talmudic observation that "most bastards are bright." So *mamzer,* with its insulting reference to genealogy, maintains a measure of admiration for intellectual acuity. That's why a proud *bobe* could hold her grandchild in her arms and whisper, "*Oy*, you cute little *mamzer.*"

➤ *Makhasheyfe*—A witch

The Bible forbids going to a *makhasheyfe* for advice. Sorcery and witchcraft are blasphemous. Too bad that every so often a man unwittingly marries a *makhasheyfe* and has to listen to her for the rest of his days.

➤ *Meshugener*—A mad person, an eccentric

Meshugener is more of a fun word than a condemnation. Every person, goes the Yiddish proverb, has his or her own *meshugas*. It's a way of acknowledging that "it's a mad, mad world," and we all have to be a little bit *meshuge* to survive.

➤ *Miskayt*—An ugly person

No, that's not quite right. A *miskayt* isn't just ugly. In a beauty contest, she'd come in fourth if there were only three contestants. A *miskayt* is someone whose own mother doesn't call him beautiful. A *miskayt* is so ugly that if as a baby he's compared to Winston Churchill, Churchill would be offended.

➤ *Moyshekapoyer*—Literally, Moses upside-down; a person who does everything in reverse

A *Moyshekapoyer* would put his hat on his feet and his socks on his head if he were able to do so. A *Moyshekapoyer* as a waiter gets every order at the table mixed up, even if there's only one person eating. A *Moishekapoyer* would ask the Pope how his wife is feeling.

➤ *Moyser*—A squealer, an informer

A *moyser* is the most detested of all Jews. He informs against his own people. A special blessing was added to the Silent Devotion, the prayer recited three times every day by observant Jews, that slanderers be eradicated and that there be no hope for them.

N *Is For ...*

➤ *Nafke*—A prostitute

Also known as *a kurve*, a whore can be a professional or any woman of loose morals who doesn't charge for her services. Calling someone a *nafke* or *kurve* can get you severely beaten up by a woman's husband, boyfriend, or pimp.

➤ *Nar*—Fool

The original Hebrew word on which this is based simply meant "young person." It's the foolishness of youth and the naivete of the inexperienced that's being derided. The word *nar* gives us the word *narish* (foolish) and *narishkayt* (foolishness).

➤ *Neb, nebish, nebishel*—A weakling, a pitiable person; a shy, drab, awkward person

Remember the *neb* of your high school class: the one with the geeky look, the funny glasses, the acne face who stuttered whenever he approached a girl. Of course, today he's a computer nerd, making billions from his software company and married to one of Hollywood's most famous actresses. Don't ever feel too sorry for a *neb*. Invariably, he's got something else going for him.

➤ *Nokhshleper*—A hanger-on, an unwanted follower

A *nokhshleper* thinks that "Goodbye" means "Welcome," and that "Get out of here" is just another way of saying, "Won't you be my friend?" A *nokhshleper* not only can't take a hint, but he also doesn't understand simple English—or Yiddish, for that matter.

➤ *Nudnik*—A nuisance, a bore

I know, I know, we already talked about a *nudnik* before. But here he is again. I guess that's because he's such a *nudnik*.

O Is For ...

➤ *Oisgetsatsket*—An overdressed woman

So what if it's 100° weather in Miami Beach. She still has to wear her mink coat so that everyone will know she has one. The diamonds will go well over the rainbow-colored dress, with the slit from the bosom to the *pupik* (belly button). The *oisgetsatskete* woman believes she's making a fashion statement. She is—and the word is *tasteless*.

➤ *Opnarer*—A trickster, a shady operator

When you shake hands with an *opnarer*, count your fingers afterward to make sure you still have 10 of them. The minute the *opnarer* says, "Trust me," be forewarned that he's out to get you.

➤ *Oyverbotel*—Senile, over the hill, someone who lost his faculties

To say it about an old man is disrespectful. Used for a younger person, it's another way of suggesting that he has "lost all his marbles."

➤ *Oysvurf*—An outcast

An *oysvurf* doesn't belong in school, in the synagogue, or among a social group. We'd excommunicate him if we could—at the least we won't talk to him.

With a Shmaykhel

Sarah says to her husband, "Should I wear the mink or the sable? Should I put on the tiara or the brooch? Should I wear this necklace or that one?" "Any one you want, darling, but please hurry or we'll miss breakfast altogether."

P Is For ...

➤ *Paskudnik, paskudnyak*—A revolting, disgusting, mean, evil person

The term is derived from a Polish/Ukrainian root and sounds just like what it means. All the syllables allow you to linger over your revulsion.

➤ *Parekh*—literally, having scabs on the head; a lowlife

The scabs of the *parekh* were considered contagious. So too, a *parekh*'s behavior presents an environmental threat to all those around him.

➤ *Pitshetsh*—A chronic complainer

A *pitshetsh* belongs with a *kvetsh* and a *krekhtser* and finds even smaller things than they do to complain about.

➤ *Prostak*—A boorish, coarse person

Prost alone says it as well. Not just a person, but actions as well can be swiftly summarized—and put down as *prost*, common, and vulgar.

231

A Gut Vort

Seder, literally "order," is the name of the festive meal celebrated on the night of Passover, so called because it follows a fixed sequence and order. Christianity's Last Supper was actually a *Seder.*

R Is For ...

➤ *Roshe*—A wicked person

At the Passover *Seder,* the liturgy speaks of four different kinds of children. One is wise, the second wicked, the third simple, and the fourth not even able to ask a question. The word for the wicked son is *roshe.* It's the shortest, most concise, and most powerful way to describe a really bad person.

S Is For ...

➤ *Sheygets*—A non-Jew; a Jew acting like a non-Jew

Morris was horrified to see his rabbi walk by the restaurant where he was eating pig with a baked apple in its mouth. Afraid everyone would call him a *sheygets,* he immediately called out, "Is this the way you serve me the apple I ordered?"

➤ *Shiker*—A drunkard

To be a *shiker* is bad every day of the year except one. On *Purim,* Jews are commanded to drink until "they don't know the difference between 'blessed be Mordecai' (the hero of the story) and 'cursed be Haman' (the villain)" (Babylonian Talmud).

➤ *Shmendrik*—A pipsqueak, a weaker version of a *shlemiel*

Based on the name of a character in an operetta by Abraham Goldfaden, *shmendrik* lives on as an ineffectual nobody, henpecked by his wife, and walked all over by his "friends."

➤ *Shmo*—A boob, a jerk

This is a shortened, more acceptable version of the vulgar word that starts the same way, *shm-,* but ends with *-ok* and means penis. Not only has *shmo* made it into English, but not too many years ago it also gained national recognition when Al Capp (born Caplan), the cartoonist and originator of the *L'il Abner* comic strip, created the shmoo: a lovable creature who adores being kicked and gives milk as a reward for being abused. (Talk about a subconscious symbol of the Jewish people.)

➤ *Shnorer*—A beggar, a sponger, a moocher

A *shnorer* can be respectable. Someone down on his luck is entitled to ask others to help him. It's only when he chooses this as a lifestyle and a profession instead of work that it gives the word a bad reputation.

T *Is For ...*

➤ *Treyfnyak*—An irreligious person; someone who eats non-kosher food

Derived from the word *treyf* (non-kosher), a *treyfnyak* just refuses to follow the rules. Usually the implication is specifically someone who ignores ritual laws, but it could also be extended to an immoral person or to someone who considers himself above the law.

➤ *Trombenik*—A blowhard, a braggart

From the Polish and Yiddish *tromba* (trumpet), it's somebody who blows his own horn with self-praise he doesn't deserve.

➤ *Tsedreyter*—A nut; a crazy, screwed-up person

When a spool of wool gets *tsedereyt*, it becomes all tangled up and extremely difficult to straighten out. That's just what a *tsedereyter* is like!

With a Shmaykhel

Yankel has been coming for years to a rich man for a donation. This time he has another young man alongside for whom he also asks alms. "Who is this?" asks the rich man. "That's my new son-in-law," answers Yankel. "I promised to support him for the next two years."

U *Is For ...*

➤ *Umglik*—A born loser; an unlucky person

Glik is *mazel*, success, good fortune. The letters *um* negate it. An *umglik* is a person who's an accident waiting to happen.

➤ *Unterveltmentsh*—Literally, an underworld person, a racketeer

So Jews didn't start the Mafia, but they still had their Bugsy Siegals and their Meyer Lanskys.

V *Is For ...*

➤ *Vayzuso*—An idiot

You're right—I almost couldn't find one for V. Thank God for the youngest son of Haman, who foolishly followed his father's genocidal plan against the Jews in ancient Persia. A *vayzuso* is a follower, not a leader, but is extremely unwise in his choice of heroes.

X Is For ...

X-rated words that won't appear in this book, as well as Yiddish words, none of which begin with an X.

Y Is For ...

➤ *Yente*—A female blabbermouth

Yente used to be a common and acceptable name until the humorous writer B. Kovner (pen name of Jacob Adler) popularized *Yente Telebente* in a Yiddish newspaper, a made-up character who couldn't control her tongue. I don't know if Yentes of the times changed their names, but today I know of no one who willingly goes by it. *Yente* is no longer a name but a title. It's given not by parents, but by long-suffering friends—and only to the truly deserving. For Yentes, gossip is air, and their mouths have discovered the secret of perpetual motion.

Z Is For ...

➤ *Zhlob*—An insensitive, gauche, ill-mannered person

A *zhlob* needs his hands to eat with, to point with, and to wipe his nose with. Otherwise, they're too clumsy to hold on to anything and too uncultured to shake hands with.

The Least You Need to Know

➤ Almost every letter of the alphabet begins a Yiddish word for a uniquely Jewish character.

➤ There are no uniquely Jewish characters that start with the letters Q or X.

Mentshen and Meyvinim

Everybody knows that Adam and Eve had two sons, Cain and Abel. Most people are unaware, though, that they also had a third boy named Seth. Why are so few people aware of his existence? It has been widely suggested that the reason Seth remains so much of an unknown biblical character is because he alone of all the first couple's original children didn't get into any trouble!

It's an ironic truth that sinners get much more publicity than saints. The bad guys make the headlines. Good people live quiet lives of anonymity. Remarkably enough, this slanted emphasis is evident even in the vocabulary of languages. We have far more words to describe the misfits than we do for the *mentshen*. We just completed a lengthy chapter becoming familiar with descriptions of imperfect individuals. We were overwhelmed with the quantity of words in Yiddish that allow us to express our distaste and our condemnation for "peculiar" people. Guess what? The list for the sane, the good, and the normal is far, far, shorter. Let's meet them next and then talk about how Yiddish folk sayings view the collective human scene.

When the Saints Come Marching In

No, of course, Jews don't have saints. A people whose gift to the world is monotheism—the belief in one God, and one God alone—can never elevate a human being to a level where that person is to be worshipped. However, that doesn't mean that Jews don't have their own kind of heroes. There are people to be looked up to for virtuous character, for specific traits, for particular strengths and talents. We'll get to those in a moment, but there's one word which tops the list that we have to single out all on its own. The word, of course, is *mentsh*.

Who is a *mentsh*? To borrow a line from the Supreme Court in a totally different context, you'll know him when you see him. You want a brief definition? That's impossible.

Khap a Nash

A mystical tradition teaches that in every generation there are 36 *tsadikim* (particularly holy people) whose righteousness, unrecognized by those around them, is responsible for preserving the world. If they did not exist, God would immediately be forced to destroy the earth.

A *mentsh* is a human being in the finest sense of the word. A *mentsh* doesn't have to be Jewish. A *mentsh* isn't even necessarily religious. There are extremely pious people who aren't *mentshen*; there are atheists who are. A *mentsh* lives by a code of honor, goes against his self-interest to act with nobility and decency, and is more concerned with pursuing his convictions than success.

The fact that "be a *mentsh*" has been the parental commandment for countless generations proves not only its primacy, but also shows that it was taken for granted that children would readily understand what was required of them. In English, the expression "I'm only human" is used as an excuse to explain away failings. The Yiddish *Zay a mentsh* declares that a person's humanity, implying that we are created in the image of God, places obligations upon us that we dare not violate.

Wise Sayings

"A home is blessed only on the wife's account."

—Babylonian Talmud

Meeting *Mentshen*

Here are some people who deserve a measure of respect for specific qualities or professions—people who hopefully also aspire to be a *mentsh*:

Frumer—A person who is *frum*, observant of the law, religious.

Kluger—A smart person; a wise individual, one of sharp intellect.

Khokhem—The Yiddish word from the Hebrew meaning wise, smart. Remarkably enough, a scholar is almost never referred to with just the word *khokhem*. Instead, the phrase used is *talmid khokhem*—a *student* of wisdom. To think you're already all wise proves that you're not. A truly wise person is always in pursuit of more wisdom, hence *talmid khokhem*.

Lamden—From the Hebrew word for learning or studying, it's used specifically for a genius in areas of religious scholarship.

Khoshever-mentsh—The super word *mentsh* is here prefaced by the word for *worthy*. You can imagine how worthy a person has to be to merit this description.

Tsadik—A holy person; one who goes beyond what is required by law.

Obegehitener—Someone scrupulous about observing every detail of Jewish law.

Balmlokhe—A master craftsman, a skilled workman; someone who earns his fee.

Balaboste—An excellent homemaker, an industrious housewife. "She's a real *Balaboste*" is considered a precious compliment.

Balebos—Literally, "master of the house"; the head of the family, the "boss."

With a Shmaykhel

The shrewish wife chased her husband around the house until he found safety hiding under the bed. "Come out right now," she shouted to her quivering mate. "*Ikh kum nit* (I'm not coming)," he muttered. "*Ikh bin der balebos do* (I'm the boss here)."

Wise Sayings

"To him who has the means and refuses the needy, the Holy One says: Bear in mind fortune *is* a wheel!"

—Babylonian Talmud

Baltsedoko—a dispenser of charity; someone who contributes frequently and significantly to the poor.

Baltshuve—Someone who returns to the faith; a repentant, a newly religious Jew. Jews commonly refer to *baleytshuve* as BTs, as opposed to FFBs, those who are *Froom* From Birth.

Mashgiakh—(Not to be confused with *moshiakh*, Messiah). The inspector and religious supervisor of Jewish dietary laws (*kashrut*) in restaurants, hotels, and catering establishments.

Rov/Rebbe—Rabbi, spiritual leader, from the Hebrew word that means teacher. A rabbi, unlike a priest, has no special spiritual status other than that bestowed upon him by his scholarship.

Rebitsen—The wife of the rabbi. In the Jewish denominations that permit women to serve as rabbis, we still don't have a good word to describe the female rabbi's husband. (The *rebitsene* just doesn't sound right. Any suggestions?)

Yakhsen—A person of distinguished lineage; someone with *yikhus.*

Meyven—an expert, an authority; someone who recognizes quality. A *meyven* understands that everybody on this list is superior to those mentioned in the previous chapter.

A Gut Vort

Gehenem, the Jewish name for Hell, comes from a valley in Israel where people would sacrifice their children to their gods. *Ganeydn* is the Yiddish version of the Hebrew *Gan Eden* (the Garden of Eden), the original Paradise.

The Good, the Bad, and the Beautiful

The world's a stage, as Shakespeare told us, and its actors are a diverse mixture of all types of people. Yiddish proverbs make sure we remember who is to be pitied and who is to be emulated; who is to be humored and who is to be honored; who are the villains and who are the heroes. I'm sure you'll enjoy these wise and witty observations:

Yiddish	English
A groyse oylem, un nito eyn mentsh.	A crowd of people, and not one real person among them.
A nar blaybt a nar.	A fool remains a fool.
A nar ken a mol zogn a klug vort.	Sometimes even a fool can say a smart word.
A nar vakst on regn.	A fool grows without rain.
A tsadik vos veyst az er iz a tsadik is keyn tsadik nit.	A saintly man who knows he is a saintly man is not a saintly man.
Az a nar shvaygt, veyst men nit tsi er iz a nar oder a khokhem.	When a fool keeps quiet, you can't tell whether he's foolish or clever.
A fremder nar iz a gelekhter, an eygener a shande.	A strange fool is laughable, but your own fool is shameful.
Az m'is tsu klug, ligt men in drerd.	When you're too smart, you ruin yourself.
Beser mit a klugn in gehenem eyder mit a nar in ganeydn.	Better to be with a wise person in Hell than with a fool in Paradise.

Yiddish	English
Der vos farshteyt zayn narishkayt iz a kluger mensch.	He who is aware of his foolishness is a wise person.
Di greste narishkayt fun a nar iz az er meynt az er iz klug.	The greatest folly of the fool is that he thinks he is smart.
Eyn nar ken mer fregn eyder tsen kluge kenen entfern.	One fool can ask more than ten smart men can answer.
Fun a nar hot men tsar.	From a fool one has grief.
Dem roshe geyt gut oyf der velt, dem tsadik oyf yener velt.	The wicked person fares well in this world, the saint in the life to come.
Beser mit a klugn tsu farlirn, eyder mit a nar tsu gevinen.	Better to lose with a wise man than to win with a fool.
Mit a nar tor men nit handlen.	Don't do business with a fool.
Nor naronim farlozn zikh oyf nisim.	Only fools rely on miracles.
Of a shaynem iz gut tsu kukn, mit a klugn iz gut tsu lebn.	On a beautiful person it's good to look, with a smart person it's good to live.
Seykhl iz an eydele zakh.	Wisdom is a precious thing.
Vos a nar ken kalye makhn, kenen tsen khakhomim nit farrikhtn.	What a fool can spoil, ten wise men cannot repair.
Ven der nar volt nit geven mayner, volt ikh oykh gelakht.	If the fool didn't belong to me, I'd be laughing too.

The Terrible "D" Word

There's one person and one descriptive word we have left out until now. To be honest, I didn't think the word would make it into this book. But a court case that recently came to my attention made me realize that it must be included, if only as a primer on practical Yiddish for lawyers.

The word, often considered taboo as too vulgar, is Yiddish for *excrement*. It's used not only to describe the real thing, but also to describe inferior merchandise, as well as a person who's considered truly worthless. Here's how it came to be the subject of a legal debate in the United States District Court of Massachusetts.

Defense attorneys arguing in a summary judgement motion in federal court in Boston wrote, in a responsive pleading, "It is unfortunate that this court must wade through the *drek* of plaintiff's

Khap a Nash

Miracles happen only after we do as much as we can on our own. The rabbis teach that God didn't split the waters of the Red Sea for the Jews as they were fleeing from the Egyptians until they walked into the raging water up to their necks. Only when they could do no more themselves did God intervene!

original and supplemental statement of undisputed facts." In response to this characterization using the offensive *drek* the plaintiff's attorneys filed this motion:

UNITED STATES DISTRICT COURT OF MASSACHUSETTS

MONICA SANTIAGO, Plaintiff

v.

SHERWIN-WILLIAMS COMPANY, et al.

Defendants.

Civ. No. 87-2799-T

PLAINTIFF'S MOTION TO STRIKE IMPERTINENT AND SCANDALOUS MATTER

Plaintiff, by her attorneys, hereby moves this Court pursuant to Rule 12(f) of the Federal Rules of Civil Procedure to strike as impertinent and scandalous the characterization of her factual submission as "drek" on page 11 of Defendant's Rule 56.1 Supplemental statement of Disputed Facts (a copy of which is attached hereto as Exhibit A). As grounds thereof, plaintiff states:

1. For almost four years now, plaintiff and her attorneys have been subjected to the constant *kvetshing* by defendants' counsel, who have made a big *tsimes* about the quantity and quality of plaintiff's responses to discovery requests. This has been the source of much *tsores* among plaintiff's counsel and a big *megille* for the Court.

2. Now that plaintiff's counsel has, after much time and effort, provided defendants with a specific comprehensive statement of plaintiff's claims and the factual basis thereof, defendants' counsel have the *chutzpe* to call it "drek" and to urge the Court to ignore it.

3. Plaintiff moves that this language be stricken for several reasons. First, we think it is impertinent to refer to the work of a fellow member of the bar of this Court with the Yiddish term "drek" as it would be to use "the sibilant four-letter English word for excrement."

(Rosten, The Joys of Yiddish (Simon & Schuster, New York, NY 1968) p.103.)

Second,

Defendants are in no position to deprecate plaintiff's counsel in view of the *khazeray*, which they have filed over the course of this litigation. Finally, since not all of plaintiff's lawyers are *yeshiva khurum*, defendants should not have assumed that they would all be conversant in Yiddish.

WHEREFORE, plaintiff prays that the Court put an end to the *mishegas* and strike "drek."

Say It Ain't So

We've talked about "negative" people. Let's spend a little time clarifying the grammar for expressing the negative. From the many quotes you have read, you have noticed the word *nit* inserted after the verb. For example:

Yiddish	English
Der bokher filt gut.	The young man feels well.
Der bokher filt nit gut.	The young man doesn't feel well.
Zey zenen gute mentshen.	They are good people.
Zey zenen nit gute mentshn.	They are not good people.

Sometimes, instead of the word *nit* you'll see the word *nisht*. The two are interchangeable.

Now here comes the tricky part. If the verb is followed by an object preceded by an indefinite article—for example, the girl has a beautiful dress—then for the negative case, the indefinite article—*a* or *an*—is eliminated and the phrase used is *nit keyn*. So, for example:

Yiddish	English
Zi hot a sheyn kleyd.	She has a beautiful dress.
Zi hot nit keyn sheyn kleyd.	She hasn't got a beautiful dress.

Another example:

Yiddish	English
Ikh bin a doktor.	I am a doctor.
Ikh bin nit keyn doktor.	I am not a doctor.

If the object of the sentence is preceded by a definite article, singular or plural—such as *der*, *di*, *dos*, or *dem*—retain the article and simply add *nit* to make the sentence negative:

Yiddish	English
Der talmid hot dos bukh.	The student has the book.
Der talmid hot nit dos bukh.	The student doesn't have the book.
Ikh darf dos getrank.	I need the drink.
Ikh darf nit dos getrank.	I don't need the drink.

One more thing. The negative of *es iz do* (there is) is *es iz nito keyn:*

Yiddish	English
Es iz do a lerer in klas.	There is a teacher in the classroom.
Es iz nito keyn lerer in klas.	There is no teacher in the classroom.
Es zaynen do flesher oyfen tish.	There are bottles on the table.
Es zaynen nito kayn flesher oyfen tish.	There are no bottles on the table.

Note that like *nit* and *nisht, nito* and *nishto* are also interchangeable.

The Least You Need to Know

➤ Words describing good and heroic individuals are not as numerous as those describing the bad ones.

➤ Yiddish proverbs stress the importance of wisdom and the superiority of the sage over the foolish.

➤ The negative *nit* or *nisht* appears alone in a sentence with no object or predicate noun.

➤ *Nit keyn* replaces the indefinite article *a* or *an* in a negative sentence.

➤ The negative of *es iz do* is *es iz nito keyn.*

Part 7

Yiddish Selections

"You want me to describe *chicken soup?" asked Sholom Aleichem. "That's* meshuge. *There's only one way to really know what it is. Taste it." You want a whole book to* talk *about Yiddish and not really let you get the* tam *(flavor) of this inimitable language?*

Part 7 treats you like an honored guest and offers you a delectable sampling of Yiddish "dishes." To make it easier, I'll offer you selections from many passages and phrases that you already know in English, and then tell you what they sound like when said in Yiddish. You'll get a chance to read Shakespeare the way people of the shtetel *would have understood him. You'll laugh at how sound bytes that are part of American culture, such as Richard Nixon's "I am not a crook," get a really Yiddish flavor when they become translated into phrases such as "Ikh bin keyn ganef." You'll snack on short pieces from some of the greatest Yiddish literary giants, including Nobel prize winner Isaac Bashevis Singer.*

To end on a happy note, you'll get a little overview of Yiddish humor. All that will, hopefully, allow you to leave this book with such love for Yiddish that you'll keep crying, "Ikh vil mer!"—which by now you've got to know means, "I want more!"

Chapter 22

The Wisdom of Proverbs

In This Chapter

➤ Yiddish proverbs about love and marriage

➤ Wise words about food and feasting

➤ Insights on family life and the bonds between parents and children

➤ Good counsel to guide you through life's many challenges

➤ Understanding the blessings and perils of age

➤ The grammar of reflexive words

The *Midrash*, an ancient collection of stories and interpretations of the Bible, tells us this tale: A king once said to his favorite counselor, "Ask of me whatever you wish, and I will grant it." The counselor thought for a brief moment and then asked the king for the hand of his daughter in marriage. He knew that, having her, everything else that he desired would be his as well. So, too, concludes the *Midrash*, God asked Solomon what it is that he wanted above all, and He would fulfill his request. That is why Solomon asked that he be given wisdom, knowing that once he possessed this great gift, all the king's riches would automatically follow.

Solomon wrote the biblical Book of Proverbs. Its insights and wise sayings are still studied and treasured to this day. In the course of time, Yiddish, as the expression of the soul of the Jewish people, also created its proverbs. These proverbs reflect the wisdom not of one man but of many. They capture the collective genius of a people as they thought about life and death, love and God, wealth and honor, as well as all the other issues that have long fascinated mankind.

A Gut Vort

Bashert is the Yiddish word for "predestined." Although Judaism believes strongly in free will, a mate is believed to be predestined by heavenly decree from a time preceding even birth.

Proverbs are the most succinct summaries of profound ideas. They are the sound bytes of a culture, the key to understanding a people. We've seen a number of these *shprikhverter* scattered throughout previous chapters. This time, I'll give them their due with a chapter all to themselves. Read them not only to absorb more of the Yiddish language, but also to laugh, to weep, and to be inspired by their insights.

Love Is a Many-Splendored Thing

What better way to start than with love. After all, love does make the world go round. As you'll soon see, that's not just an English point of view; Yiddish strongly agrees with it.

Yiddish	English
Kleyne meydlekh tseraysn di shertsn, groyse meydlekh tseraysn di hertser.	Little girls tear aprons, big girls tear hearts.
Kalte hent—varme libe.	Cold hands—warm love.
Ganovim un farlibte hobn lib fintsternish.	Thieves and those in love both love darkness.
A tropn libe brengt amol a yam trern.	A drop of love sometimes brings a sea of tears.
Hob mikh veyniker lib, nor hob mikh lang lib.	Love me a little less, but love me longer.
Tsuzogn un lib hoben kostn kayn gelt nisht.	To make promises and to love don't cost any money.
Durkh der libe farlirn mankhe dem farshtand; durkh dem farshtand, mankhe di libe.	Through love some lose understanding; through understanding, some love.
A harts iz a shlos; men darf dem rikhtiken shlisel.	A heart is a lock; you need the right key to it.
A meydel darf zikh putsen far fremde bokharim un a vaybel far'n eygenem man.	A maiden should pretty herself for strangers, and a young wife for her husband.
A meydel iz vi samet—aderabe gib a glet!	A maiden is like velvet—come on, give a fondle!
A meeseh moyd hot faynt dem shpigel.	A homely girl hates the mirror.
Ale kales zenen sheyn; ale meysim zenen frum.	All brides are beautiful; all the dead are pious.

Yiddish	English
Az di kale ken nit tantsen, zogt zi az di klezmorim kenen nit shpilen.	If the bride can't dance, she finds fault with the musicians.
Az es kumt der basherter, vert es in tsvey verter.	When the predestined one comes, it happens in two words (on the first date).
Az es zenen nito keyn andere mayles, iz a zumer-shprinkele oykh a mayle.	If a girl has no other virtues, even a freckle can be considered one.
Az me kumt treysten a yunge almone, trakht men zikh nit tsu fardinen a mitsve.	When someone comes to comfort a young widow, he doesn't think about performing a good deed.
Kheyn geyt iber sheyn.	Charm is better than beauty.
Der bester ferd darf hoben a baytsh, der klugster man an eytse, un di frumste nekeyve a man.	The best horse needs a whip, the wisest man advice, and the chastest woman a man.
Di libe iz zis nor zi iz gut mit broyt.	Love is sweet, but it's good with bread.
Dray zakhen ken men nit bahalten: libe, hisen un dales.	Three things can't be hidden: love, coughing, and poverty.
Es nit di lokshen far Shabes.	Don't eat the noodles before Sabbath (don't have sex before you're married).
Far a bisel libe batsolt men miten gantsen leben.	For a little love you pay all your life.
Far zise reydelekh tsegeyen di meydelekh.	For sweet talk, the girls melt.
Fun an alte moid vert a getraye vayb.	From an old maid you get a faithful wife.
Gey farshtey a meydel: Zi vart oyf di khasene un veynt tsu der khupeh.	Go understand a girl: She looks forward to her wedding and she cries as she walks to the marriage canopy.
Nit dos iz sheyn vos iz sheyn, nor dos vos gefelt.	Not that which is beautiful is beautiful, but that which pleases.
Nokh der khupe iz shpet di kharote.	After the wedding it's too late to have regrets.

Es, Es—Eat, Eat

"Bread," said Jonathan Swift, "is the stuff of life." Without food, we can't survive. Without feasts, who would want to survive? Food is the subject of fantasy, of fine conversation, and, of course, of profound proverbs and insights. See if the following proverbs don't speak to your soul as well as your stomach:

A Gut Vort

Hagode (in Hebrew, **haggadah**), literally "the telling," is the name of the book used at the Passover Seder that recounts the entire story of the exodus from Egypt.

A Gut Vort

Zmires (in Hebrew, **zmirot**), are the tunes sung at the Sabbath meal praising God and expressing the spiritual joy of the day.

Yiddish	English
Az men est khazer, zol rinen ariber der bord.	If one eats pig, let it run over his beard. (If you're going to do something wrong, enjoy it!)
Az men est nisht kayn knobl, shtinkt men nit.	If you don't eat garlic, you won't smell bad.
Az men trinkt ale mol esik, veyst men nit az es iz do a zisere zakh.	When one always drinks vinegar, he doesn't know that anything sweeter exists.
Az men iz hungerik, est men afile trukn broyt.	If you're hungry enough, you'll eat dry bread.
Az in hartsn iz biter, helft nit in moyl arayn tsuker.	If there's a bitterness in the heart, sugar in the mouth won't make life sweeter.
Di kats hot lib fish, nor zi vil zikh di fis nit aynnetsn.	The cat likes fish, but she doesn't want to wet her paws.
Geshmak iz der fish fun yenems tish.	Tasty is the fish on someone else's table.
Kreplakh esn vert oykh nimes.	One even gets tired of eating only *kreplekh* (dumplings).
Tsores mit yoykh iz gringer vi tsores on yoykh.	Troubles with soup is easier than troubles without soup.
Me ken khapn mer flign mit honik vi mit esik.	You can catch more flies with honey than with vinegar.
Mit shney ken men nit makhn gomolkes.	You can't make cheesecakes out of snow.
Me meynt nit di hagode, nor di kneydlekh.	You don't mean the hagode, but the dumplings. (You're not interested in the religion aspect, just in the food.)

Yiddish	English
A mayse on a moshl iz vi a moltsayt on a tsimes.	A story without a moral is like a meal without a sweet-flavored side dish.
Beser bay zikh krupnik, eyder bay yenem gebrotns.	Better barley soup at home than a roast at someone else's home.
A sakh zmires, un veynik kneydlekh.	Many songs, but few dumplings.
Men meg esn, nit fresn.	You may eat, but don't gorge yourself.
Az men hot nekhtn gegesn, iz me haynt nit zat.	If you ate yesterday, you're not full today.

Wise Sayings

"You eat to live, you do not live to eat."

—Saadia Gaon of Sura, Babylonian sage of the ninth century

All in the Family

Family is civilization in miniature. Family is our introduction to the world. Its members are the saints and the sinners, the heroes and the villains, the wise and the foolish of our earliest encounters. The following proverbs help us to grasp the special meaning of this all-important part of our lives:

Yiddish	English
A gute tokhter iz a gute shnur.	A good daughter makes a good daughter-in-law.
A shlekhte mame iz nito.	There is no such thing as a bad mother.
Az der tate shenkt dem zun, lakhn beyde; az der zun shenkt dem taten, veynen beyde.	When the father supports the son, both laugh;when the son supports the father, both cry.
Az di muter shrayt oyf'n kind "mamzer," meg men ir gloybn.	When a mother screams "bastard" at her child, you can believe her.
Bay tog tsum get, bay nakht tsum bet.	By day they're ready to divorce, by night they're ready for bed.

Oy Vey

Don't let the fear of having bad children deter you from propagating. The Talmud warns, "He who brings no children into the world is like a murderer." We must fulfill the commandment to "be fruitful and multiply." (Genesis 1:28) The rest is in God's hands.

249

With a Shmaykhel

What's **G.N.P.?** For countries, it defines success as the gross national product. For grandparents, it's the gross *nakhes* production.

Yiddish	English
Beser oyf der velt nit tsu lebn, eyder onkumen tsu kinder.	Better not to live than to become dependent on children.
Blut iz diker fun vaser.	Blood is thicker than water.
Eltern kenen alts geben, nor keyn mazl kenen zey nit gebn.	Parents can provide everything, but they can't give good luck.
Fun a muter's klap, vert dem kind nit keyn lokh in kop.	A mother's slap won't give a child a hole in the head.
Fun krume shidukhim kumen aroys glaykhe kinder.	From bad matches come good children.
Kinder brengen glik, kinder brengen umglik.	Children bring good fortune, children bring misfortune.
Kleyne kinder, kleyne freydn; groyse kinder, groyse zorgn.	Little children, little joys; big children, big worries.
Kleyne kinder trogt men oyf di hent; groyse kinder oyfn kop.	Little children are a load for the hands; big children are a load on the mind.
Nakhes fun kinder iz tayerer fun gelt.	Joy from children is more precious than money.
Oyf eygene kinder iz yederer a blinder.	When it comes to one's own children, everyone is blind.

Good Advice

Advice is a funny thing: The wise don't need it, and the foolish won't take it. Yet, it's probably one of the most important commodities in the world. Samuel Coleridge, the early eighteenth-century English poet, said it well: "Advice is like snow: The softer it falls, the longer it dwells upon and the deeper it sinks into the mind." See what you think of these observations:

Yiddish	English
A shlekhter sholem iz beser vi a guter krig.	A bad peace is better than a good war.
Ale mayles in eynem, iz nito bay keynem.	No one person possesses all the virtues.
Az a leyb shloft, loz im shlofn.	When a lion is sleeping, let him sleep.
Az es brent, iz a fayer.	When something's burning, there's a fire.
Beser a krumer fus eyder a krumer kop.	Better a crooked foot than a crooked mind.
Beser a yid on a bord vi a bord on a yid.	Better a Jew without a beard than a beard without a Jew.
Der emes iz der bester lign.	The truth is the best lie.
Der emes ken arumgeyn a naketer; dem lign darf men bakleydn.	The truth can walk around naked; the lie has to be clothed.
Der vos hot lib tsu nemen, hot nit lib tsu gebn.	He who likes to take does not like to give.
Di klenste nekome farsamt di neshome.	The smallest vengeance poisons the soul.
Emes iz nor in sider.	Truth is found only in the prayer book.
Ganve nit un fast nit.	Steal not and repent not.
Host du, halt; veyst du, shvayg; kenst du, tu.	If you have it, hold it; if you know it, be silent; if you can do it, do it!
Krikh nit tsu hoykh, vest du nit darfn faln.	Don't climb too high, and you won't have to fall.
Kuk arop, vest du visn vi hoykh du shteyst.	Look down, and you'll know how high up you are.
Loyf nit nokh koved, vet es aleyn kumen.	Don't run after honor; it will come by itself.
Me darf nit zayn hoykh tsu zayn groys.	You don't have to be tall to be great.
Biz zibetsik yor lernt men seykhl, un me shtarbt a nar.	Up to seventy we learn wisdom, yet we die fools.

Khap a Nash

The letters that form the word *emes* (truth) are the first, the middle, and the last letters of the Hebrew alphabet. For something to be true, it must be true from beginning to end, including the middle.

A Gut Vort

Sider (Hebrew, **Sidur**) is the name of the Hebrew prayer book. The word literally means "order" and refers to the fact that the prayers are in a systematically arranged order.

251

With a Shmaykhel

Before the High Holy Days, the painter was filled with remorse. He had knowingly watered down his paint and had overcharged his clients. Weeping, he prayed to God for guidance and forgiveness. Suddenly, he heard a heavenly voice: "Repaint, repaint—and thin no more!"

With a Shmaykhel

Here's a Jewish conversation from beginning to end. "*Nu?*" "*Nu?*" "*Nu?*" "*Nu?*" "*Nu?*" "*Nu?*" "*Nu?*" "*Nu?*" "All right. Monday I'll send the check."

Yiddish	English
Der iz klug vemes mazl geyt im nokh.	He is smart whose good luck accompanies him.
Der seykhl kumt nokh di yorn.	Wisdom comes with the years.
Di velt iz ful mit tsores, ober yederer filt nor zayne.	The world is full of troubles, but each person feels only his own.
Dos lebn iz nit mer vi a kholem, ober vek mikh nit oyf.	Life is no more than a dream, but don't wake me up.
Eynems mazl is an anderens shlimazl.	One's good luck is another's misfortune.
Farlorene yorn iz erger vi farlorene gelt.	Lost years are worse than lost dollars.
Fun glik tsum umglik iz nor a shpan; fun umglik tsum glik iz a shtik veg.	From fortune to misfortune is but a short span; from misfortune to fortune is a long way.
Got iz a foter; doz mazl iz a shtiffoter.	God is a father, fortune a stepfather.
Gute tsoln, shlekhte monen.	The good ones pay up; the bad ones demand.
Keyner veyst nit vemens morgn es vet zayn.	No one knows whose tomorrow it will be.
Mit mazl ken men alts ton.	With luck one can do anything.
Oyb er volt gehandelt mit likht, volt di zun nit untergegangen.	If he dealt in candles, the sun wouldn't set.

Friends and Enemies

Friendship is the equivalent of God's affection for man. Friendship is truly the best ship to come in for any person. Life without friendship is like the sky without the sun. Yiddish knows that all too well and gives us wonderful food for thought in these wise sayings:

Yiddish	English
An alter fraynt iz beser vi naye tsvey.	Better an old friend than two new.
Az du kenst nit baysn, tsayg nit dayne tseyner.	If you can't bite, don't show your teeth.
Az du krigst zikh, krig zikh az du zolst zikh kenen iberbetn.	When you quarrel, do it in a manner that will allow you to make up.
Az me redt zikh arop fun hartsn, vert gringer.	When you speak from your heart, you feel better.
Beser a guter soyne eyder a shlekhter fraynd.	Better a good enemy than a bad friend.
Beser der soyne zol bay mir guts zen, eyder ikh bay im shlekhts.	It is better for my enemy to see good in me than for me to see bad in him.
Beser zikh tsu vintshn, eyder yenem tsu shiltn.	Better to make a wish for oneself than to curse another.
Der ershter broygez iz der bester broygez.	The first quarrel is the best quarrel.
Fun kine vert sine.	From envy grows hate.
Fun vaytn nart men laytn, fun neont zikh aleyn.	At a distance you fool others, close at hand just yourself.
Gring iz tsu krign a soyne; shver iz tsu krign a fraynt.	It's easy to acquire an enemy; it's difficult to acquire a friend.
Hit zikh far di fraynd, nit far di faynt.	Beware of your friends, not your enemies.
Keyner iz nit azoy toyb vi der vos vil nit hern.	No one is as deaf as the one who will not listen.
Khavershaft iz shtarker vi brudershaft.	Friendship is stronger than kinship.
Ver es toyg nit far zikh, toyg nit far yenem.	He who is no good to himself is no good to another.

Grow Old Along with Me

An English proverb has it that "Youth delights in wishful thinking; age in thoughtful wishing." Age, as we all too soon learn, brings with it blessings and curses. We pray to be granted length of days, and we dread the disabilities that come with the years. Happy is the person who can say, "Thank God, I'm not 80. I'm just four times 20." Yiddish proverbs help us to put age into proper perspective. Consider the message of these profound observations, and remember that growing old is the only alternative to dying:

Wise Sayings

"Some friends are like a sundial: useless when the sun sets."

—Judah Jeiteles, nineteenth-century Austrian Orientalist

Yiddish	English
A man ken zayn alt un hobn a groye bord, ober dos meynt nit az er iz a khokhem.	A man may be old and have a grey beard, but this doesn't mean that he is wise.
Az me vil nit vern alt, zol men zikh yingerheyt oyfhengen.	If you don't want to get old, hang yourself when you're young.
Tsu vos men iz gevoynt in der yugnt, azoy tut men oyf der elter.	That which is practiced in youth will be pursued in old age.
Voyl iz dem mentshn, vos vert baglikt oyf der elter.	Fortunate is the man who has a happy old age.
Di yugnt iz a feler, di menlekhe yorn a kamf, un der elter a kharote.	Youth is a mistake, middle age a battle, and old age a regret.
In lebn zaynen faran dray epokhes; yung, mitlyorik, un "du kukst oys azoy gut."	There are three stages in life: young, middle-age, and "you look so good."

Wise Sayings

"Youth is fair, a graceful stag,
Leaping, playing in a park.
Age is gray, a toothless hag,
Stumbling in the dark."

—Isaac L. Peretz

Thinking About It

Well, you've just read so many profound observations. Time now that you *batrakht zikh. Batrakht* means "think," *zikh* is "yourself." *Zikh* is a word you need whenever you're talking about something that's reflexive. A number of verbs always require the addition of *zikh* because the action reverts back to yourself. Let's conclude this chapter with a list of examples such as "think" that require the extra *zikh* word:

English	Yiddish
to get undressed	*oyston zikh*
to wake up	*oyfkhapen zikh*
to get dressed	*onton zikh*
to work one's way up	*aroyfarbeten zikh*
to hide	*bahalten zikh*
to get to know	*bakenen zikh*
to prepare oneself	*greyten zikh*
to come to know	*dervisen zikh*
to sit down	*zetsen zikh*

English	Yiddish
to meet	*trefen zikh*
to lie down	*leygen zikh*
to be happy	*freyen zikh*
to fight	*tsekrigen zikh*
to be embarrassed	*shemen zikh*

Add this list to your knowledge of Yiddish grammar, and I can only tell you that *ikh frey zikh*—I'm really happy that you've come so far in your knowledge of Yiddish!

> ## The Least You Need to Know
>
> ➤ Yiddish proverbs express profound ideas about every aspect of life.
>
> ➤ Some words require the addition of the reflexive *zikh* to indicate that their actions revolve around oneself.

Chapter 23

"Velvel" Shakespeare— and Other Classics

In This Chapter

➤ What Shakespeare sounds like in Yiddish

➤ Lincoln's Gettysburg Address—Jewish style

➤ If God spoke Yiddish

Nu, I know that William Shakespeare wasn't Jewish. In fact, some scholars even think that he was really Sir Francis Bacon, whose name would have definitely made it not *kosher* for him to be identified with our people. Yet his works are so universal in theme and his insights so relevant to all mankind that they would surely sound just as good in Yiddish as they do in Elizabethan English—which, after all, is the real mark of greatness that defines a true classic. No matter what language it's in, it can speak to our hearts and our souls.

So let's have a little fun and see what some of Shakespeare's most famous passages would have sounded like if their author's first name wasn't William, but Velvel. As long as we're fantasizing, we might just as well go even further and also Yiddish-ize some other famous works. I'm sure we'll not only get a chuckle out of the way lines so familiar to us in our native tongue come across in their camouflaged clothing, but we'll also have a great opportunity to improve our Yiddish as we encounter new words we're prepared for because of our familiarity with the passage.

Romeo, Shmomeo—What's in a Name?

Is there a dialogue in the plays of Shakespeare that speaks more poignantly and pointedly to the Jewish people throughout all the long years of their exile than the one between Romeo and Juliet that bears on hatred engendered just because of family name? The enmity between the Montagues and the Capulets is a profound metaphor for the age-old hostility of anti-Semites to the Jews.

Oy Vey

Be warned, say the rabbis, not to change your Jewish-sounding name. The only reason that the Jews of Egypt were saved was by merit of their not having assimilated because they refused to change their names to Egyptian equivalents.

With a Shmaykhel

Goldberg changed his name to O'Rourke for business reasons. Now he comes before the same judge to change his name yet again to McCarthy. "Why aren't you satisfied with your present name?" the judge asks. "Oh, it's a fine name—but everybody keeps asking me, 'What was your name before?'"

Heinrich Heine, the famous early nineteenth-century German poet, explained his conversion to Christianity based on his belief that "baptism is an entrance ticket to European society." Heine understood that the siren call of his society seductively pleaded, as did Juliet, "Deny thy father and refuse thy name." Every Moses, like a Montague, had to face this challenge. Should a Cohen change his name to Kane to be more readily accepted? What, after all, *is* in a name? And would "that which we call a rose by any other word … smell as sweet"?

Let's read the passage in the original English and reflect upon some of the deeper meanings the words would have for Jews. Remember the backdrop against which this dialog takes place—lovers, doomed by their different family backgrounds, hoping to find redemption by renouncing their heritage:

Juliet: O Romeo, Romeo, wherefore art thou Romeo?
Deny thy father and refuse thy name;
Or if thou wilt not, be but sworn my love,
And I'll no longer be a Capulet.

Romeo: (aside) Shall I hear more, or shall I speak at this?

Juliet: 'Tis but thy name that is my enemy;
Thou art thyself, though not a Montague.
What's Montague? It is nor hand nor foot,
Nor arm nor face, nor any other part
Belonging to a man. O be some other name!
What's in a name? That which we call a rose
By any other word would smell as sweet;
So Romeo would, were he not Romeo called,
Retain that dear perfection which he owes
Without that title. Romeo, doff thy name,
And for the name, which is no part of thee,
Take all myself.

Romeo: *I take thee at thy word:*
Call me but love, and I'll be new baptized;
Henceforth I never will be Romeo.

Juliet: *What man art thou that thus*
bescreened in night
So stumblest on my counsel?

Romeo: *By a name*
I know not how to tell thee who I am.
My name, dear saint, is hateful to myself,
Because it is an enemy to thee;
Had I it written, I would tear the word.

Wise Sayings

"A good name is better than precious ointment."

—Ecclesiastes 7:1

Now, let's do it one more time, with the lovers speaking in Yiddish. For maximum effect, read the words aloud. Pretend you're a Shakespearean actor, and don't be afraid to emote. Yes, you can even take both parts—just speak in a little higher pitch when you're doing Juliet.

Dzuli'et: *Rome'o, oy, Rome'o, farvos bist du Rome'o?*
Zog zikh fun dayn foter op un varf avek dayn nomen,
Un oyb du vilst nit, shver zikh nor tsu zayn mayn libe,
Ikh vel demolt veren oys Kapulet.

Rome'o: *Tsu zol ikh vayter heren oder epes zogen?*

Dzuli'et: *S'iz nor dayn nomen mir a soyne;*
Ober du blaybst dokh du, nit zayendik kayn Montagyu
Vayl vos iz Montagyu? Keyn hant, keyn fus nit,
Keyn orm nit, keyn ponim nit, keyn ander teyl
Fun mentshen. Oy, ven s'iz nor an ander nomen!
Vos ligt azoy in nomen? Vos me ruft bay undz a royz
Volt mit an ander nomen oykh hoben dem gerukh dem zisen;
S'iz azoy Rome'o, haysendik gor andersh
Farmogt er dokh di zelbike natur
Iz tuzhe oys fun zikh dem nomen, vi a kleyd
Er iz fun dir afile nit keyn teyl
Un mikh derfar nem tsu ingantsen.

Rome'o: *Ikh khap dikh ba a vort:*
Du ruf mikh on gelibter, un ikh vel shoyn hoben gor an ander nomen
Kh'vel fun haynt on mer keynmol nit Rome'o zayn.

Dzuli'et: *Ver bistu vos du host, farborgen in der nakht*
Zikh ongeshtoysen of mayn sod?

> **Rome'o:** *Mit a nomen*
> *Veys ikh nit vi zikh on rufen*
> *Mayn nomen, libe heylike, iz mir farhast gevoren*
> *Vayl er iz dayn faynt*
> *Volt ikh dos ongeshriben, volt im gern tseflikt oyf shtiker.*

It tears out the heart, no? It grabs you in the *kishkes* (the intestines), no? *Oy*, could that Shakespeare write! More from that play I just can't quote anymore. I have enough of my own *tsores*.

Ham Is Bad, but *Hamlet*'s Great

A true genius, it has been said, isn't somebody who knows all the right answers: It's somebody who asks the right questions. Shakespeare proved himself as a first-rank philosopher with the inimitable soliloquy of Hamlet that poses the ultimate human dilemma: "To be or not to be."

The musings of Hamlet are far more than poetry. In the most profound sense of the word, they are theology. When Jewish audiences saw *Hamlet* performed in translation, they were not only moved by its dramatic power, but they also were overwhelmed by its brilliant insights that mirrored so many of the teachings of their own tradition.

For most Shakespearean scholars, the legitimacy of suicide is the theme of Hamlet's meditation. It is an issue of considerable relevance to a people who for so long suffered "the slings and arrows of outrageous fortune." For all the difficulties the world imposed upon Jews, Judaism nevertheless clearly affirmed the immorality of taking "arms against a sea of trouble, and by opposing end them."

Here's how perhaps the most famous scene in all of Shakespeare's plays reads in the original:

> **Hamlet:** *To be, or not to be, that is the question—*
> *Whether 'tis nobler in the mind to suffer*
> *The slings and arrows of outrageous fortune,*
> *Or to take arms against a sea of troubles,*
> *And by opposing end them. To die, to sleep—*
> *No more; and by a sleep to say we end*
> *The heart-ache and the thousand natural shocks*
> *That flesh is heir to—'tis a consummation*
> *Devoutly to be wished. To die, to sleep—*
> *To sleep, perchance to dream. Ay, there's the rub,*
> *For in that sleep of death what dreams may come,*
> *When we have shuffled off this mortal coil,*
> *Must give us pause. There's the respect*
> *That makes calamity of so long life,*

For who would bear the whips and scorns of time,
Th' oppressor's wrong, the proud man's contumely,
The pangs of disprized love, the law's delay,
The insolence of office, and the spurns
That patient merit of th' unworthy takes,
When he himself might his quietus make
With a bare bodkin? Who would fardels bear,
To grunt and sweat under a weary life,
But that the dread of something after death,
The undiscovered country from whose bourn
No traveler returns, puzzles the will,
And makes us rather bear those ills we have
Then fly to others that we know not of?
Thus conscience does make cowards of us all,
And thus the native hue of resolution
Is sicklied o'er with the pale cast of thought,
And enterprises of great pitch and moment
With this regard their currents turn awry
And lose the name of action. Soft you now,
The fair Ophelia.—Nymph, in thy orisons
Be all my sins remembered.

For Hamlet, suicide seems an unworthy option because of human ignorance about the afterlife. For Jews, suicide must be rejected precisely *because* what happens after death is revealed to us. We are accountable to God for our actions. It is God who gives life and only God who can take it. Suicide isn't simply a bad choice, it's an unforgivable sin.

Let's listen carefully to how Hamlet's description of the human dilemma sounds in Yiddish. Here again is a wonderful opportunity for you to improve your Yiddish and fulfill your fantasy of playing a Shakespearean lead at the same time. Stand up on a box: It will help put you in the mood. Ask your friends and family to listen, and then take a poll to see which version, the English or the Yiddish, they prefer:

> **Hamlet:** *Zayn tsi nit zayn—dos iz di frage—*
> *Vos virdiker iz far dem mentshen, layden*
> *Un oystrogen di ale faylen un shtoysen fun*
> *dem shtoorkhendiken mazel*

Wise Sayings

"A suicide is a sentinel who deserted his post."

—Bahya Ibn Pakuda, eleventh-century Spanish moralist

Tsi oyfheyben di wafen kegen a yam fun payn
Un durkh dem oyfshtand makhen a sof fun ir?
Yo, shtarben, aynshlofen
Nit mer; un kenen in shlof zikh zogen as es iz a sof
Fun harts-veytek un fun di toysent plogen
Vos ligen in natur fun kerper—dos
Iz dokh an op-ru vos me meg im vintshen
Fun gantsen hartsen. Shtarben—shlofen—
Shlofen un efshar zen khaloymes. Ot in vos
Es iz der ophelf. Ot vos tsvingt undz varten,
Der shrek, vos far khaloymes kenen zayn
In yenem shlof fun toyt, ven s'vet avekgeyn
Der lirem un di havenish fun leben.
Deriber iz tsu langer yor der elnt
Vayl on dem shrek tsi volt gor zayn a balen
Af oystsutrogen fun der tsayt di shmits un shpot
Fun a tiran dos umrekht, fun a shtoltsen dem khoysek,
Fun an opgenarter libe dem veytek
Fun gezets di shleferikayt.
Di hoze fun di amtlayt un di shtoysen
Vos es bakumt der emeser fardinst
Fun toygenikhsten? Ver volt velen layden
Oyb s'iz genug a shtokh ton mit a nodel
K'dey tsu veren ruik? Ver volt shlepen
Di lasten fun dem leben, shvitsen, krekhtsen
Ven nit der shrek far epes nokhn toyt
Far aza land vos nit andekt, funvanen
Es iz tsurik nokh keyner nit gekumen?
Vos andersh laymt dem vilen un es makht undz
Mir zolen beser trogen yene payn
Vos iz shoyn do bay undz, un nit antloyfen
Ahin, vu s'zayne naye umbakente?
Azoy makht der bavustzayn far pakhdonim undz alemen.
Un di gezunte farb fun draystkayt in bashlus vert obgetsert
Tsulib dem blaykhkayt, opglents fun gedank
Un s'krikhen maysim fun gevikht un shnelkayt
Tsulib der vaklenish, arop fun veg
Dem nomen fun a handlung—ober shtil!
Ofeliya di sheyne.—Nimfe, nem arayn
In dayne tfiles ale mayne zind!

Hamlet's closing words ask Ophelia to remember "all my sins." For those who heard the passage in Yiddish, the very contemplation of suicide may well be one of the sins to which he made reference.

"Avrohom" Lincoln

Jewish history begins with the story of a people redeemed from slavery. Moses freed the Jews from their bondage in Egypt. Many centuries later, a man whose first name was Abraham emancipated those who were still slaves in nineteenth-century America. Abraham Lincoln is revered as probably the greatest of all American presidents. Jews know Abraham as a human partner with God who chose to identify Himself as the Lord who "took you out of the land of Egypt, the house of bondage," in the first of the Ten Commandments.

Khap a Nash

When a delegation of Jews from Paducah, Kentucky, came to President Lincoln to beg that he rescind an anti-Semitic order of General Grant, the head of the delegation, Cesar Kaskel, pleaded, "That is why we have come unto Father Abraham's bosom, asking protection." To that Abraham Lincoln replied, "And this protection they shall have at once."

In the midst of the great Civil War that tested the American ideal of equality for all men, Lincoln gave one of the greatest speeches of history, immortalized as the Gettysburg Address. In all of three short paragraphs, Lincoln was able to sum-marize the ideals of this nation, "conceived in lib-erty and dedicated to the proposition that all men are created equal." Its message and its mean-ing speak to us to this day. I'm grateful to Marie B. Jaffe for her magnificent transla-tion (in her wonderful book, *Gut Yuntif Gut Yohr: A Collection in Yiddish of Original Holiday Verses and Popular English Classics in Translation*), which allows us to read words so relevant to Jews in their own beloved tongue.

The Gettysburg Address (Original Version)

"Four score and seven years ago, our fathers brought forth on this continent a new nation, conceived in liberty and dedicated to the proposition that all men are created equal.

"Now we are engaged in a great civil war, testing whether that nation, or any nation so conceived and so dedicated, can long endure. We are met on a great battlefield of that war. We have come to dedicate a portion of that field as a final resting place for those who here gave their lives that that nation might live. It is altogether fitting and proper that we do this.

"But in a larger sense, we cannot dedicate—we cannot consecrate—we cannot hallow this ground. The brave men, living and dead, who struggled here, have consecrated it, far above our poor power to add or detract. The world will little note, nor long remem-ber, what we say here, but it can never forget what they did here. It is for us the living, rather, to be dedicated here to the great task remaining before us—that from these

honored dead we take increased devotion to that cause for which they gave the last full measure of devotion. That we here highly resolve that these dead shall not have died in vain—that this nation, under God, shall have a new birth of freedom—and that the government of the people, by the people, for the people, shall not perish from the earth.

And Now for the Yiddish

"Zieben-und-akhtzik yohr tzurik, hoben unzereh elteren beshtelt af diesen velt-teil ah nayen folk, begrayft in frayhayt, und gevidmet tzu die forshlageh as alleh mentshen zaynen beshafen glaykh.

"Yetzt fieren mir ohn a shveren birger-krig, tzu probiren oyb dieser folk, oder velkher es is folk, vos is azoi begrayft und azoi gevidmet, ken lang doieren. Mir zaynen zikh tzuzamen gekumen tzu vidmen ah teyl fun dem feld als ah beysoilem far dee neshomes vos hoben geshonken zeyer leben as der folk zol oishalten. Es iz zehr rikhtig, es past zikh, as mir zolen dos tohn.

"Ober fun ah gresseren shtandpunkt, kennen mir nit vidmen—mir kenen nit beheiligen—mir kennen nit m'kadish zayn diesen ort. Dee helden vos hoben doh gekemft—dee vos leben, un dee vos zenen geshtorben—zey hoben shoin dem ort haylig gemakht. Unzereh oremeh koikhes kennen datzu gornit tzulegen. Dee gantzeh velt vet kam bemerken vos mir zogen doh; ober zee vet keynmol nit fergessen vos zey hoben doh oisgefirt. Mir, dee lebedigeh, mussen zikh doh vidmen tzu dee groiseh oifgabeh vos blaybt doh—as fun deezeh be'erteh neshomes vet uns tzukumen ah gresserer kheyshik oistzufiren dee oifgabeh, far velkheh zey hoben tzugelegt mit zeyer leben. Mir mussen doh beshleesen az unzere toyte zenen nit geshtorben umzist—und as unzer folk, mit Got's hilf, vet nokhamol zayn fray. Und as dee regirung fun dee mentshen, bay dee mentshen, und far dee mentshen, zol nit umkumen fun der velt."

I can't help but share with you the story of the time I read this in Yiddish to a large group of newly arrived immigrants and discovered to my amazement, as I concluded, that there was not a dry eye in the audience. What a masterpiece to evoke such emotion almost a century and a half after the words were first spoken!

Some Phrases to Remember

You've read the entire text of the Gettysburg Address in Yiddish, following the English. You surely understood the meaning of the words as you realized the context. As a further exercise, I'd like you to hone in on some all-important phrases and memorize them because of their importance.

These are the expressions I hope you'll never forget:

Yiddish	English
begrayft in frayhayt	conceived in liberty
ale mentshen zenen beshafen glaykh	all men are created equal
a shveren birger-krig	a great Civil War
es iz zehr rikhtig, es past zikh	it is altogether fitting and proper
di vos leben un di vos zenen geshtorben	the living and the dead
unzere toyte zenen nit geshtorben umzist	these dead shall not have died in vain
di regirung fun di mentshen, bay di mentshen	that government of the people, by the people, for the people
zol nit umkumen fun der velt	shall not perish from the earth

As a final exercise, see if you can move from the recitation of an English sentence to its repetition in Yiddish for the entire passage. Look at the Yiddish version, close your eyes, and then try to say it by heart. If you can do the whole thing correctly, consider yourself well on the way to becoming a fluent Yiddish speaker.

The *Tzen* Commandments

I admit that it's quite a stretch for Shakespeare and Lincoln to be quoted in Yiddish. Yet no one, I think, can argue that God surely knows the language of His people. True, He chose to write the Bible in Hebrew. But for centuries, Jews have been teaching their children the text translated into Yiddish. You probably are familiar with the original, so let's use the Ten Commandments as another excellent practice to broaden our knowledge and learn some important Yiddish words.

I'll alternate between the Yiddish and the English for every one of the Commandments. That will let you get a better grasp of the exact translation phrase by phrase and sentence by sentence. You might want to read a few words in Yiddish and then go down to the English as you move along and try to memorize the meanings of words you do not yet know. As always, I suggest reading aloud. Adding your mouth and ears to the input for your mind will help considerably to let you acquire and retain the information.

The First Commandment

"Ikh bin Hashem dayn Got vos hot dikh aroysgetsoygen fun land mitsrayim, fun dem hoyz fun knekhtshaft."

"I am the Lord your God, who brought you out of the land of Egypt, out of the house of bondage."

The Second Commandment

"Zolst nit hoben andere geter far mayn ponim, zolst dir nit makhen a geshnits oder a shum geshtalt fun vos in himmel oyben, oder vos oyf der erd unten, oder vos in vaser unter der erd. Zolst zikh nit buken tsu zey, un zolst zey nit dinen, varum ikh, hashem, dayn Got bin a tserndiker Got, vos rekhent zikh far di zind fun di foters mit di kinder, mitn driten un mit'n firten dor fun di vos hoben mikh faynt, un tu khesed mit'n toyzenten glid fun di vos hoben mikh lib, un fun di vos hiten mayne gebot."

"You shall have no other gods before me. You shall not make unto yourself a graven image, nor any manner of likeness of anything that is in Heaven above or that is in the earth beneath or that is in the water under the earth. You shall not bow down unto them, nor serve them, for I, the Lord your God, am a jealous God, remembering the sins of the fathers upon the children unto the third and fourth generation of them that hate me, and showing mercy unto the thousandth generation of them that love me and keep my commandments."

The Third Commandment

"Zolst nit aroyfbrengen dem nomen fun Hashem dayn Got tsum falshen, varum Hashem shenkt nit dem vos brengt aroyf zayn nomen tsum falshen."

"You shall not take the name of the Lord your God in vain, for the Lord will not hold him guiltless who takes His name in vain."

The Fourth Commandment

"Gedenk dem tog fun shabes, im tsu halten haylik. Zeks teg zolstu arbeten un ton ale dayne melokhes, ober der zibeter tog iz shabes tsu hashem dayn Got. Zolstu nit ton keyn melohka, du un dayn zoon un dayn tokhter, dayn knekht, un dayn dinst, un dayn bheyme, un dayn fremder vos in dayne toyren, vayl zeks teg hot Got gemakht dem himel un di erd, dem yam, un alts vos iz in zey, un oyfen zibeten tog hot er gerut, drum hot Got gebentsht dem tog fun shabes un hot im gehaylikt."

A Gut Vort

Shabes comes from the Hebrew word "rest." It describes what God did on that day after creating the world in the first six. The name itself also conveys God's command to rest on this day.

"Remember the Sabbath day to keep it holy. Six days shall you labor and do all your work, but the seventh day is a Sabbath unto the Lord your God, and in it you shall not do any manner of work, you, nor your son, nor your daughter, nor your manservant, nor your maidservant, nor your cattle, nor your stranger that is within your gates. For in six days the Lord made heaven and earth, the sea, and all that is in them, and rested on the seventh day. Wherefore the Lord blessed the Sabbath day and hallowed it."

The Fifth Commandment

"Halt in koved dayn foter un dayn muter, kdey dayne teg zoln zikh lengeren oyf der erd vos Hashem dayn Got git dir."

"Honor your father and your mother, so that your days may be long upon the land that the Lord your God gives you."

The Sixth Commandment

"Zolst nit hargenen."

"You shall not murder."

The Seventh Commandment

"Zolst nit mezane zayn."

"You shall not commit adultery."

The Eighth Commandment

"Zolst nit ganvenen."

"You shall not steal."

The Ninth Commandment

"Zolst nit zogen oyf dayn khaver falshe eydus."

"You shall not bear false witness against your neighbor."

The Tenth Commandment

"Zolst nit glusten dayn khaver's hoyz. Zolst nit glusten dayn khaver's vayb, oder zayn knekht, oder zayn dinst, oder zayn oks, oder zayn eyzel, oder vos nor es iz dayn khavers."

"You shall not covet your neighbor's house. You shall not covet your neighbor's wife, nor his manservant, nor his maidservant, nor his ox, nor his ass, nor anything that is your neighbor's."

Khap a Nash

The Ten Commandments were given on two tablets because they are divided into two categories: laws between man and God, and laws between man and fellow man. The Fifth Commandment, to honor parents, appears on the tablet of human obligations to God because parents, as our creators, are to be afforded the same respect as the Almighty Himself.

With a Shmaykhel

Asked to recite the Seventh Commandment, little Abie must have had contemporary morality in mind when he expressed the law as, "Thou shalt not admit adultery." He, of course, is the same kid who claimed that the Bible teaches, "You shall not covet your neighbor's wife in vain."

Khap a Nash

The Talmud teaches that the gravest form of stealing is kidnapping. Long before the Lindbergh baby trial, the rabbis taught that kidnapping is a capital crime.

Exercising Your Mind

You've got to admit that this chapter had an incredible lineup of speakers. How can you beat William Shakespeare, Abraham Lincoln, and God Himself? That's why it would be a real insult to them if we didn't make certain that we leave these pages with a firm grasp of some of their major pronouncements. As a final exercise, let's see how well you do by providing the Yiddish for these lines. If you have any problems, go back to the place in this chapter where they appeared, and then fill in the correct response. (I don't want you moving on to the next chapter until you get a 100 percent on this exam!)

From Shakespeare

1. "Deny thy father and refuse thy name."

   _____

2. "What's in a name?"

   _____

3. "That which we call a rose by any other word would smell as sweet."

   _____

4. "Call me but love"

   _____

5. "To be or not to be"

   _____

6. "To die, to sleep"

   _____

7. "Be all my sins remembered"

   _____

From Abraham Lincoln

1. "Four score and seven years ago"

   _____

2. "A new nation"

   _____

3. "Conceived in liberty"

_____

4. "All men are created equal."

_____

5. "That that nation might live"

_____

6. "The brave men, living and dead"

_____

7. "It is for us the living"

_____

8. "This nation under God"

_____

9. "That government of the people, by the people, for the people"

_____

10. "Shall not perish from the earth"

_____

From God

1. "I am the Lord your God."

_____

2. "You shall not bow down to them."

_____

3. "Showing mercy"

_____

4. "Them that love me"

_____

5. "Six days shall you labor."

_____

6. "And rested on the seventh day"

_____

7. "Honor your father and your mother."

_____

8. "You shall not murder."

   _____

9. "You shall not steal."

   _____

10. "You shall not covet."

   _____

And don't forget the Eleventh Commandment for this book: You shall keep studying Yiddish until you know it well—and then you'll tell everyone that you learned it from this book!

The Least You Need to Know

➤ A passage from *Romeo and Juliet*—"What's in a name?"—has special meaning for Jews, who often had to face the temptation of changing their names to conceal their identities.

➤ Hamlet's soliloquy—"To be or not to be"—is equally powerful in its Yiddish version.

➤ The ideals of heroism, freedom, and holiness find eloquent expression in the Yiddish translation of Lincoln's Gettysburg Address.

➤ The Ten Commandments summarize the moral code of the Bible in every language into which they have been translated.

Chapter 24

Pop Culture in Yiddish Clothing

In This Chapter

➤ What famous movie lines sound like in Yiddish

➤ Translating slogans and sayings

➤ Playing fun games with famous quotes

Let's really have some fun now. Contemporary culture is filled with countless expressions, slogans, and sayings that are immediately recognizable to everyone. Their sources can be nursery rhymes ("Three Blind Mice"), anonymous graffiti ("Kilroy was here"), unattributed metaphors ("eyeball to eyeball"), or famous White House transcripts ("expletive deleted"). The media, the movies, and television introduced us to the politicians, writers, statesmen, and athletes, such as Yogi Berra with his inimitable malapropisms whose quotes are an integral part of contemporary American "folk wisdom."

Because you already are familiar with the originals, you should have little trouble recognizing them in Yiddish translation. If I say, *"shvarts iz sheyn,"* remembering either one of the Yiddish words will allow you to correctly guess that the whole phrase is of course, "black is beautiful." In most cases, you will only know part of a phrase in its Yiddish format, but you can inductively figure out the rest, and you can enjoy the same kind of pleasure as when you successfully complete a crossword puzzle. This chapter is truly interactive learning. We'll test your wits—and after you've solved all the questions, why not try them on your friends?

The Top Ten Movie Quotes

Someone eventually had to do it. Now at last we can thank the editors of *The Guinness Book of Film* for drawing up a list of the ten greatest movie quotes ever heard on screen. The compilers, a prominent group of film critics and experts, had more than seventy years and thousands of movies from which to glean the winners.

Before we start, you might want to see if your picks match theirs. Choose your own top ten. Now let me present you with their choices—but with a slight change that will make it more interesting. I'll give them to you in Yiddish and then see if you can not only figure out the original quote, but also add who said it and in which movie.

Here goes:

1. *"Bond—Yossel Bond."*

2. *"Fun ale kretshmees oyf der velt, kumt zi arayn in mayne."*

3. *"Es zaynen nisht di mener in dayn leben vos zaynen der iker, nor dos leben in dayn mener."*

4. *"Ikh vel zayn tsurik."*

5. *"Vost du geven dershtoynt oyb ikh vot zikh ongeton a bisel mer bakver?"*

6. *"Dos leben is punkt vi a kestel fun shokoladen: Du veyst keynmol nit vos du vest krigen."*

7. *"Ikh ken tantsen mit dir biz di ki kumen aheym. Oyf dem tsveyten blik, ikh vil beser tantsen mit di ki biz du kumst aheym."*

8. *"Tsu zogen dem emes, mayn tayere, es hart mikh gornit."*

9. *"Du redst tsu mir?"*

10. *"Gib mir a shnappsel mit a bisel sodevaser oyf der zayt—un zay nish keyn kabtsen, mayn kind."*

And the correct answers are:

1. "Bond—James Bond." The line, of course, is James Bond's introduction, the first utterance by Sean Connery as Agent 007, repeated in the 17 subsequent Bond films. That one was a throw-away and doesn't count for your quiz.

2. "Of all the gin joints in all the towns in all the world, she walks into mine."—Humphrey Bogart, *Casablanca* (1942)

3. "It's not the men in your life that count, it's the life in your men."—Mae West, *I'm No Angel* (1933)

With a Shmaykhel

When an anti-Semitic country club refused to admit Groucho Marx and his family as members, he wrote them: "Since my little son is only half Jewish, would it be all right if he went into the pool only up to his waist?"

4. "I'll be back."—Arnold Schwartzenegger, *The Terminator* (1984)

5. "Would you be shocked if I changed into something more comfortable?"—Jean Harlow, *Hell's Angels* (1930)

6. "Life is like a box of chocolates: you never know what you're gonna get."—Tom Hanks, *Forest Gump* (1994)

7. "I could dance with you 'til the cows come home. On second thought, I'd rather dance with the cows until you came home."—Groucho Marx, *Duck Soup* (1933)

8. "Frankly, my dear, I don't give a damn."—Clark Gable, *Gone With the Wind* (1939)

9. "You talking to me?"—Robert DeNiro, *Taxi Driver* (1976)

10. "Gimme a visky with a ginger ale on the side—and don't be stinchy, beby."—Greta Garbo, *Anna Christie* (1930)

Khap a Nash

The first full-length talking picture—*The Jazz Singer* (1927), starring Al Jolson—told the story of a young man who rejected the wish of his father, a cantor, to follow in his footsteps. Instead of singing to God in the temple, the cantor's son chose to become a popular singer. The movie was really the story of Al Jolson's life.

By the way, the line they didn't allow in the competition, because it was in a class all by itself, consists of the first words of the first talkie, *The Jazz Singer,* uttered by Al Jolson: *"Vart a minut! Vart a minut! Ir hot nokh gornisht gehert."* ("Wait a minute! Wait a minute! You ain't heard nothing yet!")

Slogans and Famous Sayings

Now let's try some really well-known quotes. Under each one, see how many words you can put down in English and how many you can complete.

1. *Amerika—hob es lib, oder loz es iber.*

   _____

2. *Haynt iz der ershter tog fun dem resht fun dayn leben.*

   _____

3. *Shik mikh aroyf, skottee—s'iz nit do keyn lebedike mit seykhel do.*

   _____

4. *A kop iz a shreklikhe zakh avekzuwarfn.*

   _____

5. *Vos du zest iz vos du krigst.*

---

6. *Azoy tsebrekelt zikh dos kikhel.*

---

7. *"Der din fun Murphy:" vos als ken kale veren, vet es ton.*

---

8. *Gevinen iz nit als, es iz di eyntsige zakh.*

---

9. *Vos, ikh zol zikh zorgen?*

---

10. *Mir velen iberkumen.*

---

11. *Di shvere zakhen tu'en mir bald. Di ummeglikhe zakhen nemen a bisel lenger.*

---

12. *Keyn mayse fun khesed gayt ongeshtroft.*

---

13. *Zog az es iz nit emes, yosel.*

---

14. *Fiftsig milyon frantsoysen kenen nish zayn umgerekht.*

---

15. *Eyn bild iz vert toysent verter.*

---

16. *Keyn froy ken zayn tsu raykh oder tsu din.*

---

17. *Epes alt, epes nay, epes geborgt, epes bloy.*

---

18. *Itst iz di tsayt far ale gute mener tsu kumen tsum hilf far zeyer partey.*

---

19. *An epel a tog halt dem doktor avek.*

---

20. *Froyen un kinder tsumershten.*

---

21. *Gey nisht iber der brik eyder du kumst dertsu.*

_____

22. *Es iz als in a tog arbet.*

_____

23. *Der man ken arbeten fun zun tsu zun ober di arbet fun a froy iz keynmol nit geendikt.*

_____

24. *Lebun loz leben.*

_____

25. *Es regent kets un hint.*

_____

And in the original:

1. "America, love it or leave it."—Slogan, 1960s
2. "Today is the first day of the rest of your life."—Slogan, 1970s
3. "Beam me up, Scotty. There's no intelligent life down here."—Invented in the early 1970s by fans of the *Star Trek* television series
4. "A mind is a terrible thing to waste."—United Negro College Fund advertising slogan, 1972

With a Shmaykhel

What do you get when it rains cats and dogs? Poodles on the ground, of course!

5. "What you see is what you get."—Computer users' aphorism, 1980s
6. "That's the way the cookie crumbles."—Saying, 1950s
7. "Murphy's Law: If anything can go wrong, it will."—Saying, 1950s
8. "Winning isn't everything, it's the only thing."—Saying, often attributed to Vanderbilt University coach Red Sanders, 1953
9. "What, me worry?"—*Mad Magazine* motto, 1955, adapted from a turn-of-the-century advertising slogan used by cartoon character Alfred E. Newman
10. "We shall overcome."—Adapted for the Civil Rights movement from an old religious song, 1960s
11. "The difficult we do immediately; the impossible takes a little longer."—Slogan of the U.S. Army
12. "No good deed goes unpunished."—Anonymous saying

13. "Say it ain't so, Joe."—Small boy to "Shoeless" Joe Jackson of the Chicago White Sox, as he emerged from a Grand Jury session in 1920 on corruption in the 1919 World Series

14. "Fifty million Frenchmen can't be wrong."—Saying popular with American soldiers during World War I, 1917–1918

15. "One picture is worth a thousand words."—A misattributed Chinese proverb

16. "No woman can be too rich or too thin."—A saying popularly attributed to the Duchess of Windsor

17. "Something old, something new; Something borrowed, something blue."—Wedding rhyme

18. "Now is the time for all good men to come to the aid of the party."—Practice sentence used in typewriting

19. "An apple a day keeps the doctor away."—Popular saying since the nineteenth century

20. "Women and children first."—From the Birkenhead Drill, February 26, 1852

21. "Don't cross the bridge until you come to it."—Popular proverb

22. "It's all in a day's work."—Popular saying since the eighteenth century

23. "Man may work from sun to sun, but woman's work is never done."—Popular saying

24. "Live and let live."—Scottish proverb

25. "Raining cats and dogs."—Popular saying

So what do you think? Would these sayings have become as popular if they originated in Yiddish? Guess we'll never know, but you can amuse your friends and assuredly bring a smile to their faces as you offer them this different perspective. And if anyone thinks what you're doing is too much *khutspe*, just tell them, *"Leb un loz leben"* (live and let live).

Guess Who Said It?

Grab a piece of paper and get ready for twenty questions that will test not only your knowledge of Yiddish, but also your trivia quotient. If I wrote them in English, I'm sure you'd probably get more than 80 percent right. In Yiddish, the challenge is first to figure out what the phrase means and then to tell me who said it. For example, if I said, *"Ikh bin keyn ganef,"* you'd certainly recognize the word for "I," "am," "not," and "crook"—"I am not a crook"—and answer Richard Nixon.

Now, jog your memory and see how you do on the following twenty questions:

1. *Ikh vil kikhel.*

   _____

2. *S'iz nish azoy laykht tsu zayn green.*

   _____

3. *Mir zenen di velt*
   Mir zenen di velt
   Mir zenen di mentshen
   Tsu makhen a beseren tog.

   _____

   _____

4. *E.T., telefonir aheym.*

   _____

5. *Kum mayn kind, tsind on mayn fayer*

   _____

6. *Gey, makh mayn tog.*

   _____

7. *Kenst krigen vos du vilst baym restoran fun Aliss.*

   _____

8. *Gir iz gut.*

   _____

9. *Zol der koyakh zayn mit deer.*

   _____

10. *Vuhin bist du gegangen, Yossel Dimazheeo?*

    _____

11. *Azoy vi a brik iber umruike vaser*

    _____

12. *Sholom Aleykhem, finsternish, mayn alter khaver.*

    _____

13. *Dos iz di nayes, vi ale froyen zenen shtark, ale mener*
    sheyn, ale kinder beser vi normal.

    _____

    _____

14. *Ikh bin der grester.*

    _____

15. *Der entfer, mayn khaver, blost in dem vint, der entfer blost in dem vint.*

   _____

16. *Ikh gay dir zogen epes*

   Ikh meyn du vest farshteyn

   Demols gey ikh dos zogen

   Ikh vil halten dayn hant

   _____

   _____

   _____

17. *In himel mit brilianten*

   _____

18. *Vi filt dos tsu zayn fun di sheyne mentshen?*

   _____

19. *Libe meynt men darf keynmol nit zogen me hot faribel.*

   _____

20. *Shpil dos nokh amol Sam.*

   _____

Oy Vey

Jewish tradition disagrees with Eric Segal. Don't believe that love means never having to say you're sorry. Every year, before the High Holy Days, Jews are expected to say they're sorry and to beg forgiveness from all those they may have hurt, either overtly or indirectly.

The Envelope, Please

Let's see how you did as I give you the correct answers:

1. The Cookie Monster.
2. "Green," sung by Kermit the Frog.
3. Michael Jackson and Lionel Ritchie, from the song "We Are The World."
4. Melinda Mathison, from the movie *E.T.: The Extra-Terrestrial*. (Okay, Melinda Mathison isn't a household name, so if you just said this was from the movie *E.T.*, mark yourself correct.)
5. The Doors, from the song "Light My Fire."
6. Clint Eastwood, from the movie *Sudden Impact*. (You also get credit if you said Ronald Reagan, who stole the line when he said, "I have only one thing to say to the tax increasers: 'Go ahead and make my day.'")

7. Arlo Guthrie, from the song "Alice's Restaurant."

8. Michael Douglas, in the movie *Wall Street*, written by Oliver Stone.

9. George W. Lucas, Jr., from the movie *Star Wars*.

10. Paul Simon, from "Mrs. Robinson."

11. Paul Simon, from "Bridge Over Troubled Water."

12. Paul Simon, from "The Sound of Silence."

13. Garrison Keillor, signature line from *A Prairie Home Companion*.

14. Mohammed Ali.

15. Bob Dylan (née Robert Zimmerman).

16. John Lennon and Paul McCartney, from "I Want To Hold Your Hand."

17. John Lennon and Paul McCartney.

18. John Lennon and Paul McCartney, from "Baby, You're A Rich Man."

19. Eric Segal, from *A Love Story*.

20. *Play It Again, Sam;* title of a Woody Allen film.

What Did They Say?

This is a two-part quiz. Now that you know who said all the above, take another sheet of paper and see if you can translate all the quotes in their entirety. Knowing the author as well as the context should help you considerably. When you're done, you can look at the list that follows, which gives you the complete translations:

1. "Me want cookie."

2. "It's not that easy bein' green."

3. "We are the world.
   We are the children.
   We are the ones
   To make a better day."

4. "E.T., phone home."

5. "Come on, baby, light my fire."

6. "Go ahead, make my day."

7. "You can get anything you want, at Alice's Restaurant."

8. "Greed is good."

9. "May the Force be with you."

10. "Where have you gone, Joe DiMaggio?"

Khap a Nash

Leonard Nimoy, the actor who plays Mr. Spock in *Star Trek*, is Jewish. The "Vulcan" hand gestures he uses are based on the biblical priestly blessing.

Khap a Nash

Steven Spielberg tells how he was made to feel like "a man from another planet" by anti-Semitic peers as a teenager. Could this be the source of his identification with E.T. and space aliens?

11. "Like a bridge over troubled water"

12. "Hello, darkness, my old friend."

13. "That's the news from Lake Wobegon, where all the men are strong, the women are good-looking, and all the children are above average."

14. "I am the greatest."

15. "The answer, my friend, is blowin' in the wind. The answer is blowin' in the wind."

16. "I'll tell you something
I think you'll understand,
Then I'll say that something,
I want to hold your hand."

17. "Lucy in the Sky with Diamonds"

18. "How does it feel to be one of the beautiful people?"

19. "Love means never having to say you're sorry."

20. "Play it again, Sam."

You might want to single out the following words to remember on their own:

Yiddish	English
laykht	easy
velt	world
krigen	get
koyakh	strength
vaser	water
nayes	news
shtark	strong
entfer	answer
vint	wind
farshteyn	understand
shpil	play

How about saying something noteworthy yourself, so that you may be quoted?

The Man and the Message

Now that you have the hang of it, let's try it the hard way and see if you can get both at the same time. Prepare yourself for the last quiz in this chapter. For the next 20 questions, see if you can translate as well as identify the speaker:

1. *Akhtsik protsent fun hatslokha iz nor az men zol zikh bavayzen.*

   Translation:_____

   Speaker:_____

2. *Dos iz eyn kleiner trot far a man, a groyser shprung far mentshhayt.*

   Translation:_____

   Speaker:_____

3. *Trots ales, gloyb ikh nokh als as mentshen zenen take gut in hartsen.*

   Translation:_____

   Speaker:_____

4. *Ikh hob a kholem.*

   Translation:_____

   Speaker:_____

5. *In tsukunft, vet yeder eyner sayn barimt far fuftsen minut.*

   Translation:_____

   Speaker:_____

6. *Es iz nish fariber biz es iz fariber.*

   Translation:_____

   Speaker:_____

7. *Bist a guter man, Khayim Braun.*

   Translation:_____

   Speaker:_____

8. *Mentshen vos darfen andere mentschen zenen di gliklikhster mentshen oyf der velt.*

   Translation:_____

   Speaker:_____

9. *Ikh vel em makhen a forshlag fun vos er vet zikh nit kenen opzogen.*

   Translation:_____

   Speaker:_____

10. *Ikh ken nish krigen keyn koved.*

    Translation:_____

    Speaker:_____

11. *Ikh hob geveynt dem gantsen veg tsu der bank.*

    Translation:_____

    Speaker:_____

12. *Freg nit vos dayn land ken ton far dir; freg vos du kenst ton far dayn land.*

    Translation:_____

    Speaker:_____

13. *Un azoy geyt dos!*

    Translation:_____

    Speaker:_____

14. *Kukdort in himel—s'iz a foygel, s'iz an eroplan, s'iz Superman.*

    Translation:_____

    Speaker:_____

15. *Er ken loyfen, ober er ken zikh nit bahalten.*

    Translation:_____

    Speaker:_____

16. *Ikh bin bseder, du bist bseder.*

    Translation:_____

    Speaker:_____

17. *Nem mayn froy—ikh bet dir.*

    Translation:_____

    Speaker:_____

18. *Ikh vil zayn aleyn.*

    Translation:_____

    Speaker:_____

19. *Fayne mentshen kumen arayn tsum sof.*

    Translation:_____

    Speaker:_____

20. *Tsukerl is zis, ober shnaps iz shneler.*

    Translation:_____

    Speaker:_____

The correct answers are these:

1. "Eighty percent of success is showing up."—Woody Allen

2. "That's one small step for man, one giant leap for mankind."—Neil Alden Armstrong

3. "In spite of everything, I still believe that people are really good at heart." —Anne Frank

4. "I have a dream."—Martin Luther King Jr.

5. "In the future, everyone will be world-famous for fifteen minutes."—Andy Warhol

6. "It ain't over 'til it's over."—Yogi Berra

7. "You're a good man, Charlie Brown."—Charles Monroe Schulz, *Peanuts* comic strip

8. "People, people who need people, are the luckiest people in the world."—Bob Merrill, sung by Barbra Streisand

9. "I'll make him an offer he can't refuse."—Mario Puzo, in *The Godfather*

10. "I can't get no respect."—Rodney Dangerfield

11. "I cried all the way to the bank."—Liberace

12. "Ask not what your country can do for you; ask what you can do for your country."—John Fitzgerald Kennedy

13. "And that's the way it is."—Walter Cronkite, sign-off sentence, *CBS Evening News*

14. "Look, up there in the sky, it's a bird, it's a plane, it's Superman!"—(Jerry Siegel and Joe Shuster)

15. "He can run, but he can't hide."—Joe Louis

16. "I'm okay—you're okay."—Thomas Anthony Harris

17. "Take my wife … please!"—Henny Youngman

18. "I want to be alone."—Greta Garbo

19. "Nice guys finish last."—Leo Durocher

20. "Candy is dandy, but liquor is quicker."—Ogden Nash

> **Wise Sayings**
>
> "I draw meaning for my life not from Marxism or any other secular philosophy, but from the prophets of Israel, from their passion for justice and cry for righteousness."
>
> —Martin Luther King Jr.

Take Note of These

You might also want to take special note of some frequently used words that appeared in these quotes:

Yiddish	English
hatslokhe	success
tret	step
menshhayt	mankind
trots	in spite of

continues

continued

Yiddish	English
gloyb	believe
take	really
barimt	famous
darfen	need
gliklikh	lucky
geveynt	cried
kuk	look
bseder	okay
sof	last

With all the words you've learned in this chapter, I guarantee that you'll not only be able to quote the eloquent, but you'll also be eloquently quoted.

The Least You Need to Know

➤ The ten greatest lines of movie history sound almost as great in Yiddish.

➤ Slogans and famous sayings offer a great opportunity to learn Yiddish words in the context of something familiar.

➤ Famous quotes translated into Yiddish make us smile and teach us at the same time.

Chapter 25

Voices of
the Masters

In This Chapter

➤ The wisdom of Sholom Aleichem

➤ The genius of Isaac Leibush Peretz

➤ The vivid portraits of Isaac Bashevis Singer

➤ The lullaby of Abraham Goldfaden

➤ The optimism of the partisans

To really appreciate Yiddish, you've got to hear it used by the masters. Don't ever think that just because you've heard someone say *shlep* or *shlemazel*, use a Yiddish expression such as *vey iz mir* (woe is me), or even put a few sentences together to express an opinion, that you've experienced the real flavor of this remarkable language. Just as Shakespeare showed what could be done with English, so too there are giants of Jewish prose, novelists, essayists, playwrights, and lyricists who have demonstrated how Yiddish words could convey the deepest secrets of the soul and the most profound messages of the heart.

Languages are the containers into which we place our ideas. If they are not large enough to hold them, our efforts to communicate suffer. Yiddish was sometimes dismissed as an unworthy language incapable of bearing the weight of profundity, sensitivity, and universal themes. With a burst of literary creativity culminating in a Nobel prize for the work of Isaac Bashevis Singer in Yiddish in 1978, it has become abundantly clear that the language of the street and the masses has achieved well-deserved respectability. To understand why this is so, I invite you to share in a little *nash* from the works of those who made Yiddish sing—both metaphorically and literally.

Hello, Sholom Aleichem

Beloved by the masses during his lifetime, Sholom Aleichem's reputation has soared among serious critics and scholars since his death in 1916. Prolific beyond belief, this journalist, novelist, playwright, and humorist leaves a legacy of hundreds of works with a kaleidoscopic overview of the foibles of life and the perils of his people.

The ruthlessness of Jewish existence, the absurdity of life, the combination of madness and logic that pervade human existence, and the cycles of birth and death, success and failure, joy and pain—all these serve as the framework for the entertaining and timeless works of this master craftsman. In the first chapter, we identified him as the leading figure of Jewish literature.

In a short selection, it's almost impossible to do justice to the scope and the brilliance of his writings. The modern world knows him best for his sympathetic portrayal of Tevye, the milkman, who became the hero of the long-running play on Broadway, *Fiddler on the Roof.* Tevye epitomized the Jewish people's desire for survival. With this simple character who spent much of his day in direct dialogue with God, we could clearly see the giant canvas of Jewish society at the time of the great historical transition from the old order of traditional life in Eastern Europe to modern times.

Sholom Aleichem perceived that the Jewish people, with all their failings, had something noble and precious to bring to the world. He realized that the people who first broached the idea of a world brought to perfection in a Messianic era have a special role in helping to bring that time closer to realization. Rather than emphasizing Sholom Aleichem's comic talents, the following piece focuses instead on his vision of an idealized future and his recognition of the greatest impediment to its fulfillment: the lack of Jewish unity.

A Gut Vort

A ***beys-hamedrash,*** literally "a house of study," is another name for a synagogue. At a time when books were scarce, the synagogue served as a public library, a school, and the equivalent of an intellectual ***salon*** for Jews of all ages.

The Treasure

In Yiddish, a treasure is an *oytser.* What's in it? Sholom Aleichem won't tell you. Think of it as the answer to your own three wishes that the magic genie will grant you when you help him escape from the bottle. What Sholom Aleichem wants to do is explain what's preventing us from realizing our dreams and fulfilling our wishes. To make it easier for you, I'll put the English translation alongside the Yiddish:

Yiddish	English
Oyf yener zayt berg, hinteren alten beyshamedrash, gefint zikh an oytser.	On that side of the mountain, behind the old house of study, there is to be found a treasure.
Azoy hot men geshmust bay undz in shtetel. Nor kumen tsum oytser iz nit azoy gring. Az ale yiden in shtetel velen leben b'sholom, un velen zikh nemen ale im zukhen, demolt vet men im gefinen. Azoy hot men geshmust bay undz in shtetel.	That's what they used to say among us in the *shtetel*. But getting to the treasure is not so easy. When all the Jews in the *shtetel* will live together in peace and will come together to seek it, then it will be found. That's what people said among us in the *shtetel*.
Un az ale yiden velen leben tsufriden, es vet nit zayn keyn kine bay yiden, keyn sine, keyn krig, keyn loshen-hore, keyn rekhilus, un men vet zikh nemen ale, vet men opzukhen dem oytser, un az nit— vet er arayn tif-tif in der erd arayn.	And when all Jews will live contentedly, there will be no jealousy by Jews, no hatred, no conflict, no evil talk, no tale-bearing, and all will come together, the treasure will be found, and if not, it will sink deep, deep into the ground.
Azoy hot men geshmust bay undz in shtetel.	That's what they said among us in *shtetel*.
Un men hot ongehoyben zikh tsu shparen un ibershparen, tsu zidlen un tsu krigen zikh, vos vayter als merer, als shtarker, un als iberen oytser. Der hot gezogt: dorten … un me hot nit oyfgehert zikh tsu shparen un ibershparen, tsu zidlen un tsu krigen zikh, vos vayter als merer, als shtarker, un als iberen oytser.	And people began to argue and argue some more, to curse and to fight, the longer the greater, ever stronger, and all over the treasure. This one said, there … and they didn't stop quarreling and fighting, cursing and battling, the longer the greater, ever stronger, and all over the treasure.
Un der oytser … hot gezunken alts tifer un tifer in der erd arayn.	And the treasure … sunk ever deeper and deeper into the ground.

Try This Test

You'll notice the style was purposely repetitious. The impact came from the seeming redundancy. See if you can remember some of the phrases. Fill in the blanks alongside the English:

1. That's what they said

   _____

2. Coming to the treasure

   _____

3. Is not so easy

   _____

Oy Vey

Be careful not to use the words *in drerd arayn* loosely. While literally they mean "into the ground," they're the Yiddish slang version of "go to Hell."

287

4. Will live in peace   _____

5. By us in the *shtetel*   _____

6. Live contentedly   _____

7. No jealousy   _____

8. No hatred   _____

9. Deep, deep in the ground   _____

10. Ever stronger   _____

Well, what do you think, was this exercise *gring* (easy) or not?

The Popular Peretz

Isaac Leibush Peretz began his literary career as a poet. Eventually a novelist, a critic, and a playwright, he retained the poetic strain in all his writings. As you learned in the first chapter, this Polish-born writer is also ranked as one of the founders of modern Yiddish literature. His works, too, span the gamut of Jewish life and capture the ethos of his people. Perhaps best known of all his works is a short story that highlights the tension between two approaches to Judaism and offers a startling and inspirational conclusion.

To understand the deeper meaning of the tale, titled *"If Not Higher"*, a little background is necessary.

A Gut Vort

Rebbe is not the same as *rabbi.* A *rebbe* is the title of a Hassidic spiritual leader who usually has a devoted following of disciples. A *rabbi* is someone who has received ordination attesting to his knowledge of Jewish law and may, if he chooses, not accept a post as leader of a congregation.

The Head or the Heart?

By the late nineteenth century, the rift between the two approaches to religious practice in Judaism had reached serious proportions. The Hassidic movement, founded by the Ba'al Shem Tov ("Master of the Good Name," 1700–1760), introduced a new emphasis to spirituality. Whereas Jewish law had always stressed observance as the most important requirement and strict adherence to every nuance of law as the definition of Judaism, Hassidism taught that feeling was more crucial than performance, fervor more significant than mindless following of legalistic procedures.

For Hassidim and their revered teachers, the *rebbes*, the heart was more important than the head in the service of God. For this belief, the *Mitnagdim* (literally, the "opponents"), followers of the great Talmudist Rabbi Elijah, known as the *Gaon* (genius) of Vilna

(1720–1797), placed the Hassidim under a ban of excommunication. The readiness of Hassidim to set aside punctilious observance of ritual was for *Mitnagdim* no less than heresy.

For Hassidim, it was possible to set aside the performance of a law for the sake of a nobler goal. Hassidic masters were condemned by others for laxity of observance as they happily forsook serving God for the joy of helping another human being. That is the theme of the Peretz story from which we will read a small concluding portion.

A Gut Vort

Slikhes is the name of the special prayers recited before the High Holy Days. Literally, "forgiveness," they express the hope that God will overlook human failings and grant the supplicants a good year in spite of their sins.

Introducing the Cast

The story starts in a little village called Nemirov. There is a Hassidic *rebbe*, the Nemirover, revered by his disciples. Enter also a cynic, a doubter of the *rebbe*'s holiness, a man identified only as a "Litvak"—a Lithuanian Jew steeped in the traditions of the *Misnagdim*.

The time is before *Rosh Hoshanah,* the Jewish New Year. Jews are commanded by law to appear early every morning at the synagogue to recite special *slikhes*, penitential prayers, prior to the awesome Day of Judgment. Remarkably enough, the holy rabbi, the Nemirover, is nowhere to be seen at these daily services. Did he simply oversleep? Impossible, say his disciples. Indeed, the *rebbe* is not at synagogue, not in the house of study, and not in his home. The only conclusion? The Hassidim knew that their *rebbe* must have ascended to the heavens to plead before God on their behalf.

The Litvak could only laugh at this assumption. He would find out the truth. So he hid himself under the *rebbe*'s bed early at night. He waited patiently until he heard a stirring and then followed noiselessly as the *rebbe* left his home, walked into the nearby woods, and chopped a tree to make pieces of lumber. With them, he walked back to town and knocked on the door of a poor widow's decrepit shack.

It is now that we begin to learn the secret of the *rebbe*'s absence from synagogue services.

How High Is High?

With the *rebbe* at the door, dressed in peasant's clothes, and the Litvak at a distance observing the strange encounter, the story continues.

Yiddish	English
"Ver iz?" fregt men dershroken fun shtub aroys. Der Litvak derkent, es iz a kol fun a yidene, fun a kranker yidene.	"Who is it?" someone asks with fright from the room. The Litvak recognizes that it is the voice of an old Jewish woman, of a sick Jewish woman.
"Ikh!" entfert der Rebbe oyf poyerish loshon.	"I!" answers the rabbi in the accent of a peasant.
"Ver ikh?" fregt men vayter fun shtub.	"Who I?" comes the question again from the room.
Un der Rebbe entfert vayter, oyf malorusish loshon: "Vassil!"	And the rabbi answers again in altered accent: "Vassil!"
"Vos far a Vassil, un vos vilst du Vassil?"	"What kind of Vassil, and what do you want, Vassil?"
"Holts," zogt der fashtelter Vassil, "hob ikh tsu farkoyfen!	"Wood," says the masquerading Vassil, "I have to sell!
Zeyer bilig—bekhotso khinom holts!"	Very cheap—wood almost for nothing."
Un nish vartendik oyf a tshuva, nemt er zikh in shtub arayn.	And not waiting for an answer, he enters the room.
Der Litvak ganvet zikh oykh arayn un, baym groyen likht fun frien morgen, zet er an orme shtub, tsubrokhen, oreme kley-bayis. In bet ligt a kranke yidene, farvikelt mit shmates, un zi zogt mit a bitter kol:	The Litvak also steals himself in, by the great light of early morning, and sees an impoverished room, and broken, cheap furniture. In bed lies a sick Jewish woman, wrapped with torn clothing, and she says with a bitter voice:
"Koyfen? Mit vos zol ikh koyfen? Vu hob ikh, orme almone, gelt?"	"Buy? With what should I buy? Where do I, poor widow, have any money?"
"Ikh vel dir borgen!" entfert der farshteler Vassil. "Ingantsen zeks groshen!"	"I will lend you!" answers the masquerading Vassil. "Altogether six groshen!"
"Funvanen vel ikh dir batsolen?" krekhtst di orme yidene.	"How will I pay you?" croaks the poor old Jewish woman.
"Narish mentsh," mussert zi der Rebbe. "Ze, du bist an orme kranke yidene un ikh getroy dir dos bisel holts. Ikh bin botuakh az du vest batsolen. Un du host aza shtarken, groysen Got, un getroyst em nish—un host oyf em oyf narishe zeks groshen faren bintel holts keyn bitokhen nisht!"	"Foolish person," the rabbi scolds her. "See, you are a poor sick old woman, and I trust you with a little bit of wood. I am confident that you will pay me back. And you have such a strong, great God, and you don't trust Him—and for six stupid groshen for a bundle of wood you don't have trust in Him!"
"Un ver vet mir onheytsen?" krekhtst di almone. "Ikh hob den koyakh oyftsuteyn? Mayn zun iz oyf der arbet gebliben."	"Light the fire for me?" croaks the widow, "Do I then have strength to get up? My son remains at work."
"Ikh vel dir aynhetsen oykh," zogt der Rebbe.	"I will light the fire for you," says the *rebbe.*

Yiddish	English
Un araynlegendik dos holts in oyven, hot der Rebbe, krekhtsendik, gezogt fun Slikhes dem ershten pizmon.	And putting the wood in the oven, the *rebbe*, with a sigh, recited the first chapter of the penitential prayers.
Un az er hot untergetsunden, un dos holts hot freylikh gebrent, hot er gezogt, shoyn a bisel lustiger, fun di Slikhes dem tsveiten pizmon.	And when he lit the fire, and the wood happily burned, he said, somewhat more lustily, the second chapter of the penitential prayers.
Dem driten pizmon hot er gezogt, ven es hot zikh oysgebrent un er hot di blekh farmakht.	The third paragraph he said, with the fire fully caught and he closed the iron cover.
Der Litvak, vos hot dos alts gezen, iz shoyn gebliben a Nemirover Khosid.	The Litvak, who saw all this, became a Nemirover disciple.
Un shpeter, oyb a Khosid hot amol dertseylt az der Nemirover heybt zikh oyf, Slikhes-tsayt, yeden frimorgen, un flit in himel arayn, flegt shoyn der litvak nisht lakhen, nor tsugeben shtilerheyt: "*Oyb nisht nokh hekher!*"	And later, if a disciple ever said that the Nemirover arose, during the time of penitential prayers, early every morning, and flew to heaven, the Litvak would no longer laugh, but would add in a whisper: "If not even higher!"

Fill in the Missing Word

Try your hand now at filling in the missing Yiddish word (I give you the English one in parentheses). After you try all 10, go back to the original story, find the phrase, and check your answers.

1. *Der Litvak* _____ (recognizes)
2. _____ *yidener* (sick)
3. _____ *men vayter fun shtub* (ask)
4. *Hob ikh tsu* _____ (sell)
5. *In bet* _____ *a kranke yidene* (lies)
6. *Orme* _____ (widow)
7. *Ikh vel dir* _____ (lend)
8. *Fuvanen vel ikh dir* _____ (pay)
9. *Un dos holts* _____ *gebrent* (happily)
10. *Oyb nish nokh* _____ (higher)

A Nobel Singer

The Nobel prize didn't change Isaac Bashevis Singer's self-image. "I never forget," he said of himself, "that I am only a storyteller." Yet, we the readers know how little that description tells us about his genius. Because of him, Yiddish was honored with the greatest prize the world has to offer. Reading him is to realize how a thousand-year-old language can express ideas in ways that its younger counterparts cannot imitate.

I can only hope that your Yiddish eventually becomes good enough to allow you to read Singer's powerful narratives in the original. Until then, here's a little *forshpayz* (appetizer) to give you a clue for understanding his universal appeal.

With a Shmaykhel

It was a bitter, cold night in winter, and Abie lay on his bed close to death. "Please call a priest for me to offer a prayer," he whispers to his wife. "A priest? All your life you've been a good Jew, and now as you prepare to meet your Maker, you ask me to get you a priest? Why in the world would you do that?"

"To tell you the truth," Abie responds, "on a night like this, *nu*, I should make a rabbi come out in this weather?"

The Washer Woman

Jews weren't always the only downtrodden, impoverished victims. Their gentile neighbors often suffered as they did from the difficulties of eking out the minimum needed for their daily existence. One of Singer's powerful descriptions in his opus *From My Father's Court* is the moving story of their family's non-Jewish neighbor who served as a washer woman.

Faithfully, this aged, sickly woman would carry a laundry load on her back that seemed heavier than she was and would diligently clean it with the primitive methods then available, all for a few coins. Once, in the midst of a severe winter storm, she trudged home carrying her usual pack but failed to return. Singer's family was sure that she had passed away, that the burdens she had assumed were simply too much for her. Months later, unexpectedly, the washer woman miraculously showed up at their door once more. We pick up the story as Singer recounts what happened:

Yiddish	English
Zi iz gevoren azoy krank az emitser hot gerufen dem doktor un hot geheysen brengen dem galakh. Emitser hot tsuvissen geton ir zun un yener hot tsushtayer gegeben oyf a bagrebenish. Ober Got der almekhtiger hot nish gevolt nemen tsu zikh di farpaynikte neshomo. S'iz ir gevoren beser, zi iz gevoren gezunt, un ven zi hot vider gekent shteyn of di fis, hot zi zekh genumen tsu der vesh. Nish bloys unzer vesh, nor di vesh fun etlikhe shtiber.	She became so sick that someone called the doctor, and the doctor told them to call for a priest. Someone notified her son, and he sent some funds for a burial. But God the Almighty didn't want to take this pained soul. She became better, she became healthy, and when she was again able to stand on her feet, she took herself to the task of the laundry. Not just our laundry, but the laundry of several homes.

Yiddish	English
"Ikh hob nit gekent in bet aynligen tsulib der doziger vesh," hot di alte getaynet. "Di dozige vesh hoben mir nish gelost shtarben."	"I couldn't rest in bed because of this wash," the old woman explained. "This wash did not allow me to die."
"Mit Got's hilf vet ir leben hundert un tsvontsik yor," hot di mame ir ongevuntshen.	"With God's help you'll live to 120," mamma wished her.
"Zol Got bashiremen! Vos toyg meer azoy lang tsu leben? Di arbet vert alts shverer ... di koykhes lozen zikh oys ... ikh vil nisht falen keynem tsu last!"	"May God spare me! What do I need to live so long? The work becomes ever harder ... strength fails me ... I don't want to become dependent on anyone!"
Azoy hot di alte geplepelt, un oyfgehoyben di oygen tsum himel. S'iz grad geven gelt in shtub un di mame hot ir oysgetseylt ir getsolts. Ikh hob gehat a modne gefil: Glaykh di matbeyes volten gevoren in ire oysgevashene hent punkt azoy mid un reyn un frum vi zi aleyn. Zi hot zey epes vi opgeblozen un farbunden in a tikhel. Dernokh iz zee avek un tsugezogt tsu kumen in a por vokhen arum nokh frisher vesh.	So the old woman rattled and stammered, and opened her eyes to the heavens. There just happened to be some money at home, and mamma counted out her payment. I had a peculiar feeling: as if the coins became in her washed hands so clean and pious as she herself. She blew them off and bound them in a kerchief. Then she left and promised to return in a few weeks for fresh laundry.
Ober zi iz mer keynmol nisht gekumen. Di dozige vesh vos zi hot obgrebakht iz geven ir letste onshtrengung oyf der doziger erd. S'iz geven der vilen optsugeben yenem zayn aygentum, tsu ton di arbet vos zi hot oyf zikh genumen.	But she never came back. The wash she had returned was her last struggle on this earth. It was her will to return to everyone their possessions, to complete the work that she had taken upon herself.
Gefalen iz der guf, vos iz shoyn lang geven a tsebrokhener sharben, un zikh oyfgehalten bloyz mit'n koyakh fun erlikhkayt un farantvortlekhkayt. Di Neshomo iz avek in yene sferen voo s'kumen zekh tsunoyf ale heylike neshomes, on untershid vos far a rol zey hoben geshpilt oyf der erd, fun voser shprakh, fun voser gloyben. Ikh ken mir nisht forshtelen a velt vu s'iz nisht faran keyn loyn far aza bamiung.	The body failed, indeed it had long been a broken vessel, and only maintained itself with the strength of faithfulness and responsibility. The soul departed to those spheres where there come together all holy souls, without distinction as to what kind of role they played on earth, which language they spoke, or which faith they professed. I cannot imagine to myself a world where there is no reward for such effort.

Try to Write Like a Singer

See how close you can come to the original text by writing these phrases in Yiddish:

1. Called the doctor

   _____

2. Bring the priest

   _____

3. Pained soul

   _____

4. She became better

   _____

5. The wash didn't let me die

   _____

6. With God's help you'll live to 120

   _____

7. I had a peculiar feeling

   _____

8. As pious as she herself

_____

9. But she never came back

   _____

10. The soul departed

    _____

Khap a Nash

Zion is the name for the mountain on which the Holy Temple stood, as well as for Jerusalem. In a broader sense, it can also be used as a synonym for the entire land of Israel. And that's how we got the name **Zionism** for the movement that emphasized a return of Jews from all over the world to their ancient homeland.

Go back to the story now and see how well you did. Got them all? I'm proud of you!

The universal message of love and feeling for the ethical nobility of others is a theme to which Singer often returned. Even as he loved the world, so did the world reciprocate its love to him.

With a Song in My Heart

Yiddish has been blessed not only with its Singers, but also with its singers, bringing lyrics to melodies that had been passed on through the generations. Jewish mothers rocked their babies to sleep, crooning lullabies that were sung to them as infants. One of these folk songs was adapted by Abraham Goldfaden, the Ukrainian-born Father of the Yiddish Theatre (1840–1908), and became universally beloved in almost every Jewish home. Simply titled "Rozhinkes Mit Mandlen" ("Raisins and Almonds"), it poetically depicts the hopes and prayers of Jewish mothers for their offspring—dreams of riches and prosperity coupled with remembrance of the past of their people. Try to get a recording of this song in the original, and sing along with its haunting melody after you've learned the translation.

Yiddish	English
Rozhinkes Mit Mandlen	**Raisins and Almonds**
In dem beys hamikdosh, in a vinklkheyder,	In the Holy Temple, in a quiet nook,
Zitst di almone Bas-Tsioyn aleyn;	I see the widowed daughter of Zion rock
Ir benyokhidl, Yidele, vigt zi keseyder	Her little infant Judah. I
Un zingt im tsum shlofn a lidele sheyn:	Hear her sing this lullaby:
"Unter Yideles vigele	"Under little Judah's cot
Shloft a klor vays tsigele,	Stands a snow-white little goat,
Dos tsigele iz geforn handlen,	The goat goes selling merchandise,
Vos vet zayn dayn beruf:	Which is what you, my child, will do.
Roshinkes mit mandlen	Almonds and raisins
Shlof zhe, Yidele, shlof!	Sleep, my baby, sleep.
In dem lidl, mayn kind, ligt fil nayes	In this song, my child, it is prophesied
Az du vest a mol zayn tsezeyt oyf der velt,	That you will be scattered far and wide,
A soykher vestu zayn fun ale tvues	A big corn merchant you will be,
Un vest fardinen in dem oykh fil gelt."	And will earn a lot of money."
Refren	Refrain
Un az du vest vern raykh, Yidele,	And when you are rich I hope you may
Zolstu zikh dermonen in dem lidele:	Remember this song I sing today:
Rozhinkes mit mandlen	Almonds and raisins are very nice,
Dos vet zayn dayn baruf,	You will sell all kinds of merchandise,
Yidele vet alts handlen.	This is what you my child will do.
Shlof zhe, Yidele, shlof!	Sleep, my baby, sleep.
Es vet kumen a tsayt fun vertpapirn,	There will come a time of stocks and shares,
Kantorn veln zayn in der gantser velt;	Big offices for exchanging wares,
Der grester vestu zayn fun ale bankirn	And a big banker you will be,
Un vest in dem oykh fardinen fil gelt	And will have lots of money.
A-a-a-a-a!	

Yiddish	English
(Refren)	(Refrain)
Es vet kumen a tsayt fun ayznbanen,	There will come a time when railways run
Zey veln farfleytsn di gantse velt;	All over the world, my little one,
Aayzerne vegn vestu oysshpanen	Iron wagons will loaded be,
Un vest in dem oykh fardinen fil gelt.	And you will earn lots of money.
A-a-a-a-a!	
(Refren)	(Refrain)

Khap a Nash

The partisans give the lie to the ugly libel that Jews went like sheep to slaughter during the Holocaust. With almost no access to arms and mightily outnumbered, the partisans demonstrated incredible courage in the face of impossible odds against them.

You can almost feel the mixed emotion as the mother prophesizes material abundance and pleads that her children retain the memory of a life lived simply and honorably.

Out of the Depths of Despair

The twentieth century imposed upon Yiddish the obligation to find words for a tragedy that rendered speech almost impossible. A people who had survived the cruelties of all past barbaric ages were almost exterminated entirely as victims of Hitler's program of genocide. The song of the partisans, expressing hope in the face of death camps and crematoria, stands as a striking testimonial to the strength of the human spirit. By an unknown author, its words inspire us to this day.

Song of the Partisans

Yiddish	English
Zog nit keyn mol, az du geyst dem letstn veg,	Never say that there is only death for you
Khotsh himlen blayene farshteln bloye teg,	Though leaden clouds may be concealing skies of blue,
Kumen vet nokh undzer oysgebenkte sho,	Because the hour that we have hungered for is near;
S'vet a poyk ton undzer trot: Mir zaynen do!	Beneath our tread the earth shall tremble: We are here!
Fun grinem palmenland biz vaysn land fun shney,	From land of palm-tree to the far-off land of snow

Yiddish	English
Mir kumen on mit undzer payn, mit undzer vey;	We shall be coming with our torment and our woe,
Un vu gefaln iz a shprits fun undzer blut,	And everywhere our blood has sunk into the earth
Shpritsn vet dort undzer gvure, undzer mut!	Shall our bravery, our vigor blossom forth!
S'vet di morgnzun bagildn undz dem haynt,	We'll have the morning sun to set our day aglow,
Un der nekhtn vet farshvindn mit dem faynt;	And all our yesterdays shall vanish with the foe,
Nor oyb farzamen vet di zun un der kayor,	And if the time is long before the sun appears,
Vi a parol zol geyn dos lid fun dor tsu dor!	Then let this song go like a signal through the years.
Dos lid geshribn iz mit blut, un nit mit blay,	This song was written with our blood and not with lead;
S'iz nit keyn lidl fun a foygl oyf der fray,	It's not a song that birds sing overhead.
Dos hot a folk tsvishn falndike vent	It was a people, among toppling barricades,
Dos lid gezungen mit naganes in di hent!	That sang this song of ours with pistols and grenades.
To zog nit keyn mol, as du geyst dem letstn veg,	So never say that there is only death for you
Khotsh himlen blayene farshteln bloye teg;	For leaden clouds may be concealing skies of blue
Kumen vet nokh undzer oysbebenkte sho	And yet the hour that we have hungered for is near;
Es vet a poyk ton undzer trot: mir zaynen do!	Beneath our tread the earth shall tremble: We are here!

For many who sang this song, the words were their last on earth. Thankfully, there remained some survivors for whom the lyrics were prophetic: "We are here!"

The Least You Need to Know

➤ Sholom Aleichem is an *oytser* of Yiddish, a national treasure whose stories continue to delight us.

➤ Isaac Leibush Peretz captured the beauty of the Hassidic movement in its emphasis on the good deed over adherence to strict ritual.

➤ Isaac Bashevis Singer elevated the stature of Yiddish when he received a Nobel prize for his work.

➤ Yiddish folk songs express the hopes and the prayers of the Jewish people.

Chapter 26

Now
That's Funny

In This Chapter

➤ Why Yiddish stresses humor

➤ How Yiddish improves jokes and stories

➤ Making Yiddish and English merge for hilarious results

➤ Reading exercises to make you laugh and learn

If language has personality, then Yiddish is funny. Comedians realize it, and that's why they so frequently throw Yiddish words into their acts. "I'm *farklempt*" gets a huge laugh on *Saturday Night Live*, while "I'm all choked up" wouldn't draw a titter. What makes *farklempt* such a funny word, and why is *farblondjet* more humorous than "lost," *fartshadet* more delightful than "confused," *farpetshket* more entertaining than "messed up"? Linguists have a field day trying to figure it out. Whatever the reason, anyone who has a feel for Yiddish just knows it's true.

Perhaps one explanation that's offered carries the most weight. Yiddish is funny because it has been used for a thousand years by a people who treasure humor and who have come to believe that laughter is one of the major keys to their survival. Life without humor, it has been said, is like an automobile without shock absorbers. And who needed shock absorbers more than all those Yiddish speakers who found themselves at the mercy of anti-Semites in every age who sought to destroy them?

Let's see how Yiddish adds a new dimension to humor with its special brand of Jewish jokes.

The Punch Line Is Yiddish

Now that you know a lot of Yiddish words, you'll be able to laugh when the punch line is a Yiddish word or phrase. Why not simply say it all in English? Okay, try to tell the following story without using the Yiddish word:

> Yankel gets a new dog and he can't wait to show him off to his neighbor. So when the neighbor comes over, the guy calls the dog into the house, bragging about how smart the critter is. The dog quickly comes running and stands looking up at his master, tail wagging furiously, mouth open in classic doggie-smile position, eyes bright with anticipation. The guy points to the newspaper on the couch and commands, "Fetch!" Immediately, the dog sits down, the tail wagging stops, the doggie-smile disappears; he hangs his head, looks balefully up at his master, and says in a whiney voice, "Oy! My tail hurts from wagging so much. And that dog food you're feeding me tastes absolutely terrible. And I can't remember the last time you took me out for a walk."
>
> The neighbor looks puzzled. "Oh," explains the dog owner, "he thought I said '*kvetsh*!'"

If you don't remember that *kvetsh* means to constantly gripe and complain, you won't get it. And if you're going to *kvetsh* that you don't think it's funny, maybe you should fetch a book on how to develop a sense of humor.

Say It Again, Sarah

What makes this one a Jewish joke? Sure, the Yiddish punch line could just as easily be said in English. But somehow I have the feeling that it's so much more powerful in Yiddish—don't you agree?

> Abie, proving to his wife that women talk more than men, showed her a study that indicated that men use on the average only 15,000 words a day, whereas women use 30,000 words a day. She thought about this for a while and then told her husband that women use twice as many words as men because they have to repeat everything they say.
>
> He said, "*Vos host du gezogt?*" (What did you say?)

The First Jewish President

Let me give you another example with the story of the Jewish mother who had so much reason to be proud of her children. One of them even reached the highest office of the land. Just listen to her reaction:

The first Jewish President of the United States calls his mother in Queens and invites her to come down for Thanksgiving. She says, "I'd like to, but it's so much trouble—I mean, I have to get a cab to the airport, and I hate waiting on Queens Boulevard."

He replies, "Mom! I'm the President! You won't need a cab! I'll send a limousine for you!"

His mother replies, "I know, but then I'll have to get my ticket at the airport, and try to get a seat on the plane, and I hate to sit in the middle—it's just too much trouble."

He replies, "Mom! I'm the President of the United States! I'll send Air Force One for you—it's my private jet!"

To which she replies, "Oh, well, but then when we land, I'll have to carry my luggage through the airport and try to get a cab—it's really too much trouble."

He replies, "Mom! I'm the President! I'll send a helicopter for you! You won't have to lift a finger."

She answers, "Yes, that's nice—but, you know, I still need a hotel room, and the rooms are so expensive, and I really don't like the rooms."

Exasperated, he answers, "Mom! I'm the President! You'll stay at the White House!"

She responds, "Well, all right. I guess I'll come."

The next day she's on the phone with her friend Betty.

Betty: "Hello, Sylvia—so what's new?"

Sylvia: "I'm visiting my son for Thanksgiving!"

Betty: "The doctor?"

Sylvia: "No—*der anderer*." (the other one).

It's the dismissive tone of the Yiddish *der anderer* that makes the line really funny.

Khap a Nash

On Passover, Jews are forbidden to eat or to own not only bread, but all leavened foods, grains that have become exposed to water and started to ferment or to become "sour."

A Gut Vort

The **afikomen** is a piece of matso, the permissible unleavened bread for Passover, which is set aside for children to find as part of the Passover ritual.

The Yid-English Dictionary

Try these wacky definitions—and if you don't get any one of them, it's probably because you've forgotten a Yiddish word and you should be "shamed yourself." Here goes:

Chutspapa: A father who wakes his wife at 4 A.M. so that she can change the baby's diaper.

Disoriyenta: When Aunt Sadie gets lost in a department store and strikes up a conversation with everyone she passes.

Deja Nu: Having the feeling that you've seen the same exasperated look on your mother's face, but not knowing exactly when.

Impasta: Someone who eats leavened foods during Passover while maintaining that he is observant.

Jewdo: A traditional form of self-defense based on talking one's way out of a tight spot.

Afikomments: Adult arguing that occurs as children search for hidden Passover matzo.

Ashkeshnozzim: A nose the shape of Florida and the size of a medium potato.

Torahfied: Inability to remember one's lines when called to read from the Torah at one's Bar or Bat Mitzvah.

Trayffic Accident: An appetizer one finds out has pork in it after one has eaten it.

Jewbilation: Pride in finding out that one's favorite celebrity is Jewish.

Yentility: A deceptively sweet manner used to extract information. Key phrases include, "trust me," "your secret is safe with me," and "if you can't tell me, who can you tell?"

Yidentify: To be able to determine ethnic origins of celebrities even though their names might be St. John, Curtis, Davis, or Taylor.

Kinderschlep: To be called on to carpool more children than one has fingers, in a car that was made in Japan.

Mamatzah Balls: Matzo balls that are as good as mother used to make.

Matzilation: Smashing a piece of matzo to bits while trying to butter it.

A Gut Vort

A *minyan* is the required number of ten for synagogue services.

Blintzkrieg: A late-night assault on the refrigerator in search of leftovers even though "I won't be able to eat for a week!" Particularly common four to six hours after special occasion gluttony.

Bobbegum: Candy one's mother gives to her grandchildren that she never gave to her own children.

Minyastics: Going to incredible lengths and troubles to find a tenth person to complete a minyan.

Meinstein: Slang for "My son, the genius."

Bris and Tell: A detailed description given by parents of their child's circumcision, generally spoken quite loud in front of the grown child and those people he would least like to hear the story.

Discahkentude: Looking like one isn't involved while one's dog goes to the bathroom on a neighbor's lawn.

Diskvellified: To drop out of law school, medical school, or business school, as seen through the eyes of parents, grandparents, and Uncle Sid. (In extreme cases, simply choosing to major in art history when Irv's son, David, is majoring in biology, is sufficient grounds for *diskvellification*.)

Feelawful: Indigestion from eating Israeli street food.

Goyfer: A gentile messenger.

Hebort: To forget all the Hebrew one ever learned immediately after one's Bar Mitzvah.

Hebrute: Israeli aftershave.

A Gut Vort

Rosh Hashanah (literally, "head of the year"), on the first day of the Hebrew annual calendar, is a day set aside for divine judgment and introspection.

A Gut Vort

Shofar (literally, "a ram's horn") is blown on the High Holy Days. At the conclusion of the Day of Atonement, Yom Kippur, it signals the end of the ten-day period of repentance.

Hindstein: A Semitic smart aleck.

Isroyalty: Major contributors to the UJA, the JUF, or the IEF.

Mishpokhamarks: The assorted lipstick and makeup stains found on one's face and collar after kissing all one's aunts and cousins at a reception.

Re-Shtetlement: Moving from Brooklyn to Miami and finding that all your old neighbors live in the same condo as you.

Rosh Hashanana: A rock 'n' roll band from Brooklyn.

Santashmanta: The explanation Jewish children get for when they celebrate Chanuka while the rest of humanity celebrates Christmas.

Shiksabob: A special meal that Muffy O'Brien prepares for Morris Greenblatt.

Shofarsogut: The relief you feel when, after many attempts, the *shofar* is finally blown at the end of Yom Kippur.

Bagela: A gay Jewish baker.

Bialyache: The result of lunch at your mother's and dinner at your mother-in-law's.

If you didn't get at least 90 percent of these daffy definitions, I recommend that you reread the previous chapters!

Yiddish Types

Some jokes are funny because they're so typical of a kind of "character." We laugh because we can acknowledge human foibles and do it at someone else's expense. Many of them are so distinctively Jewish that we can almost hear the Yiddish accent even though the words are pure English. If you've ever been to a Jewish restaurant, you must know that the waiters are a breed all to themselves:

"Waiter!" Cohen yells out.

"Whatsa madda, you have a heart attack maybe? You calling me for a reason in the middle of my working day?"

"Of course I got a reason. I need to tell you this fish looks sick."

"So what do I look like, a doctor?"

Or how about the proud English-speaking immigrant who still has a little trouble with his pronunciation:

The chairlady at the PTA meeting puts forth her proposal:

"We feel we should raise teachers' salaries on a strictly merit basis."

Kaplan is furious. "I disagree *mit* 100 percent. Maybe more. I don't believe it should be on a strictly merit basis. What's the difference if they're merit or single? They should be treated the same."

There's even a Yiddish approach to how to become a success in business. This next story probably says it best:

The boss called one of his employees into the office. "Paul," he said, "you've been with the company for a year. You started off in the post room, one week later you were promoted to a sales position, and one month after that you were promoted to district manager of the sales department. Just four short months later, you were promoted to vice chairman. Now it's time for me to retire, and I want you to take over the company. What do you say to that?"

"Thanks," says the employee.

"Thanks?" the boss replied. "Is that all you can say?"

"I suppose not," the employee said. "Thanks, *tate* (dad)."

Ah, what a *brokheh* (blessing) to have a familial foot in the door!

Oy, Vey, the Rabbi

Obviously, of all the specifically Jewish characters, the rabbi is the most Yiddish. As an authority figure, he also gets a disproportionate amount of attention in Yiddish humor—for good and for bad.

Of course, the rabbi is very smart. Sometimes that makes him shrewd in a somewhat questionable manner, as in the following:

> A rabbi, while driving, smacks into another car. Getting out to survey the damage, he sees that the other driver is a priest. Hugging him, he says to his fellow clergyman, "Before we get excited, this is a time for us, as men of the cloth, to demonstrate our brotherhood instead of conflict. Cars can be fixed, but human relationships are more important than anything. As a sign of my respect for you, let me offer you a drink and a toast of *L'khayim*."
>
> The priest is delighted by the rabbi's gesture of friendship and takes the proffered drink. "And why don't you join me?" asks the priest.
>
> "Of course, I will, but let me just wait a few minutes until after the police get here."

A Gut Vort

Shames is the sexton of the synagogue, in charge of a multitude of tasks relating to the services.

A Gut Vort

Tshuve means repentance, and **baal tshuve** (literally "master of repentance") is the name given to contemporary returnees to faith. The *baal tshuve* movement is an important religious phenomenon of the twentieth century.

The rabbi as sermonizer often didn't fare as well. Every *Shabes*, the congregation was at the rabbi's mercy as he might preach about eternity for an almost equal length of time. The next story makes the point well:

> The rabbi was upset and stopped in the middle of his sermon to call the *shames*. "Look, there, right in front of me, is a man who has the *khutspe* to sleep in the middle of my sermon. Go wake him up."
>
> "No, I don't think it's fair. I don't think I should do it."
>
> "What do you mean, not fair? How dare you not listen to your rabbi?"
>
> "It's not fair because you put him to sleep. You should be the one to wake him up."

Listen to Your Rabbi

The rabbi was the source of inspiration, of instruction, and of guidance. To him, those who were sinners came to be given a suitable form of penance. The next story, in Yiddish, is a delightful example of the humor to be found in the interplay between the spiritual leader and his disciples (courtesy of Ruth Levitan, from her wonderful book *Lakht a Bissel, Lakht a Sakh*):

Yiddish	English
Viln Tshuve Ton	***Wanting to Repent***
Tsvey yeshive bokherim zaynen gekumen tsu zeyer rebn, un zikh moyde geven az zey zenen bagangen a zind—an aveyre.	Two Yeshiva boys came to their rabbi and confessed that they had committed a sin, a religious transgression.
Vos far a zind?	What kind of a sin?
Zey hobn aruntergelozt di oygn farshemt.	They both lowered their eyes in embarrassment.
"Mir hobn mitn yeytser-hore gekukt oyf a froy."	"Out of evil desire, we looked at a woman."
"Doz iz take zeyer a groyse aveyre."	"That is indeed a very grave religious violation."
"Rebe, vi azoy konen mir tshuve ton?"	"Rabbi, how can we repent?"
"Oyb ir vilt beemes tshuve ton, heys ikh aykh araynleygn arbes in di shikh, un azoy arumgeyn far tsen teg. Efsher vet ir vider nit zindikn."	"If you really want to repent, I order you to put peas in your shoes and walk around in that manner for ten days. Perhaps you will no longer sin."
Di tsvey yunge layt zaynen aheymgegangen, un geton vi der rebe hot zey geheysn. A por teg shpeter hobn zikh di baaley-tshuve bagegnt oyf der gas.	The two young men went home and did as the rabbi commanded them. A few days later, the penitents met on the street.
Eyner hot untergehinkt in groyse veytikn, ober der anderer iz arumgegangen azoy vi im meynt men nisht, un er hot geshmeykhlt.	One of them was limping in great pain, but the other one went about as if it didn't bother him, and he smiled.
"Azoy folgstu dem rebn?"—hot der ershter yeshive bokher gehat taynes tsum tsveytn. "Ikh ze az du herst dem rebn vi dem koter. Host nisht arayngeleygt kayn arbes in dayne shikh."	"That's how you listened to the rabbi," the first Yeshiva boy reproached the second. "I see that you listen to the rabbi like to the cat. You didn't put peas in your shoes."
"Ver zogt as neyn? Ikh hob geton akurat vi der rebe hot mir geheysn, nor ikh hob frier opgekokht di arbes."	"Who says no? I did exactly what the rabbi told me, but I first cooked the peas."
Dos iz, az me hot a kop oyf di pleytses, azoy tut men.	That shows, if someone has a head on their shoulders, that's what he does.

Some Words to Remember

Here are some words you might want to single out from the story that you'll probably hear in other contexts as well:

Yiddish	English
moyde zayn	to confess
di baaleytshuve	penitents
di aveyre(s)	sin(s)
unterhinken	to limp
der yeytserhore	evil desire
di tayne(s)	reproach(es)
di tshuve(s)	penance
der koter(s)	cat(s)

Fill in the Missing Word

How about trying your hand at reconstructing some of the Yiddish phrases? Write them in the lines provided alongside the English:

1. Two Yeshiva boys

   _____

2. A sin, a religious transgression

   _____

3. Looked at a woman

   _____

4. Put peas in your shoes

   _____

5. A few days later

   _____

6. Met on the street

   _____

7. In great pain

   _____

8. That's how you listen?

   _____

9. Like the cat

   _____

10. Exactly what the rabbi told me

    _____

Only in America

Yiddish had its most fascinating encounter as it tried to come to grips with the American experience. The clash of cultures between the *shtetl* of old and the American metropolis was profound. The reaction of immigrants to the changes they saw around them provided fodder for charming and humorous essays. A good example is this cry-from-the-heart story about teeth and the different reactions to toothaches in the Old World and the New World:

Yiddish	English
Tseyner	*Teeth*
"Oykh a land, Amerike!	"Oh, what a land, America!
"A land vu yeder muz hobn tsu ton mit di tseyner," hot tsu mir getaynet an elterer yid.	"A land where everybody has to be bothered with teeth," complained to me an elderly Jew.
"In der heym hot men opgelebt a lebn, un geshtorbn mit eygene tseyner in moyl, un do, az me vet kumen oyf yener velt, vet men dokh avade fregn:	"Back home one lived one's life, and died with one's own teeth in the mouth, and here, when we will come to the other world, they will surely ask:
"'Reb yid, vu hot ir ahingeton ayere tseyner?'"	"'Sir Jew, where did you put your teeth?'"
Ver un vos zaynen shuldik in tseynveytik un farfoylte tseyner?	Who and what are responsible for toothaches and decayed teeth?
Dos iz dokh a land ayngetunken in kendi.	This is really a land awash in candy.
Nokhdem zaynen shuldik di tut-piks. Me kalupet azoy lang in moyl, biz me firt iber ti tseyner.	After that, the guilt lies with toothpicks. People keep picking their mouths for so long until they ruin their teeth.

continues

continued

Yiddish	English
Doz iz dokh a medine mit azoy fil dentistn, un yederer muz makhn a lebn. Muz men raysn tseyner, rekhts un links.	This is a country with so many dentists, and every one has to make a living. They have to pull teeth right and left.
Bay undz in der heym hobn amol vey geton di tseyner, nor vos? Me hot gevust az me muz laydn. A tson tut vey, biz es hert oyf. Me hot gelitn eyn tog, tsvey teg, dray teg, biz me hot zikh ibergemutshet.	By us at home teeth hurt sometimes, but so what? We knew we had to suffer. A tooth hurts until it stops hurting. We suffered one day, two days, three days, until we suffered through.
A tson iz vi a vayb. A vayb shrayt, biz zi shrayt zikh iber. Azoy oykh mit a tson— tut vey, biz es hert oyf. Der iker iz az me muz hobn geduld, nisht ayln zikh. Ober do in Amerike hot men dokh nisht kayn geduld. Teykef, vi es git zikh a shokl a tson, loyft men shoyn tsum dentist. Vil dokh der dentist parnose, nemt er un rayst!"	A tooth is like a wife. A wife screams until she finishes screaming. So, too, with a tooth—it hurts until it stops. The most important thing is that you have to have patience, not to hurry. But here in America nobody has any patience. Immediately, as soon as a tooth makes a move, people already run to the dentist. The dentist wants to make a living, so he goes and he pulls."

Can You Figure It Out?

Next to each of these Yiddish words that appeared in the story, see if you can put the English translation:

1. *farfoylt* _____
2. *oyfhern* _____
3. *di geduld* _____
4. *teykef* _____
5. *di parnose* _____
6. *a medine* _____
7. *nokhdem* _____
8. *geshtorbn* _____
9. *yener velt* _____
10. *rayst* _____

Wise Sayings

"Women are a distinct race."

—Babylonian Talmud

Let's check your answers now and see how well you did with the story:

1. rotten
2. to stop
3. patience
4. immediately
5. a living
6. country
7. afterward
8. died
9. the other world
10. pulls

Now that you've got that, see if you can tell the story to someone in Yiddish!

You Figure Out the Punch Line

Let's see how well you're doing. Let's close with a few stories for which I'll give you the punch lines in Yiddish and see if you can understand them well enough to translate on your own. (I'll give you the correct answers after you've finished trying all three.)

The Jewish Atheist

A secular, assimilated Jewish family moved to a little town where the best school was the Catholic private school. With just the slightest hesitation, the father enrolled his youngest child. After the first day, the youngster comes home and tells his father, "Daddy, did you know that God is really three and he has a Son and then there's also a Holy Ghost?"

The father angrily replies: *"Her zikh gut tsu. Es iz do nor eyn Got, un mir gloyben nisht in im."*

The punch line in English is:

_____

With a Shmaykhel

You think it's easy for a Jew to be an atheist? Sholom Aleichem tells of his friend, who says, "I don't know about you, but I'm an atheist, thank God!"

How Moses Won

A little boy comes home excitedly from *cheder* (Hebrew school). "You'll never guess what I learned today," he tells his parents. "The teacher told us about General Moses, the leader of the Jewish people. He explained how Moses took all the Jews out of Egypt. The Egyptians came charging after them, and the Jews were really frightened because in front of them was the Red Sea and they had nowhere to go. Well, Moses wasn't worried. He dropped an atomic bomb on the Egyptians, the waters parted in front of him, the Jews got across, and the Egyptians were all drowned."

"Is that really what the teacher told you?" gasped the father.

The boy shrugged, *"Neyn, ober oyb ikh volt dir dertseylt di mayse vi er hot es gezogt vost du es keynmol nisht gegloybt."*

The punch line of the story is:

_____

Khap a Nash

According to Jewish teaching, there is a Satan, but he has no independent power. He can do only what God allows him to do. If Satan could mess people up on his own, that would make him a God—and Jews believe there's only one God, not two.

Taking No Chances

The rabbi sat with the ailing man, and it soon became clear that these would be his final moments on earth. Whispering firmly in his ear, the rabbi told his congregant to use this opportunity to denounce the devil. "Now is the time to let him know how little you think of evil. Now is the moment to condemn the enemy of God."

The dying man said nothing. The rabbi repeated his request. Still there was only silence.

The rabbi couldn't contain himself. "Why do you refuse to denounce the devil before you leave this earth?"

The dying man responded: *"Biz ikh bin zikher vu ikh gey, heyb ikh nit on mit keynem."*

The punch line of the story is

_____

Getting the Last Laugh

Did you get them all? Here are the correct answers—and I hope that if you didn't laugh before, you'll have the last laugh now:

312

1. Listen well: There's only one God, and we don't believe in Him.

2. No, but if I told you the story the way he said it, you'd never believe it.

3. Until I'm sure where I'm going, I won't start up with anyone.

Why Always Jews?

Are you starting to wonder why so many jokes speak only of Jews? You remind me of the story of the man who began to tell a joke with the words, "These two Jews were standing and talking ...." Before he could get any further, his friend cut in and began to complain. "Jews, Jews, Jews. I'm sick and tired of you always telling stories and making Jews the main characters. Can't you ever tell a joke about two Chinamen, for example?"

"Okay, have it your way," said the storyteller. "Two Chinamen were on their way to their sons' bar mitsves ...."

Which only goes to prove that some stories just can't be converted. They're Jewish through and through—told with some Yiddish words thrown in or entirely in Yiddish, they become so much better. A chapter certainly couldn't do justice to a subject that has been voluminously covered in countless books. Jewish humor is something you'll want to pursue on your own for many years to come. Hopefully, though, with the background in Yiddish that this book has given you, you'll be able to enjoy Yiddish humor so much more that you'll never stop *lakhen.*

The Least You Need to Know

➤ Yiddish has developed an extraordinary ability to give expression to the humor of a people who needed laughter to preserve their sanity in order to ensure their survival.

➤ Some Yiddish words just sound funny, although no one can really explain why that is.

➤ Mixing English and Yiddish produces some hilarious word combinations.

➤ Yiddish humor centers around themes important in Jewish life, such as family, synagogue, and concern with the afterlife.

➤ Stories capture cultural nuances with words and expressions that deserve to be memorized.

Chapter 27

A Little Exercise Wouldn't Hurt You

In This Chapter

➤ Short exercises to test yourself

➤ Fill-in, complete, and choose the right words

As you surely realize, this chapter is our farewell. We've shared a great deal as you've hopefully come to a much broader appreciation of Yiddish. I've taught you words, phrases, and proverbs, as well as rules of grammar. At this point, you should be able to understand a lot as well as make yourself understood.

The best way to make sure that you've succeeded in absorbing what you've learned until now is with some exercises that will review most of the previous chapters. Use this as a self-test. If you find yourself a little hazy about any subject, review the chapter in which you first studied it—I'll always remind you exactly where you can find it. You won't need your gym shorts for these exercises. Just get a *feyder* (pen) or a *blayer* (pencil), and *hob nisht keyn moyre* (don't be afraid). I'm certain this final chapter will give you an opportunity to prove that you are really a *talmid khokhom* (a wise person). You'll find the answers to these exercises in Appendix D, "Answer Key."

It Sounds Just Like It (Chapter 3)

When you play charades, you touch your ear and everyone knows what you're trying to say is "sounds like." As you remember from Chapter 3, "So Who Says You Don't Know Yiddish Already?" cognates are words that help make Yiddish easy. They sound just like the words we know as their equivalents in English. They do, however, have a slightly different pronunciation. See how well you do with these as you fill in the blanks alongside the English words with their close-sounding relatives in Yiddish. Be sure to include the definite article as well:

1. the actor   _____
2. the music   _____
3. the paper   _____
4. the contract   _____
5. the hunger   _____
6. the apple   _____
7. the book   _____
8. the captain   _____
9. the concert   _____
10. the singer   _____

That's a Good Idea (Chapter 4)

You, too, can be a philosopher if you offhandedly toss off these observations. Let's see if you can fill in the missing word in Yiddish:

1. *A klap _____, a vort bashteyt.*

   (A blow passes on, a spoken word lingers on.)

2. _____ *farshtayt fun ain vort tsvey.*

   (A wise man hears one word and understands two.)

3. _____ *darf hoben a guten zikoren.*

   (A liar must have a good memory.)

4. *A mentsh iz a mol shtarker fun ayzn un a mol _____ fun a flig.*

   (Man is sometimes stronger than iron and at other times weaker than a fly.)

5. *Az me hot nit tsu entfern, muz men _____.*

   (If one has nothing to answer, it is best to shut up.)

6. *Az me leygt arayn, nemt men _____.*

   (If you put something in, you can take something out.)

7. *A mentsh _____ un Got lakht.*

   (Man plans and God laughs.)

8. *Az me redt zikh arop fun hartsen, vert _____.*

   (When one pours out his heart, he feels lighter.)

I Do Declare (Chapter 5)

You'll never survive without remembering the exclamations for some of the most important moments of life. I'll set up a scene, and you tell me the one Yiddish word that's most suitable as your reaction:

1. The first prize in the lottery is an all-expense-paid trip to Israel. I bought ten tickets. You think maybe I'll win?

   _____

2. I'm collecting for the United Jewish Appeal. I don't need you to contribute a fortune. All I'm asking is that you give:

   _____

3. You saw the dress she was wearing? The cleavage was down to the *pupik*. What do I think of it?

   _____

4. What a nerve. He ate half the smorgasbord. And what does he want?

   _____

5. Will I be able to meet you? I have another appointment. The best I can do is to tell you:

   _____

6. I hate going to the movies. Everybody in the audience is so noisy that I spend most of my time saying:

   _____

Let's Have Sex Again (Chapter 5)

It's easy in English when you don't have to make any decisions about the sexual identity of a word. Yiddish, however, forces us to distinguish among masculine, feminine, and neuter words. You've learned that there are no hard and fast rules to determine gender. Yiddish speakers intuitively know when to use the masculine *der*, the feminine *di*, or the neuter *dos*. Let's see how you do for this list of words, some of which you've had and some of which are new and allow you to test your gut reactions:

1. the acquaintance: _____ *bakanter*
2. the advice: _____ *eytse*
3. the riches: _____ *ashires*
4. the roll: _____ *zemel*
5. the rug: _____ *tepekh*

6. the salt: _____ *zalts*

7. the wedding: _____ *khasene*

8. the forest: _____ *vald*

9. the wood: _____ *holts*

10. the writer: _____ *shrayber*

11. the window: _____ *fenster*

12. the sock: _____ *zok*

13. the song: _____ *lid*

14. the soup: _____ *zup*

15. the robber: _____ *gazlen*

16. the reason: _____ *tam*

17. the picture: _____ *bild*

18. the card: _____ *kort*

19. the nation: _____ *folk*

20. the pauper: _____ *kabtsen*

Living in the Present (Chapter 5)

Of course you know Yiddish. Why not use that phrase to conjugate in the present tense not just for yourself, but together with all the personal pronouns. Alongside each of the sentences write the Yiddish translation.

1. I know Yiddish.

   _____

2. You know Yiddish.

   _____

3. He knows Yiddish.

   _____

4. She knows Yiddish.

   _____

5. We know Yiddish.

   _____

6. You [pl.] know Yiddish.

   _____

7. They know Yiddish.

   _____

Objectively Speaking (Chapter 5)

The object of this exercise is to identify the objects. We're talking about people here, so supply the correct pronoun:

1. Help him: *Helf* _____
2. Pay us: *Batsol* _____
3. Give her: *Gib* _____
4. Study with me: *Lern mit* _____
5. Call them: *Ruf* _____

I Can't Live Without You (Chapter 5)

Some words are indispensable. You can't have a conversation without them. Try these ten as a quick review:

1. with: _____
2. without: _____
3. enough: _____
4. bad: _____
5. thanks: _____
6. here: _____
7. yes: _____
8. no: _____
9. many: _____
10. later: _____

Meet and Greet (Chapter 6)

So what do you say? You can't just stand there without saying a word. I'll describe the scene, and you fill in the appropriate response:

1. You want to wish the person a good holiday.

   _____

2. You're bidding your friend a good night.

   _____

3. You've just met, and you want to say hello.

   _____

4. You'd like to find out what's new.

_____

5. You've never met before, and you would like to know the person's name. (You're still somewhat formal.)

_____

6. You've just been asked how you feel, and you want to assure your friend that, thank God, you're fine.

_____

7. You're only feeling so-so, and you want to tell the truth.

_____

8. You're feeling philosophical, and you want to assure your friend that it could always be worse.

_____

9. You want to introduce your friend Abie to a beautiful woman.

_____

10. You want to offer congratulations.

_____

Infinitives Aren't Infinite (Chapter 6)

Sure, we learned a lot of infinitives, but, thank God, they are limited. They're limited by the number of verbs, and of course you remember how to form them. Try these just to make sure you remember the rule:

1. Kiss is *kush*, kissing is _____.

2. Swallow is *shling*, swallowing is _____.

3. Expect is *ervart*, expecting is _____.

4. Know is *ken*, knowing is _____.

5. Answer is *entfer*, answering is _____.

Got the Time? (Chapter 7)

Be polite. If people ask you what time it is, help them out and give them the right answer. Look at your watch and for each of the following times you see there, say it in Yiddish:

1. 8:10 _____
2. 7:30 _____
3. 2:00 _____
4. 3:45 _____
5. 10:00 PM _____

Countdown (Chapter 7)

We live in a world of numbers. Quantities of items we buy, numbers of years in our lives—almost everything we encounter gets counted. See if you remember these numbers:

1. 50 _____
2. 17 _____
3. 20 _____
4. 1,000 _____
5. 30 _____
6. 90 _____
7. 22 _____
8. 120 _____
9. 365 _____
10. 33 _____

You Can't Choose Your Relatives (Chapter 8)

The Mamas and the Papas make sweet music. The rest of your relatives can often make you crazy. But, love them or hate them, they're still *mishpokhe*. Let's see if you can identify every one of these:

1. *der shvoger* _____
2. *di shvegerin* _____
3. *di mekhutonim* _____
4. *der shver* _____
5. *der eydem* _____
6. *di shviger* _____
7. *di shnur* _____
8. *der khosen* _____

9. *di kale* _____

10. *di tokhter* _____

Clothes Make the Man and Woman (Chapter 9)

You want to be comfortable and always look your best. Let's see how well you remember important items of clothing. I'll give you the first five in English, and you'll tell me what they are in Yiddish. For the next five, we'll reverse it: I'll say it in Yiddish, and you tell me what we call it in English.

1. a raincoat _____

2. a hat _____

3. a shirt _____

4. a robe _____

5. a dress _____

6. a *shnips* _____

7. a *por shponkes* _____

8. a *por zoken* _____

9. a *sharfal* _____

10. A *por hoyzen* _____

A Rainbow Coalition (Chapter 9)

Without colors, the world is a drab place indeed. Thank God we have the gift of seeing things in Technicolor. Let's see if you can describe every one of these in Yiddish:

1. Colors of the American flag:

_____

2. What your lawn should look like if you water it regularly:

_____

3. What your mature understanding of life is when you realize it's not all black and white:

_____

4. The color you become when you stay out in the sun for a long time:

_____

5. Before color TV, you were only able to watch shows in these hues:

_____

Coming Right Up (Chapter 10)

You know you're going to do it eventually. Why not commit yourself to doing it right now? Remember that the future tense in Yiddish distinguishes between actions you plan to commence immediately and those you'll get to—but not right away. Fill in the blanks for these statements about you and your friends who are out for a night on the town and are about to go dancing:

1. *Er _____ tantsen.*

   He is going to dance.

2. *Mir _____ tantsen.*

   We are going to dance.

3. *Zey _____ tantsen.*

   They are going to dance.

4. *Ir _____ tantsen.*

   You [pl.] are going to dance.

5. *Ikh _____ tantsen.*

   I'm going to dance.

6. *Du _____ tantsen.*

   You are going to dance.

7. *Zey _____ tantsen.*

   They are going to dance.

I'll Get to It (Chapter 10)

Sure, you're never supposed to put off until tomorrow what you can do today. But we're only human. Some things will be done, but not right now. You promised the family to go on a trip. Everybody's anxious to travel. It's just that you can't do it today. Let's see how you reassure everyone that they will in the not-too-distant future be able to travel.

1. *Ikh _____ foren.*

   I will travel.

2. *Ir _____ foren.*

   You [pl.] will travel.

3. *Du _____ foren.*

   You [sing.] will travel.

4. *Mir* _____ *foren.*

We will travel.

5. *Zey* _____ *foren.*

I will travel.

6. *Er* _____ *foren.*

He will travel.

7. *Zi* _____ *foren.*

She will travel.

What's the Problem? (Chapter 11)

Can you identify the problem if someone tells you he's having trouble with each of the following with his car?

1. There's something wrong with the *tormoz*. What is it?

   _____

2. He doesn't like the looks of the *rayfen*. What will you look at?

   _____

3. He tells you he has a *geplatsten rayfen*. What happened?

   _____

4. There seems to be a *klop*. What's the difficulty?

   _____

5. The complaint is *"es raybt zikh."* What's the matter?

   _____

6. The car is stopped at the side of a road because it's *ibergehitst*. What's wrong?

   _____

7. He needs your help for *unterheyben di car*. Which tool would you get?

   _____

8. If he's low on *luft*, where would you put it?

   _____

9. If he asked for a *karte*, what does he want?

   _____

10. If he requests oil that's *laykht*, what kind is he asking for?

   _____

What's Past Is Past (Chapter 11)

You've learned so much. Now, *trakht*—think about it a little. Finished? Then, of course, *du host getrakht*. How about telling me the conjugation of the past tense for the word *arbeten*, to work. After all, doing these exercises is a little work, and you probably want to talk about it:

1. *Ikh* _____ (I worked)
2. *Du* _____ (You worked)
3. *Ir* _____ (You [formal] worked)
4. *Er* _____ (He worked)
5. *Zi* _____ (She worked)
6. *Mir* _____ (We worked)
7. *Ir* _____ (You [plural] worked)
8. *Zey* _____ (They worked)

Let's Compare (Chapter 13)

Here are some words that are comparative and superlative. Pick the right one from among them for each of the sentences that follow:

kelter	*yingster*	*kligster*	*hekher*
greser	*noenter*	*kirtser*	*reynigst*
elster	*raykhster*		

1. If he's the richest of all, then he's the _____.
2. If that basketball player is taller, then he is _____.
3. The boy who's the brightest in the class is the _____.
4. New York is _____ than Miami Beach in the winter.
5. The one who's shorter is _____.
6. The one who's standing right next to the phone is _____.
7. The youngest child in the family is the _____.
8. The one who just showered is the _____.
9. Between Grandpa and Daddy, Grandpa is the _____.
10. A yard is _____ than a foot.

You'll Find It At ... (Chapter 13)

You need to go shopping. Here's a list of stores you'll be going to:

di shpayzkrom

di opteyk

der universalkrom

der kleyderkrom

der bikherkrom

di bekeray

di shnayderke

di ayzenvargkrom

di hut-krom

di tsirungkrom

der fleyshmark

der kosherer katsev

di shukhkrom

der shuster

dos antikengesheft

di tsukernye

di shnayderay

di shpilkkrom

der zeygermakher

Now here's your to-do list. After each of the following, fill in the name of the store you'll be going to:

1. To buy a chicken for *Shabes*

   _____

2. To pick up the latest bestseller recommended by the book club

   _____

3. To pick up some medicine

   _____

4. To select the hat that will go with your new dress

   _____

5. The birthday gift for your spouse is a beautiful piece of jewelry.

   _____

6. A new season is coming. Time to pick up a sweater.

   _____

7. You need the ingredients to prepare a nice dinner.

   _____

8. The faucet is leaking. Time for new washers.

   _____

9. Steak, veal, lamb chops—you must get to the meat market.

   _____

10. Forget the diet just this once. There's nothing like a dozen doughnuts, an apple strudel, and a delicious sponge cake.

    _____

11. The wedding is just a month away. You'll only have the dress ready if you go to her.

    _____

12. Time to replace your TV for a newer model.

    _____

13. You need little candies to nibble on over the weekend.

    _____

14. Don't forget the new toy you promised to buy your child.

    _____

15. You don't want to be late. Better get your watch fixed.

    _____

16. Old things can be more beautiful than new. Time to check for antiques.

    _____

17. Your feet are hurting from all this walking. Better stop in here to see if there's something wrong with your shoe.

    _____

18. It doesn't pay to fix the old pair. Go get yourself a new pair of shoes.

    _____

19. New shoes look better with a new suit. Let's see what a tailor shop can do for you.

    _____

What Hurts? (Chapter 15)

No, you're not a hypochondriac. Something really bothers you, and you have to tell the doctor what it is. See if you recognize each of these—alongside the Yiddish, write the English:

1. *a kopveytik* _____
2. *galkrankayt* _____
3. *a penkher* _____
4. *a farkilung* _____
5. *a hust* _____
6. *shilshul* _____
7. *an oyerveytik* _____
8. *heyzerikayt* _____
9. *nitgutkayt* _____
10. *haltsveytik* _____
11. *zunshlog* _____
12. *a bis* _____
13. *a bluter* _____
14. *tsiteren* _____
15. *farshtopung* _____
16. *hits* _____
17. *boykhveytik* _____
18. *lungen-entsindung* _____
19. *an oyslinkung* _____
20. *flektifus* _____

So What Do You Do for a Living? (Chapter 16)

You'll need every one of these people. Next to the Yiddish name of the job description, write the English:

1. *der doktor* _____
2. *der advokat* _____
3. *der oygendoktor* _____
4. *der apteker* _____
5. *der bankir* _____

   6. *der stolyer* _____

   7. *der modelentsaykhener* _____

   8. *der oyfzeher* _____

   9. *der rerenshloser* _____

  10. *der lerer* _____

  11. *der tsondoktor* _____

  12. *der optiker* _____

  13. *der druker* _____

  14. *der mekler* _____

  15. *der khemiker* _____

  16. *der tsivil-dinster* _____

  17. *der katsev* _____

  18. *der mekhaniker* _____

  19. *der farkoyfer* _____

  20. *der rov* _____

Tell Me More (Chapter 16)

"Bet you can't have just one" isn't just a great ad for potato chips. Plurals are part of life. You've got to know how to turn one of something into many. See how well you do with turning these singulars into plurals:

   1. A train is a *ban*; trains are _____.

   2. A worker is an *arbeter*; workers are _____.

   3. A teacher is a *lerer*; teachers are _____.

   4. A bed is a *bet*; beds are _____.

   5. A street is a *gas*; streets are _____.

   6. A watch is a *zeyger*; watches are _____.

   7. A song is a *lid*; songs are _____.

   8. A place is a *plats*; places are _____.

   9. A picture is a *bild*; pictures are _____.

  10. A wife is a *vayb*; wives are _____.

Wise as King Solomon (Chapter 22)

You've learned so many proverbs. Let's see if you know them well enough to fill in the missing word in the list below from the choices that follow:

kheyn	*leyb*	*kine*	*tsores*
glik	*khupe*	*shlos*	*diker*
emes	*lign*	*klap*	*arop*
tayerer	*honik*	*hungerik*	*lokshen*
shpigel	*finsternish*	*getraye*	*moltsayt*

Choose the right word to complete each of these proverbs:

1. *Ganovim un farlibte hobn lib _____.*

   Thieves and those in love both love darkness.

2. *A harts is a _____; men darf dem rikhtiken shlisel.*

   A heart is a lock; you need the right key to it.

3. *A mise moyd hot faynt dem _____.*

   A homely girl hates the mirror.

4. *_____ geyt iber sheyn.*

   Charm is better than beauty.

5. *Es nit di _____ far Shabes.*

   Don't eat the noodles before Sabbath (don't have sex before you're married).

6. *Fun an alte moid vert a _____ vayb.*

   From an old maid you get a faithful wife.

7. *Nokh di _____ iz shpet di kharote.*

   After the wedding it's too late to have regrets.

8. *Az men iz _____, est men afile trukn broyt.*

   If you're hungry enough, you'll eat dry bread.

9. *Men ken khapn mer flign mit _____ vi mit esik.*

   You can catch more flies with honey than with vinegar.

10. *A mayse on a moshl iz vi a _____ on a tsimes.*

    A story without a moral is like a meal without a sweet-flavored side dish.

11. *Blut iz _____ fun vaser.*

    Blood is thicker than water.

12. *Fun a muter's _____, vert dem kind nit keyn lokh in kop.*

    A mother's slap won't give a child a hole in the head.

13. *Kinder brengen _____, kinder brengen umglik.*

    Children bring good fortune, children bring misfortune.

14. *Nakhes fun kinder iz _____ fun gelt.*

    Joy from children is more precious than money.

15. *Az a _____ shloft, loz im shlofn.*

    When a lion is sleeping, let him sleep.

16. *Der emes iz der bester _____.*

    The truth is the best lie.

17. *_____ is nor in sider.*

    Truth is found only in the prayerbook.

18. *Kuk _____, vest du visn vi hoykh du shteyst.*

    Look down, and you'll know how high up you are.

19. *Di velt iz ful mit _____, ober yederer filt nor zayne.*

    The world is full of troubles, but each person feels only his own.

20. *Fun _____ vert sine.*

    From envy grows hate.

Parting Is Such Sweet Sorrow

There's a classic line about the difference between how Jews and gentiles take leave of each other. Non-Jews leave and don't say goodbye. Jews say goodbye and don't leave. Jews tend to get very emotional when it's time to separate. It's probably a cultural trait based on Jewish insecurity. Who knows if we'll ever meet again, so let's prolong this pleasant time as much as we can.

That's pretty much how I feel as we come to the end of this book. We've shared so much—I feel as though we know each other. It's hard to find the words to say goodbye and to wish you well with your newly acquired knowledge of Yiddish. I can only try to give expression to my feelings with one of these phrases that I'm sure you'll understand and, as our very last exercise, that I'll ask you to translate:

1. *Zay gezunt.*

   _____

2. *Mir zolen zikh trefen oyf simkhes.*

   _____

3. *Zolst leben biz hundert un tzvontzik.*

   _____

4. *Zol Got dikh bentshen.*

   _____

5. *Zol reden Yidish un makhen gelt beyde zayn laykht far dir.*

   _____

6. *Zolen mir eybig zayn khaverim.*

   _____

Finally, let me thank you for being such a wonderful student. Want to make me really happy? Use the Yiddish you know as much as you can. In that way, you'll help a language that so richly deserves to live find its rightful place on the lips of millions of people who will surely come to love it as we do.

Suggested Reading

If you want to learn more about the Yiddish language and grammar, I recommend consulting these classic and standard works:

➤ *Yiddish for Beginners*, by Dr. Jean B. Jofen

➤ *Yiddish Literature for Beginners,* by Dr. Jean B. Jofen

➤ *A Grammar of Standard Yiddish*, by Yudel Mark

➤ *Yiddish II: A Textbook for Intermediate Courses*, by Mordekhe Schaechter

➤ *College Yiddish: An Introduction to the Yiddish Language and Jewish Life and Culture,* by Uriel Weinreich

For a good dictionary, try any one of the following:

➤ *Student's Dictionary: English-Yiddish and Yiddish-English*, by Aaron Bergman

➤ *Yiddish-English-Hebrew Dictionary*, by Alexander Harkavy

➤ *Great Dictionary of the Yiddish Language*, by Judah A. Joffe and Yudel Mark

➤ *Modern English-Yiddish, Yiddish-English Dictionary*, by Uriel Weinreich

For a history of Yiddish, see the entry by Uriel Weinreich on Yiddish language in the *Encyclopedia Judaica*, Vol. 16, pp. 789-798.

For a more detailed analysis, see:

➤ *History of the Yiddish Language*, by Max Weinreich

➤ *Origins of the Yiddish Language,* by David Katz

For more about Yiddish phrases and expressions, see:

> ➤ *Thesaurus of the Yiddish Language*, by Nahum Stutchkoff
>
> ➤ *Blessings, Curses, Hopes, and Fears—Psycho-ostensive Expressions in Yiddish*, by James A. Matisoff

For a history of Yiddish literature, I recommend:

> ➤ *Yiddish Literature and Major Writers*, by Charles Madison
>
> ➤ *A Shtetl of Other Yiddish Novellas*, by Ruth R. Wisse
>
> ➤ *Old Yiddish Literature from its Origins to the Haskalah*, by Israel Zinberg

For a sociology of Yiddish, as well as studies in Yiddish culture, choose any or all of the following:

> ➤ *Never Say Die! A Thousand Years of Yiddish in Jewish Life and Letters*, by Joshua A. Fishman
>
> ➤ *A Treasury of Jewish Humor*, by Nathan Ausubel
>
> ➤ *The Golden Tradition: Jewish Life and Thought in Eastern Europe*, by Lucy S. Dawidowicz
>
> ➤ *The World of Our Fathers*, by Irving Howe
>
> ➤ *In Praise of Yiddish*, by Maurice Samuel

For a collection of Yiddish folk songs, see:

> ➤ *The Anthology of Yiddish Folk Songs in Four Volumes,* by Aharon Vinkovetzky and Abba Kovner and Sinai Leichter
>
> ➤ *Voices of a People: The Story of Yiddish Folk Song*, by Ruth Rubin

For pure entertainment, I highly recommend the following authors:

> ➤ Leo Rosten, who wrote the best-selling classic *The Joys of Yiddish*. His series on the incomparable Hyman Kaplan, whose name is always spelled with stars between every letter, are an uproarious account of the travails of a native Yiddish speaker as he encounters the English language. Don't miss *The Education of H*Y*M*A*N Kaplan, The Return of H*Y*M*A*N Kaplan,* and *Oh Kaplan! My Kaplan!*
>
> ➤ Ruth Levitan has a number of very funny books written in Yiddish transliteration with sufficient vocabulary help to enable the average reader to understand—and, very often, to fall off the chair laughing. A sample of her work, from her book *Lakht a Bisl, Lakht a Sakh*, appears in Chapter 26, "Now *That's* Funny," thanks to her graciousness in making it available for our readers.

➤ Mary B. Jaffe's *Gut Yuntiff, Gut Yohr* is a hilarious collection in Yiddish of original holiday verses and popular English classics in translation. In it you'll find Yiddish versions of everything from "Old Smokey," "The Owl and the Pussycat," and "Hiawatha's Childhood" to the "Rubayat" of Omar Khayyam and selections from Emily Dickinson. I thank Carol Publishing for permission to reprint Jaffe's version of Lincoln's Gettysburg Address in Chapter 23, "'Velvel' Shakespeare and Other Classics."

➤ For those who'd like a taste of Yiddish poetry, see *Onions and Cucumbers and Plums*, 46 Yiddish poems translated and edited by Sarah Zweig Betsky. The poems appear in Yiddish script, in transliteration, and in English.

Take Me to the Movies

One of the best ways to learn a language is to watch a movie. Listen to the spoken word and read the subtitles below in English, and your mind makes the connection. A large number of good Yiddish movies are available on video cassette. You may have to search a little to find many of these, but I promise you it will be well worthwhile. Here, in alphabetical order, is a list of films I recommend:

Al Chet (1935), aka *For the Sin* (informal English title)

Almonds and Raisins (1984)

Americaner Shadchen (1940), aka *American Matchmaker*

Brivele der Mamen, A (1938), aka *Letter From Mama*

Cantor on Trial, A (1931), aka *Khazan afn Probe* (USA: Yiddish title)

Catskill Honeymoon (1950)

Chants of Sand and Stars (1996)

Daughter of Her People, A (1932), aka *Yiddishe Tochter, A*

Dybuk (1937)

Eli Eli (1940)

Eternal Fools (1930)

Eternal Jew, The (1933)

Eternal Prayer, The (1929)

Everything's For You (1989)

Feast of Passover (1933), aka *Seder Nacht, Der* (1931)

From Hell to Hell (1996)

God, Man and Devil (1950), aka *Got, Mentsh, un Tayvl*

Great Advisor, The (1994)

Green Fields (1938)

Hamartef (1963), aka *Cellar, The* (1963)

Her Second Mother (1940), aka *Ihr zweite Mame*

Hester Street (1975)

Holy Oath, The (1937)

I Want to be a Boarder (1937)

I Want to be a Mother (1937)

Jester, The (1937)

Jewish Gypsy, The (1930)

Jewish Melody, The (1940)

Jewish People Live, The (1947), aka *Am Yisroel Kay*

Jews in Poland (1957)

Joseph in the Land of Egypt (1932)

Kol Nidre (1939)

Last Klezmer: Leopold Kozlowski, His Life and Music, The (1955)

Light Ahead, The (1939)

Live and Laugh (1933)

Love and Sacrifice (1936)

Makah Hashmonim V'Echad, Ha- (1974), aka *The 81st Blow*

Mamele (1938), aka *Little Mother*

Mazel Tov Yidden (1941)

Mirele Efros (1939)

Moi Ivan, toi Abraham (1993), aka *Ivan and Abraham*

Monticelle, Here We Come (1950)

Motel the Operator (1939)

Mothers of Today (1939)

My Jewish Mother (1930), aka *Mayn Yidishe Mame*

My Son (1939), aka *Living Orphan* (USA: reissue title)

Niemandsland (1931), aka *Hell on Earth*

Our Children (1948), aka *Unzere Kinder*

Overture to Glory (1940), aka *Vilna Town Cantor, The*

Oy Doktor! (1930), aka *Oh, Doctor!*

People Eternal, A (1939)

Power of Life, The (1938), aka *Kraft von Leben, Die*

Rabbi's Power, The (1932), aka *A Vilna Legend* (1948) (USA: reissue title)

Shalosh Achayot (1998), aka *Drei Schwestern* (Germany), aka *Three Sisters*

Shoemaker's Romance (1930), aka *Schuster Liebe*

Shulamis (1931)

Shulamith (1931)

Singing Blacksmith, The (1937), aka *Yankl der Shmid*

Tevye (1939), aka *Tevya; Tevye der Milkhiker*

Three Daughters (1949), aka *Dray Tekhter*

Too Early to Be Quiet, Too Late to Sing (1995)

Two Sisters (1938), aka *Tsvaye Shvester*

Unfortunate Bride, The (1932), aka *Ungluckliche Kale, Die*

Wandering Jew, The (1933), aka *Jews in Exile* (1937) (USA: reissue title)

We Live Again (1948)

What a Mother-In-Law! (1934)

Where Is My Child? (1937), aka *Vu iz Mayn Kind?*

Yiddish King Lear, The (1934), aka *Yiddish Koenig Lear, Der* (1935)

Yidl Mitn Fidl (1935), aka *Castle in the Sky*

Yiskor (1932), aka *The Holy Oath*

Music to My Ears

On compact disc or on cassette, you can readily find some really wonderful Yiddish favorites. All these can be ordered from The Source for Everything Jewish on the Internet at www.jewishsource.com/media:

➤ *Connie Francis Sings Jewish Favorites* captures the bittersweet nuances of Yiddish song. Highlights: "Hava Nagilah," "My Yiddishe Momme," "I Love You Much Too Much," "Tzena Tzena," "Shein vi di Levone," "Mein Shtetele Belz," "Vos Is Geven," "Anniversary Song," "Eli Eli," "Sunrise Sunset," and more.

➤ *Itzhak Perlman Plays Popular Jewish Melodies* (the Israel Philharmonic Orchestra; Dov Selter, Conductor) collects warm and endearing virtuoso interpretations as only Perlman can play them. Highlights: "Reyzele," "A Dudele," "Der Rebbe Elimelech," "Oifn Pripetchok," "Rozhinkes Mit Mandlen," "Oifn Veg Shtayt a Boim."

➤ *Itzhak Perlman—In The Fiddler's House* features America's premier violinist taking a break from the concert hall to explore the vitality of contemporary klezmer music. He performs with Brave Old World ("Reb Itzik's Nign"), The Klezmatics ("Simkes Toyre Time"), The Andy Statman Klezmer Orchestra ("Flatbush Waltz"), and the Klezmer Conservatory Band ("Wedding Medley"). Both CD and audio-cassette are based on the *Great Performances* TV series.

➤ *Shalom—Music of the Jewish People* contains recorded gems by the great Jewish artists of yesteryear. In this superb technical restoration, the recordings were left in their original and properly balanced monaural state. It contains performances by Sophie Tucker ("My Yiddishe Momme"), Fannie Brice ("Second Hand Rose"), Al Jolson ("The Cantor"), Mollie Picon ("In a Yiddish Shtetele"), Eddie Cantor

("If You Knew Susie"), and Aaron Lebedeff ("Roumania"). Also featured are violinists Jasha Heifetz and Yehudi Menuhin; tenors Joseph Schmidt, Jan Peerce, and Josef Rosenblatt; The Benny Goodman Quartet; Ziggy Elman and his Orchestra; and many more. In all, 18 nostalgic selections.

➤ *Mazel Tov!—More Music of the Jewish People* is a follow-up to the best-seller, digitally remastered and meticulously restored traditional folk songs, sacred chants, patriotic anthems, and popular stage numbers. The recording features original recordings by Danny Kaye ("Dinah"), Fannie Brice ("The Sheik of Avenue B"), and Al Jolson ("Lovely Face [Liebes Punim]"). The violinist Joseph Szigeti and pianist Nikita Magaloff perform "Nigun" from Ernest Bloch's suite Baal Shem. Abe Katzman's Bessarabian Orchestra plays "Simchas Torah in Kishinev," and Jewish folk musicians of the former USSR and the Moscow State Jewish Theatre Orchestra play Jewish dances.

➤ *Yiddish Karaoke* will have you singing along with klezmer-style arrangements of popular Yiddish songs. Lyrics appear in phonetic English on a TV screen over vintage black-and-white movies of a *shtetl cheder*, a Jewish wedding, and more. Eight songs, including "Bei Mir Bistu Shein," "Belz," "Shein vi di Levone," and "Oyfen Pripetchick."

➤ *The Barry Sisters: Their Greatest Yiddish Hits* includes songs guaranteed to bring a smile and a tear! Highlights: "Hava Nagila," "Tumbalalaika," "Bublichki Bagelach," "Eishes-Chayil," "Chiribim Chiribom," "Vu a Hin Zol Ich Gayn," "Yingele Nit Vayn," "Dem Nayem Sher," "Ketzele Baroiges." Twelve songs on cassette; 16 on compact disc.

➤ *Yiddish Masterpieces* showcases vintage Jewish voices of the past. On the CD version only, The Bagelman Sisters (before they became The Barry Sisters) sing "Eyshet Chayil," and join Moishe Oysher in "Halevai." Seymour Rechtzeit sings "Misirlou." Both the CD and cassette versions include Yossele Rosenblatt singing "Mein Yiddishe Mome" and "Zog Mir Rebenu." Moshe Koussevitzky sings "A Din Tora Mit Got," and Jan Peerce performs "Rozhinkes Mit Mandlen." "A Glezele Lchaim" is sung by Mischa Alexandrovich. Selections are assembled from many sources, so sound quality will vary. Israeli import.

➤ *Bed Sidran—Life's A Lesson* features Carole King, Lee Konitz, Howard Levy, and other top stars performing Jewish music. Produced by Ben Sidran, and featuring Lynette and the Gates of Heaven Children's Choir. "Eliyahu," "Ose Shalom," "Ani Ma'amin," "Kol Nidre," "Tree of Life," "Yedid Nefesh," and more.

➤ *L'CHAIM (To Life)—The Ultimate Jewish Music Collection, London Festival* features orchestra and chorus music. Stanley Black, Conductor. "*Exodus* Main Theme", "Hava Nagila," "Raisins and Almonds," "And the Angels Sing," "Eyli Eyli," "Tzena Tzena," "Second Avenue Serenade." From *Fiddler on the Roof*, Molly Picon and Robert Merrill sing "Tradition," "To Life," and "Sunrise, Sunset." Liner notes by Alan King.

➤ *Jan Peerce On 2nd Avenue* includes love songs from the Golden Era of Yiddish theatre. Orchestra conducted by Gershon Kingsley. Highlights: "Mayn Shtetele Belz," "Mirele," "Ich Hob Dich Tzu Fil Lib."

➤ *Jan Peerce Sings Yiddish Folk Songs* features an orchestra conducted by Abraham Ellstein. Includes "Sha Shtil," "Maikomashmalon," "Vo Iz Dos Gesele," "Partizaner," "Es Brent," "Anniversary Waltz."

➤ *Theodore Bikel Sings Jewish Folk Songs* was Theodore Bikel's first recording of Yiddish folklore. Lighthearted, often humorous songs of love and everyday rituals and philosophies. Highlights: "Der Rebe Elimelekh," "Di Yontevdike Teyg," "Sha Shtil," "Di Mezinke," "Kum Aher du Filozof."

Answer Key

Here are the answers to the exercises in Chapter 27.

It Sounds Just Like It

1. *der aktyor*
2. *di muzik*
3. *dos papir*
4. *der kontrakt*
5. *der hunger*
6. *der epel*
7. *dos bukh*
8. *der kapitan*
9. *dos konsert*
10. *der zinger*

That's a Good Idea

1. *fargait*
2. *kluger*
3. *ligner*
4. *shvakher*
5. *farshvaygen*
6. *arois*
7. *trakht*
8. *gringer*

I Do Declare

1. *halevay*

2. *epes*

3. *fe*

4. *nokh*

5. *efshar*

6. *sha*

Let's Have Sex Again

1. *der*	2. *di*	3. *dos*	4. *der*
5. *der*	6. *di*	7. *di*	8. *der*
9. *dos*	10. *der*	11. *der*	12. *der*
13. *dos*	14. *di*	15. *der*	16. *der*
17. *dos*	18. *di*	19. *dos*	20. *der*

Living in the Present

1. *Ikh ken Yiddish*

2. *Du kenst Yiddish*

3. *Er ken Yiddish*

4. *Zi ken Yiddish*

5. *Mir kenen Yiddish*

6. *Ir kent Yiddish*

7. *Zey kenen Yiddish*

Objectively Speaking

1. *im*

2. *undz*

3. *ir*

4. *mir*

5. *zey*

I Can't Live Without You

1. *mit*   2. *on*

3. *genug*   4. *shlekht*

5. *dank*   6. *daw*

7. *yo*   8. *neyn*

9. *sakh*   10. *shpeter*

Meet and Greet

1. *Gut yontef*

2. *A gute nakht*

3. *Sholom aleykhem*

4. *Vos hert zikh*

5. *Vi heist ir*

6. *Borukh hashem*

7. *Azoy*

8. *Sken alemol zayn erger*

9. *Tsi ken ikh aykh forshtelen mayn khaver Avrom?*

10. *Mazel tov*

Infinitives Aren't Infinite

1. *kushen*

2. *shlingen*

3. *ervarten*

4. *kenen*

5. *entferen*

Got the Time?

1. *tsen minut nokh akht*

2. *halb nokh ziben*

3. *tzvay azayger*

4. *afertil far fir*

5. *tsen oyf der nakht*

Count-down

1. *fuftzik*
2. *zibetzen*
3. *tsvontzik*
4. *toyznt*
5. *dreisik*
6. *neintzik*
7. *tzvay un tsvontzik*
8. *hundert un tsvontzik*
9. *dray hundert un finf un zekhtzik*
10. *dray un dreisik*

You Can't Choose Your Relatives

1. the brother-in-law
2. the sister-in-law
3. the parents of your son-in-law or daughter-in-law
4. the father-in-law
5. the mother-in-law
6. the son-in-law
7. the daughter-in-law
8. the groom
9. the bride
10. the daughter

Clothes Make the Man and Woman

1. *a regen mantel*
2. *a hut*
3. *a hemd*
4. *a khalat*
5. *a kleyd*
6. a tie

7. a pair of cuff links

8. a pair of stockings

9. a scarf

10. Slacks

A Rainbow Coalition

1. *royt, vays, bloy*

2. *grin*

3. *groy*

4. *broyn*

5. *shvarts*

Coming Right Up

1. *geyt*

2. *geyen*

3. *geyen*

4. *geyt*

5. *gey*

6. *geyst*

7. *geyen*

I'll Get to It

1. *vel*

2. *vet*

3. *vest*

4. *velen*

5. *velen*

6. *vet*

7. *vet*

What's the Problem?

1. brakes
2. tires
3. flat tire
4. a noise
5. a grinding
6. overheated
7. a jack
8. tires
9. map
10. light

What's Past Is Past

1. *Ikh hob gearbet*
2. *du host gearbet*
3. *ir hot gearbet*
4. *er hot gearbet*
5. *zi hot gearbet*
6. *mir hoben gearbet*
7. *ir hot gearbet*
8. *hoben gearbet*

Let's Compare

1. *raykhster*
2. *hekher*
3. *kligster*
4. *kelter*
5. *kirtser*
6. *noenter*
7. *yingster*
8. *reynigst*
9. *elster*
10. *greser*

You'll Find It At:

1. *der kosherer katsev*
2. *der bikherkrom*
3. *di opteyk*
4. *der hutkrom*
5. *di tsirung*
6. *der kleyderkrom*
7. *di shpayzkrom*
8. *der ayzenvargkrom*
9. *der fleyshmark*
10. *di bekeray*
11. *di shnayderke*
12. *der universalkrom*
13. *di tsukernye*
14. *der shpilkrom*
15. *der zeygermakher*
16. *dos antikengesheft*
17. *der shuster*
18. *di shukhkrom*
19. *di shnayderay*

What Hurts?

1. a headache	2. gallbladder
3. a blister	4. a cold
5. a cough	6. diarrhea
7. an earache	8. hoarse
9. nausea	10. a sore throat
11. sunstroke	12. a bite
13. a boil	14. chills
15. constipation	16. fever
17. indigestion	18. pneumonia
19. a sprain	20. typhoid

So What Do You Do for a Living?

1. the doctor	2. the lawyer
3. the oculist	4. the pharmacist
5. the banker	6. the carpenter
7. the designer	8. the foreman
9. the plumber	10. the teacher
11. the dentist	12. the optometrist
13. the printer	14. the broker
15. the chemist	16. the civil servant
17. the butcher	18. the mechanic
19. the salesman	20. the rabbi

Tell Me More

1. *banen*	2. *arbeters*
3. *lerers*	4. *beten*
5. *gasen*	6. *zeygers*
7. *lider*	8. *pletser*
9. *bilder*	10. *vayber*

Wise as King Solomon

1. *finsternish*   2. *shlos*
3. *shpigel*   4. *kheyn*
5. *lokshen*   6. *getraye*
7. *khupe*   8. *hungerik*
9. *honik*   10. *moltsayt*
11. *diker*   12. *klap*
13. *glik*   14. *tayerer*
15. *leyb*   16. *lign*
17. *emes*   18. *arop*
19. *tsores*   20. *kine*

Parting Is Such Sweet Sorrow

1. Be well.
2. May we meet at happy occasions.
3. May you live until 120.
4. May God bless you.
5. May speaking Yiddish and making money both be easy for you.
6. May we always be friends.

Index

E

F

minyastics, 303
mir, 53-54
miracles, 167, 239
Mirele Efros, movie, 338
mishmash, 19-20
mishpokhamarks, 304
miskayt, 229
mit, 54
mitog, 106
Mitvokh, 66
mitzvah, 36
mitzve, 136
mizrakh, 148
Modern English-Yiddish, Yiddish-English Dictionary, book, 333
Modern German, 17-18
Modern Yiddish, 5-8, 21
money, 173-178
Monroe, Marilyn, 100
Montagues, Shakespeare, 258-260
months, Hebrew, 66-67
Monticelle, Here We Come, movie, 338
Montik, 66
morals, homosexuality, 225
morgen, 70
Moses, 38, 49, 263, 312
moshiakh, 121, 214
Motel the Operator, movie, 339
mothers, 78-79, 321-322
Mothers of Today, movie, 339
movies, 136
    81st Blow, The, 338
    A Daughter of Her People, 337
    A People Eternal, 339
    Almonds and Raisins, 337
    American Matchmaker, 337
    Blazing Saddles, 10
    Cantor on Trial, A, 337
    Castle in the Sky, 339
    Catskill Honeymoon, 337
    Cellar, The, 338
    Chants of Sands and Stars, 337
    Dybuk, 337
    Eli Eli, 337
    Eternal Fools, 337
    Eternal Jew, The, 337
    Eternal Prayer, The, 337
    Everything's For You, 337
    Feast of Passover, 338
    For the Sin, 337

    From Hell to Hell, 338
    God, Man and Devil, 338
    Great Advisor, The, 338
    Green Fields, 338
    Hell on Earth, 339
    Her Second Mother, 338
    Hester Street, 338
    Holy Oath, The, 338
    I Want to be a Boarder, 338
    I Want to be a Mother, 338
    Ivan and Abraham, 338
    Jazz Singer, The, 273
    Jester, The, 338
    Jewish Gypsy, The, 338
    Jewish Melody, The, 338
    Jewish People Live, The, 338
    Jews in Exile, 339
    Jews in Poland, 338
    Joseph in the Land of Egypt, 338
    Kol Nidre, 338
    Last Klezmer: Leopold Kozlowski, His Life and Music, The, 338
    Letter From Mama, 337
    Light Ahead, The, 338
    Little Mother, 338
    Little Orphan, 339
    Live and Laugh, 338
    Love and Sacrifice, 338
    Mazel Tov Yidden, 338
    Mirele Efros, 338
    Monticelle, Here We Come, 338
    Motel the Operator, 339
    Mothers of Today, 339
    My Jewish Mother, 339
    Oh Doctor!, 339
    Our Children, 339
    Overture to Glory, 339
    Power of Life, The, 339
    quotes, 272-273
    Rabbi's Power, The, 339
    Shoemaker's Romance, 339
    Shulamis, 339
    Shulamith, 339
    Singing Blacksmith, The, 339
    Tevya, 339
    Three Daughters, 339
    Three Sisters, 339
    Too Early to Be Quiet, Too Late to Sing, 339
    Two Sisters, 339
    Unfortunate Bride, The, 339

    We Live Again, 339
    What a Mother-In-Law, 339
    Where Is My Child?, 339
    Yiddish King Lear, The, 339
moyser, 230
music (Yiddish), 341
musicals, *Fiddler on the Roof*, 6, 286
muvis, 136
My Jewish Mother, movie, 339

N

Nag, The, stories, 5
names
    God, 181-186
    Shakespeare, 258-262
nar, 230
nash, 107
National Theater, Boris Thomashefsky, 8-10
National Yiddish Book Center, 13
nayn, 72
nayntzen, 72
Nazi Holocaust, 4
neb, 230
nebish, 9-10, 230
negev, 149
neintzik, 72
nekhten, 70
neuter. *See also* gender, 317
    definite articles, 195-197
    nouns, 137-138
    words, 50-51
Never Say Die! A Thousand Years of Yiddish in Jewish Life and Letters, book, 334
neyn, 54
Ninth Commandment, 267
nisht, 242
nishto, 242
Nissan, 67
nit, 241
nito, 242
Noah, 184-186
Nobel Prize, 12-13, 292-294
noent, 55
nokh, 50, 70
nokhshleper, 230
nominatives, 197-198

W

Y

Z